Fitting Out Ferrocement Hulls

Frontispiece   A 65 ft trawler yacht leaving the Thames for the Caribbean.

Fitting Out Ferrocement Hulls

Robert Tucker

Adlard Coles Limited
GRANADA PUBLISHING
London Toronto Sydney New York

Published by Granada Publishing
Adlard Coles Limited in 1977

Granada Publishing Limited
Frogmore, St Albans, Herts AL2 2NF
and
3 Upper James Street, London W1R 4BP
1221 Avenue of the Americas, New York, NY 10020 USA
117 York Street, Sydney, NSW 2000, Australia
100 Skyway Avenue, Toronto, Ontario, Canada M9W 3A6
Trio City, Coventry Street, Johannesburg 2001, South Africa

Reprinted 1978

ISBN 0 229 11512 8

Printed in Great Britain by
William Clowes & Sons Limited
London, Beccles and Colchester

The author gratefully acknowledges the help received from many sources, especially for permission to use material and publish photographs

Contents

Introduction

General Background

The first ferrocement boat about which much is known was built in 1849 so, despite the widely held view that the technique is very new, it has in fact a long history. True, developments were few until 1945 and were much clouded by the use of reinforced concrete for ships and barges during World War I. But from 1946, when Professor Nervi first promulgated the technology of thin shells of mortar reinforced by multiple layers of mesh,[1] development has taken place at an increasing pace.

For some reason, however, the main centre of developmental interest was Australasia rather than Europe and, because both Australia and New Zealand have few professional boat builders but many amateurs, advances in technique tend to stem from the amateur.[2] Such bias has been further helped by the labour-intensive nature of the process which exacerbates the great disparity in cost between amateur and professional construction, initially pointed by the comparatively low cost of materials themselves.

Professional building eventually started, however, and with it the need for the builder to guarantee his product. Nervi built his yachts with light steam barrel and fine chicken mesh, not so much as the outcome of technological reasoning as from the simple fact that these were the only materials available to him in Italy at the end of World War II. Moreover, Lambiot had used the same methods a century earlier. But, by the 1960s, these ideas began to be questioned increasingly throughout the world as more and more engineers turned their thoughts towards the improvement of ferrocement. With the improvement of the product came the inevitable sophistication of method, bringing with it greater awareness of the need for control of materials quality and building environment. Classification societies became involved, not always with the happiest results, and disciplines from the glass-fibre industry proved beneficial, especially in the formation of technical and aesthetic judgements. This was both logical and expected because, by 1970, glass-reinforced plastics had a dominant hold on boat building on a global basis. Logically there was bound to be an interaction, for both grp and ferrocement share the concept of mixing two individually weak materials to produce a structure with a final strength greater than the sum of its parts; moreover, the resultant membrane is homogeneous. Significantly, grp set new standards of surface finish and thus provided a yardstick by which to measure the presentability of ferro.

Ferro has a built-in problem: it has a low materials cost. This has manifested itself in a great many ways which will show up time and time again through this book. At this point let it only be stated that the cost factor has tended to obscure the excellence which ferrocement can achieve as a material when it is correctly put together by experts. It has great longevity, can survive with minimal maintenance, is little affected by changes of temperature and humidity once it is fully cured, is virtually fireproof and is impervious to rot and similar bacteriological degradation.

This panegyric sounds as if low cost is the material's only drawback; this is patent nonsense, otherwise it would be a perfect material in the fullest sense! Technically its prime drawback is that it is heavy; moreover, it is very easy, by quite minor inattention to detail, drastically to increase its weight; again, the wrong mortar–one which is too wet, too dry or too lean, or made with the wrong grade of sand or impure water–can be disastrous.

It is not the function of this book to examine in any detail the construction of ferrocement boats. This is done well elsewhere.[3,4,5] Our concern with technology lies in the assessment of hulls already built, and its effect on their completion into yachts or working craft.

In the days of conventional timber yachts, with carvel or clinker planking, a decked hull often represented a full third of the total cost of the yacht; modern methods of hull construction, coupled with greater sophistication of layout, rig and powerhouse (to say nothing of the electronics which can well cost almost as much as the hull), have greatly reduced this proportion–or greatly increased the completion cost, if you prefer it put that way–and the lower prime cost of a ferrocement hull in comparison with timber or glass-fibre only serves to exaggerate the disparity. For example, in a large yacht to the author's design the entire ferrocement work–hull, decks, tanks, bulkheads and bilge keels–accounted for only £17,000 of the finished cost of £85,000, i.e. one-fifth: and this on the basis of a professionally-built hull and superstructure but with internal fit-out by the owner.

As remarked, then, the problem of ferrocement is low materials cost. It tempts the unwary to build hulls whose fit-out costs have not been studied. When the awful truth begins to dawn it is nearly always too late and the builder either sells or botches. To return to the example above: if we accept that the breakdown of the ferro cost shows 20 per cent for materials and 80 per cent for labour, know-how and profit (which is reasonable on a labour-intensive job), our unwary builder sees himself the proud owner of a 65 ft luxury yacht for a mere £3,500, plus a fair amount of hard work. The news that he may have to find another £60,000 before he can put to sea would rightly deter him if it came before he began building, but unfortunately it seldom does. And even if he does succeed in producing a reasonably acceptable vessel (and it must be conceded that our original choice was deliberate in being to such high standards, and not by any means an average), mooring charges, etc., at £10–£15 per foot per year will daunt many an owner. It ought to be stressed at this point that the figures quoted in this book make no allowance for any tax which may be payable.

Thus it is the purpose of this book to look at all the problems involved once the ferro hull is actually there, to remove the rosy spectacles which have been proffered so often in the past (if only by implication), to try to give some idea of the work and cost involved and to point the way to solutions. It should not from this be assumed that this is a negative approach, based on the 'don't do it' concept: far from it, for its intent is to encourage the average man to go ahead and complete his ferro boat: but also, in trying to provide less optimistic guide lines and more detail, to enable him to move forward with greater surety. True, there is also an ulterior motive, namely to improve the standard of ferrocement boats. Those of us who believe deeply in the excellence of the material are often saddened by the low standards to which fine hulls are completed, with amateurish paintwork, poor joinery, secondhand spars and sails–so many shortcomings which have led to the view, 'after all it's only ferro'. That this is so wrong, such a misjudgement of the material, is shown by the really beautiful yachts which have been built, in Europe, North America and Australasia.

As already mentioned, one disadvantage of ferro is its weight per square foot of surface: this is a reducing problem as size increases, but has led to a marked reluctance among designers to produce boats under 35 ft overall. This situation is certainly changing rapidly now that newer techniques are developed, though the majority of these developments call for professional building in controlled environments and so lead to greater prime costs. Their influence on fitting-out will be examined. This weight problem leads to larger hulls, which in turn lead to higher costs of the overall completion, usually to levels well above those envisaged in the early planning stages.

From this review it can clearly be seen that there are, and probably for a long time will be, ferrocement hulls awaiting completion coming on to the market from disillusioned hopefuls. They may be professional or amateur built so they are of variable quality; but they are certainly cheap. Equally, the new medium is attracting new specialist builders; again, these hulls will be cheaper than those of most other materials and so be worthy of serious consideration for completion. We shall now look at the task of judging such hulls and of fitting them out for sea. Of course, there will also be completed vessels changing hands: these notes should provide some measure of guidance in assessing their value and quality.

Construction Variants

At the time of writing there are already several well-developed methods of building concrete hulls, and there is reason to suppose that new techniques will be available within a few years. At this stage it is not pertinent to compare and contrast, awarding points and making judgements; one can only note the differences.

Of the so-called 'straight' ferros, i.e. steel-reinforced mortars, we note:

(a) Pipe framing at regular intervals with intermediate rod frames; closely spaced longitudinal rods usually tied with soft-iron wire ties.
(b) As (a) but with 3–4 in deep web frames in place of the pipes, with or without intermediate rod frames.
(c) Either of these frameworks covered with fine-gauge 'chicken' mesh, i.e. twisted joints with hexagonal holes.
(d) Ditto, but with coverings of welded-joint square-hole mesh; in turn subdivided: (i) all meshes of the same size or (ii) meshes of varying sizes and varying lays.

Into these baskets may be placed mortars:

(e) Purely cement and sand.
(f) Cement, sand and plasticizers of pozzolanic types.
(g) Cement, sand and resinous additions.

In addition, the current development of smaller, lighter craft has led to construction over moulds; the pipe and the rod frames have been dispensed with, and–in the limit–only the mesh is left, usually welded mesh in a variety of sizes and lays. While this technique has possibilities for superstructures and bulkheads in larger craft, it is at the moment confined to dinghies and craft under 18 ft.

An entirely different approach is manifest in plastic-reinforced cement. Early successful work involving simple mixes of cement, sand and short, fine steel wires or short strands of Courlene have so far seemed applicable only to rough, massy work such as quays. However, a process combining a special glass-fibre, cement, aggregate, water and resin has produced Elkalite, a mouldable material from which boats have been built; this method, so far restricted and available from one manufacturer only, is generically grc, i.e. glass-reinforced concrete.

All these varieties of construction may be available to the prospective buyer, and all offer merit in some direction. It will be our endeavour to note such problems as each brings in selection and fitting out, where there is a pertinent departure from the norm.

Notes

1. Whitener, J. L. (1971) *Ferrocement Boat Construction.* Cambridge, Mass., Cornell Maritime Press.
2. Jackson, G. W. and Sutherland, M. (1969) *Concrete Boatbuilding.* London, Allen & Unwin.
3. Samson, J. and Wellings, G. (1968) *How to Build a Ferrocement Boat.* Ladner, British Columbia, S. M. Design Enterprises.
4. Hartley, R. (1967) *Boatbuilding with Hartley.* Takapuna North, New Zealand, Boughtwood.
5. Cairncross, C. (1972) *Ferrocement Yacht Construction.* London, Adlard Coles Ltd.

Chapter One Points for Purchasers

At this point it will be assumed that the reader has decided not to build, but opted to purchase an existing hull to fit out for himself. As remarked, this may be of professional or amateur build. If professional it may come from a specialist yard or factory, or it may have been built by professional labour on the owner's site. If amateur, it may be entirely the work of the owner and his friends, or–more likely–it will have been rendered professionally on an amateur-built framework.

On seeing the prospective purchase, the first thing which strikes is size and shape. These then lead to the first question: Is it the shape and size required? These are partly matters for individual aesthetics, but the point of cost overall hammered at in the Introduction must again be stressed, though now perhaps on a more logical basis. It is difficult to do more than draw wide comparisons at this stage, but the matter will be dealt with in more detail later. Figures 1 and 2 attempt a first comparison of power requirement and sail area against length, since these are major cost factors over which the buyer can have little real control if he is to produce a seaworthy ship. Engine costs vary widely, especially with type and maker, rising as the horsepower developed per r.p.m. rises. The smaller, lighter diesels will cost about £20–£35 per horsepower installed, the high-speed (automotive types) mid-range (70–150 h.p.) about £15–£25 and the heavy, work-boat types such as Gardner LB and Kelvin TS series probably up to £30–£35 per horsepower. In considering these figures a broad allowance has been made to cover sterngear, for this is an expensive item.

The sailing man can have even more of a headache, for he must consider not only a smallish engine, but also the cost of his rig; several well-known ferro hulls have come to grief through being fitted with a secondhand outfit which was quite unsuitable for the vessel. Comparisons are difficult because so many variables present them-

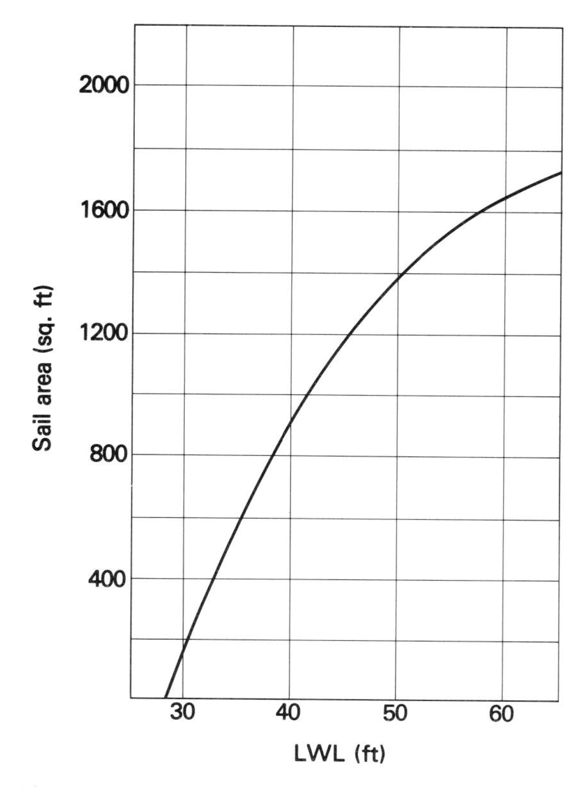

Fig. 1 Correlation between sail area and length in conventional ferro yachts.

selves, but an overall figure of £2·50 per square foot of sail will allow some judgement of the cost of spars, sails and rigging to be made in the size and type of boat normally associated with ferro. We will examine these figures in further detail in later chapters.

Design

So, having ascertained that the hull offered is of the type and size required, further aspects can be examined. Perhaps the most important question is the name of the designer. All too often the amateur builder, conscious only of his low hull-materials costs, regards professional design as an unnecessary luxury with which he is well able to dispense; so he designs his own or copies/adapts a set of hull lines published in a magazine or book. If this be so in the case of the hull under consideration, the intending purchaser can:

(a) Call off the deal
(b) Trust his own critical judgement
(c) Call in a professional designer for advice.

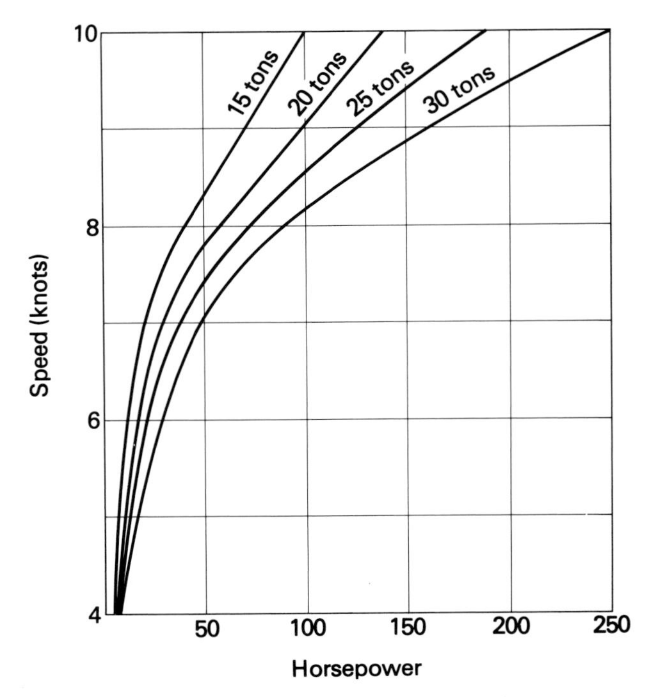

Fig. 2 Correlation between speed and horsepower in power cruisers with various displacements.

Should he adopt this last course he can choose from magazine advertisements or from lists supplied by such professional bodies as YBDSA[1] and ASSCD.[2]

Should the builder have been his own designer, ask to see the drawings and make a preliminary judgement. If there are none, not only be very wary of the product but remember that you, the purchaser, will need to acquire enough data, taken from the hull, to permit the proper calculation of ballast ratio and an effective sail plan.

Should the builder produce lines blown up from a design published in a magazine, remember that this is unethical and, if proven, will produce a demand for royalties from the original designer. In any event, check it most carefully, for if this base design is for a light-displacement hull of wood or grp construction, it will not have the displacement needed for ferrocement. Examples of such vessels have been seen, beautiful looking hulls destined to float at only half their designed freeboard or–as in a case in Florida–simply not to float at all. In saying this we are ignoring the existence of ultra-light modern methods of ferro-building which do enable such translation to be made; but the cost and complexity of such methods are such that builders are most unlikely to proceed without the benefit of an experienced designer.

In this contingency, then, the purchaser is thrown back on the courses of action listed above, except that recourse to (c) will almost certainly produce an instruction to refer back to the original designer. There is, however, one circumstance in which this plagiarism of a design without permission is justified, and this arises when the designer is dead or even unknown. For example, the design may be very old, such as a replica of a galleon or similar historic type; or it may be a committee design, such as those sponsored by fisheries boards, Admiralties and Ministries of Marine. Equally, some books of designs[3,4] have exquisitely printed lines of really lovely vessels from designers such as Gardner, Mower, Hope, Kemp and Duggan–all long dead–which could well be built again without detriment; or, indeed, with advantage. All the same, great care, and not a little skill in naval architecture, will be needed to complete such vessels.

In spite of all this, however, the truth is that there are already a number of designers selling plans to the amateur builder[5–10] at competitive prices, so that the man who does not avail himself of them may have suspect motives. If the hull is from such plans it is worth enquiring what changes the builder has made, if any. Examples of this are the substitution of ferrocement deckhouses, bulkheads and tanks where the original called for timber; the effect of the increased weight must be assessed.

From the design stage the builder proceeds to loft his sections at full size and then to bend his main frames. Some designers provide full-size drawings of these frames, greatly to the delight of the plans purchaser, but since the paper on which they are printed shrinks $\frac{1}{32}$ in per foot on printing by dry process, and more by the wet blueprint method, the accuracy of an 8×6 ft frame is likely to be suspect. If to this one adds an even greater shrinkage with humidity change, one can see how even a most careful builder may produce an unfair hull. Another way of avoiding the task of lofting now becoming available is the professionally produced frame kit, i.e. a full set of web frames, including stem, keel and stern frames, produced professionally from a yard lofting and often from a production line of similar vessels.[11]

Unmortared Baskets

If the hull is offered 'in basket', i.e. unmortared, as in Plate 1, the buyer can see for himself the fairness of the structure and what work is needed to correct unfairness. This may be little more than 'panel beating' with wooden mallet and dolly; it may be of a character which requires extra mortar thicknesses, such as inter-frame tenting (this is bad practice, for excessive mortar thickness is weakening); or it may be uncorrectable by virtue of badly shaped frames, bad setting-up,

Plate 1 An unusual hull-and-superstructure basket awaiting mortaring.

kinked longerons, etc., and as such would have a very low resale value in any condition.

It is not within our scope to examine the pros and cons of the various accepted methods of building, nor to join the weldmesh/chicken-wire controversy. If the hull is built to a ferro design, the purchaser need but check that it conforms to specification. In particular, flexibility of the basket should not be apparent; thus, if the bare hand can push the structure in by a visible amount (say $\frac{1}{8}$–$\frac{1}{4}$ in) in the flat areas of topside and deadrise between pipe or web frames, additional rod frames are needed. They can satisfactorily be added inside the existing mesh if tied to all longerons. If the movement is larger than this then consideration must be given to cause and remedy. If the cause is too light a structural design for the hull size, remedy may prove impossible; if it arises from inadequate meshing, e.g. the substitution of thinner gauges or of chicken-wire for weldmesh, additional meshing is feasible. More rod frames might be needed, as before, but more longerons are difficult to add, and a better solution would be to lay rod frames diagonally between the existing pipe or web frames, running at about 30 degrees off the vertical. For preference, the ends should be welded to main frames. Finally, flexibility may arise from inadequate tying of the mesh or failing to dress it in fully (especially prevalent with the lighter-gauge meshes). Correction is easy in both cases by rectification of the deficiencies.

A hull bought in this state will require mortaring and curing before it is available for fitting out and this poses two further questions:

(a) Can the basket be moved to be rendered elsewhere?
(b) Is the vendor prepared to allow mortaring and curing to be effected on the site as seen?

There is as yet very little evidence on which to base objective judgements on the feasibility of moving an unmortared basket. First reactions are unfavourable, if only because the structure is assumed to be adequately supported from above, and truly square. Achieving the same trueness after transport is an uncertainty, though it must be said that some baskets surveyed by the author certainly look as though they could safely be transported by experienced people if given above-average support.

Mortared Hulls

It is far more likely that the hull will be presented already mortared and cured and even partially fitted out. Efforts should be made to ascertain who did the mortaring and under what conditions, and how the shell was cured. Mortaring a hull is a skilled operation, and it is good to know that teams of specialist plasterers are now available. First-class domestic plasterers are often used and are frequently keen to learn the techniques needed, but in domestic work normally a very wet mortar is used to achieve workability, and this is dangerous in a hull for it leads to porosity. Totally amateur plastering will probably be very obvious.

The overall fairness of the hull will be clear to see, and in judging it the buyer should remember that trowel cement will fill shallow indentations but not big ones, i.e. those deeper than $\frac{1}{16}$ in, while a high-gloss paint finish will exaggerate every imperfection. Particular attention should be paid to the sheer line, which should, if at all possible, be judged from both sides and from such a distance as to enable its full sweep to be taken in. It is a critical line which can totally make or break the appearance of the boat on the water; it is a difficult line to get right, as evinced by the number of ferro hulls whose sheers have most noticeable bumps and hollows. If the station frames are all fair and true and set up to the correct heights, and if the sheer frame is of a substantial section and fastened in exactly the correct spot, all should be perfect. But sometimes the combination of frame distortion (arising perhaps from the distortion of paper patterns) and unfairness in setting up, plus over-flexible sheer piping, can lead to these errors. So often they would be apparent if the builder had room to stand back far enough. Even in this judgement the buyer must exercise caution, for small imperfections in the sheer of an otherwise very acceptable hull can be masked by the judicious handling of toe-rails and gunwale rubbing strakes.

From the general now to the particular: go over the hull with a gimlet eye, examining every square foot as far as possible. We are seeking a smooth hard surface, largely free from dust and pores, though both will be present to some extent unless the shell has been sealed.

Plastering so dry a mortar is a skilled operation often involving both steel and wooden floats and a finishing sponge; excessive floating tends to bring the finest aggregate to the surface, where it dries as dust on the cured shell; with inadequate sealing this surface dust brushes off and can expose the mesh beneath, leading to rust and to loss of strength. Therefore be wary of a dusty finish, and use a stiff brush to clean it off to solid mortar. Small areas of mesh exposure can be dealt with by the use of resin-rich repair kits,[12] but anything much over a yard square will prove troublesome.

The presence of many small pores and cracks suggests either a mix which was too wet, or too dry a cure; both can produce difficulties with little hope of solution. Too wet a mix when properly and completely dried out means porosity right through the shell, leading to leakage or–more likely–to seepage, water absorption and hence to rusted steelwork. Too dry a cure normally shows in a dusty surface and manifold cracks, and obviously can lead to the same results. It should, however, be remembered that, like timber, cement will swell enough when wet to close a few hairline cracks. Resinous sealants[13, 14] are now widely available so that fine irregularities (which can be present even on shells cast by the most experienced) can be mastered.

Trowel marks may be present; if small they will disappear when the shell is sanded over; if they are obviously too deep to be sanded out or filled after sanding, the hull will be difficult to finish. However, remember that only the topsides will have a glossy surface and show such marks; antifouling, necessary below water, is a heavy coating and does not demand a polished undersurface.

Now look at the surface for signs of mesh. In a shell with a plaster cover of $\frac{1}{16}$–$\frac{1}{8}$ in, the mesh pattern may just be discernible although with no bare steel visible. Again, good sealants plus epoxy finishes (more about these later) will give full protection, while the thin mortar cover betokens maximum flexural strength. A full $\frac{1}{8}$ in cover overall will totally hide the mesh, so that it is difficult for the eye alone to tell whether the cover is indeed as thin as this or a great deal thicker, unless this excess of mortar has already begun to craze. Even in professional building there can be a tendency to exceed the preferred thickness of the cover, since 'over building' is seldom considered to be a fault in timber or grp hulls; but it is a serious fault in a ferro shell for, despite sealers, it will craze and crack, leading to water absorption and rust. Of almost equal trouble can be the excess weight involved; a good mortar weighs between 136 and 144 lb per cu ft, so a $\frac{3}{8}$ in cover over the mesh will add 3 lb per sq ft totally useless excess weight, which is a large percentage against a shell target weight of 10–12 lb per sq ft.

Some mortars, especially those with resin binders, show a surface finish which feels like fine sandpaper coated with varnish; here the 'fines' have come well to the surface (or a very fine aggregate has been used), but so has the resin, since resin-migration is commonly experienced in these mixes, and so there is good bonding. Sanding down can produce a glass-like finish well able to take a high gloss.

External rust marks stem from corrosion of the mesh, having two main causes:

(a) Inadequate mortar cover; this shows up as mentioned above and can be treated, if not extensive, by sealers or resin-enriched mortars.
(b) Cracked or porous mortar, also dealt with above.

So far as possible, examine the underside of the keel; again, if it is straight and fair the yacht will sit well on it, but if it is bumpy (often the result of sagging when mortared because the structure is too weak), then allowing the vessel to dry out on a hard bottom will lead to severe distortional stresses and maybe to ultimate disaster. Some designers use a very heavy steel plate, often associated with an internal keelson, to provide a clear, flat solid backbone; check that the mortar joints are really good, inside and out. Despite its propensity to rust (it takes many decades to seriously corrode a $\frac{3}{4}$ in plate), this is good building practice.

Finally examine the sterngear, i.e. propeller and rudder tubes. It is anticipated that the gear itself will not be in place, but steel liner tubes most certainly should be; these should have been welded into the main framework, then meshed in and finally mortared in. Sometimes the builder has opted for sterngear complete in bronze and thus has not welded in the liner tube but made it a grease fit in the mortar and so withdrawn it later. In some constructions, notably in glass-fibre reinforced concrete (grc) the exothermic nature of the curing process precludes the normal heavy 'deadwood' equivalent, and the shell is wood-plugged for such apertures. If the builder has failed to provide for sterngear and rudder, buyer beware. It is not difficult to drill grc because the shell thickness cannot be great; but the chances of drilling through 6–15 in of steel-reinforced mortar (as is likely to be found) may be regarded as absolute zero.

In the same vein, ponder carefully on the size of the tube fitted. Figure 3 will act as a rough guide to the shaft diameter needed for the power to be transmitted. If you are determined on a big engine, don't

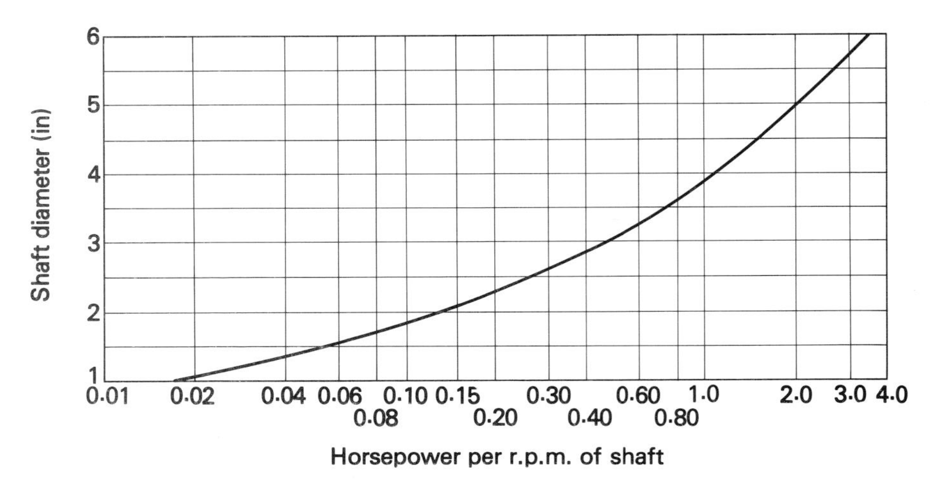

Fig. 3 Correlation between diameter of propeller shaft and horsepower transmitted by it. The effect of any reduction gearing must be included in the calculation of h.p. per r.p.m. For example, an engine developing 30 h.p. at 3000 r.p.m. driving through a 2:1 reduction gearbox will transmit 30/1500 = 0·02 h.p. per r.p.m.

buy a hull with too small an aperture. Such a situation may readily arise when the buyer is convinced that the hull is suitable for a real motor-sailer while the builder has set his sights on sailing with a small auxiliary. There can be solutions, up to a point, but these normally require the advice of a naval architect or marine engineer, at least on feasibility.

Inside the Hull

So much, then, for the outside of the hull. Now climb aboard and study the inside. In smallish vessels of light displacement the pipe frames will be held in with only half the inside meshes, and then given the minimum mortar cover; they will thus be clearly visible, as can just be seen inside the hull on Plate 2. If no frames are visible this may mean that there simply are no frames, which indicates a special form of construction, or that there is an excess of mortar.

As outside, the cover over the mesh should be minimal, and the mesh pattern just about visible. It is unlikely that the surface will have had more than a light troweling or floating, but the total absence of anything in the way of finish, leading to excess roughness, may make fitting out rather difficult and will certainly enforce ply-and-batten linings and probably prohibit integral tanks. Equally, a very smooth interior may suggest that the hull was mortared by the so-called two-shot method, wherein mortar is forced from the outside to the mesh centre, and at a later stage from the inside to the mesh centre,

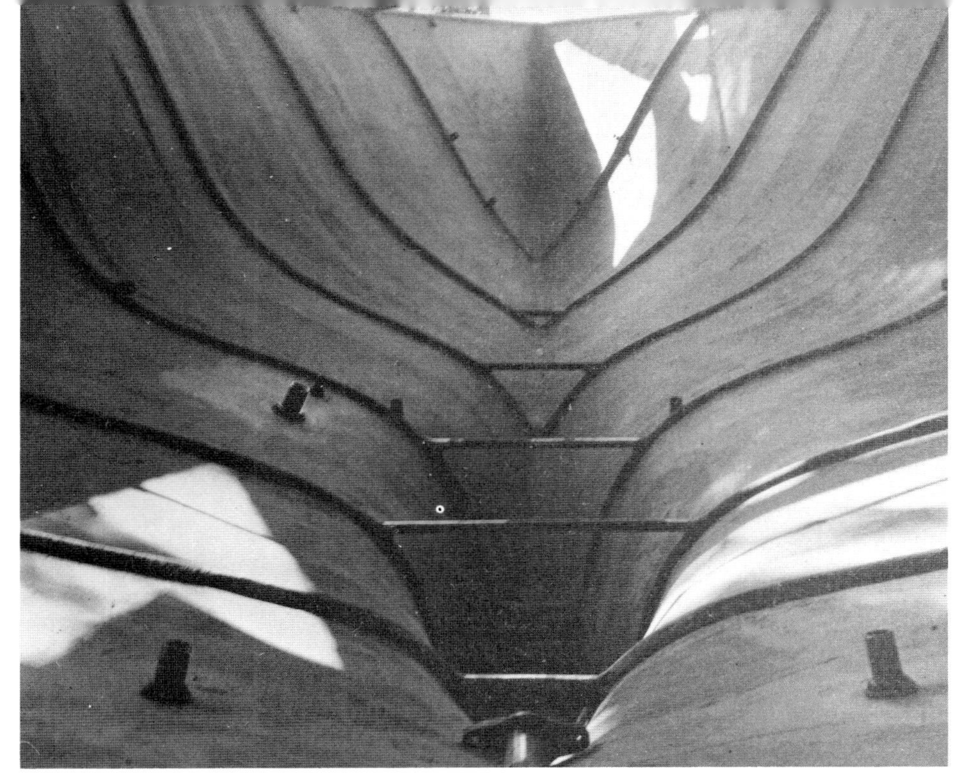

Plate 2 An Ayriel 25 *hull, fully cured and awaiting fitting out.*

in this way reducing the labour needed or man-hours worked consecutively, when compared with the one-shot method in which plastering is done continuously, in one operation. Although sponsored by experienced people, and well worthy of the effort, the two-shot method is now falling into some disrepute as the result of several hulls cracking along the joint lines when dropped.

Ferro bulkheads and floors may well be in place; any floors needed in the reverse of the keel should certainly be in, for they carry much stress, especially in a ballasted sailboat, and should be strongly welded to the frames/longerons and meshed into the hull proper; putting them in after mortaring is not likely to be successful. Bulkheads are different, however, and are normally placed later. Excessive enthusiasm for ferro, leading to many ferro bulkheads and partial bulkheads, leads in turn to excessive weight, so that a dangerous craft can result. A bridgedeck bulkhead, even in small craft, ties the vessel together well in the large cut-out which normally forms the coachroof/cockpit area, and can thus be an advantage. Ferro is often used, and correctly, for the collision bulkhead right forward, when one is fitted.

In a sailing vessel particular attention should be paid to the trough of the keel, which will carry the ballast needed to support the press of sail against capsize. When the mortar has been applied by enthusiastic amateurs, forced through by hand from the inside, small quantities fall from each handfull and roll into the keel trough. If this is not checked immediately and firmly the trough will fill with mortar (and not even compacted mortar) which needs removal–no mean task when it has set. If left in, it will seldom have density greater than 100 lb per cu ft, while the designer may have called for scrap metal and concrete at 360–400 lb per cu ft or even lead dust at 650–700 lb per cu ft. Trying to correct for this in a hull already set up and cured is a thankless task and one unlikely to be successful; at best one can chip out (with pneumatic hammer) so far as possible and then use lead ingots and lead dust in place of punchings and concrete. Sailing an over-tender boat, especially a big cruising yacht, is a frightening experience, particularly if she really gives the feeling that she may capsize if allowed to heel too far.

A final, not too easy, possibility is to have a cast iron or lead shoe of adequate weight made to fit outside the ferro hull, underneath the keel. This will put weight where it belongs but will not be easy to fasten.

A last consideration–or one of the first, perhaps–is the question of windows in the hull. If you want them and like what are provided, or if you want none and there are none, all well and good; but it is a mistake to believe that they can be cut to order later, except by the most expert use of a thermic lance.

So we have gone over the hull carefully as a prospective buyer and should now be in a position to determine whether to reject it, accept and purchase as seen, or accept subject to a professional survey. At the time of writing there are few professional surveyors specializing in ferrocement, but their numbers increase and the employment of one gives some hope of competence greater than one's own, and certainly an opinion from a man trained to look at boats critically.

Professional Builders

So far we have studied only hulls offered by amateur builders but, of course, the number of professional builders of ferrocement is increasing steadily. As yet not all are of good standard, but in the UK an effort to set minimal standards was begun by the formation of the Association of Ferro Cement Boat Builders, which had close connections with Lloyds, the British classification society. Designers and surveyors specializing in ferro are among its membership which is open (at the time of writing) only to professional builders.

Within such contexts as these it is assumed that the builder who is selling ferro hulls for completion elsewhere does so on some form of sales contract,[15] which protects the purchaser against defective materials and workmanship for an agreed period, after which such

Plate 3 Another mortared hull showing the very high standard of finish achieved in Italy. The vessel is a Yara 99.

statutory instruments as the Sale of Goods or Trade Description Acts may be invoked if needed. The prospective purchaser should need to do no more than satisfy himself that the shape, size and style are to his requirement and that he is in all respects satisfied with what is offered. Of course, even the best professionals have accidents, for they must employ labour and cannot watch all of it all the time; if anything, they tend to over-build, especially if leaned upon by classification societies, but the purchaser has the consolation that a reputable professional will stand by his work and rectify or indemnify it if and as necessary. Membership of such bodies as the Ship and Boat Builders National Federation in the UK, and its equivalents in other countries[16, 17] is normally shown on letterheadings, and indicates that the builder meets with approval from a majority of other builders in that country. The intending purchaser of a hull, whether built by professional or amateur, can therefore find advice over and above his own opinion if needed and should thus be able to avoid the bad buy.

Notes

1. YBDSA: Yacht Brokers, Designers and Surveyors Association, Haslemere, Surrey, England.

2. ASSCD: American Society of Small Craft Designers, New York.
3. SCHOETTLE, E. (*c.* 1928) *Sailing Craft.* New York, Macmillan.
4. Fox, U. (1932–37) *Sail and Power: Thoughts on Yachts and Yachting.* London, Peter Davies.
5. J. Casteleijn Inc., Oakland Avenue, Redland Bay, Queensland, Australia.
6. Seven Seas Enterprises, PO Box 2851, Cape Town, South Africa.
7. Ferro-France Marine SARL, 32 Grand Rue, Precy-sur-Maine, Paris, France.
8. Marine Plans and Agencies, 151 Manuaku Road, Epsom, Auckland, New Zealand.
9. Samson Maritime Design, Vancouver, Canada.
10. Richard Hartley Designs, Takapuna North, New Zealand.
11. Potter and Bishop Ltd, Westerham Heights, Kent, England.
12. Eponite Repair Mortar and Grout Mortar: Shell Composites Ltd, Slough, England (and world-wide).
13. Eponite Clear Sealer: Shell Composites Ltd.
14. FerroSeal: MacAlister Carvall Ltd, Hamble, Hants, England.
15. Typical contracts may be obtained from SBBNF, Great Queen Street, London WC2.
16. American Association of Boat and Engine Manufacturers, New York.
17. Registro Italiano Navale, Genoa.

Chapter Two **Suggestions for Surveyors**

The professional surveyor must be prepared to advise his client on a wide range of aspects, including the suitability of the proposed purchase; thus there is much in the previous chapter that the professional will study, and he will certainly carry out for himself the close inspection of the hull for fairness, mesh cover, keel-trough condition etc., albeit with a more jaundiced eye than either vendor or prospective purchaser.

Should there be any doubts about the fairness of the hull in the overall sense, it is best to check first on the deck plan, since this is essentially simple. A line or wire stretched from stemhead to centre of transom provides a datum centreline; measurements thence to port and starboard at selected positions will show whether there is discrepancy in plan form, while a plumb line held in contact with it (most carefully to prevent moving it off centre) will show whether the keel is central throughout, provided the hull is chocked level. A long spirit level, set if needed on a cross plank, will show this, and levels taken at several points along the hull will indicate whether there is any twist in the sheerline. It is possible that only a professional surveyor can advise just how far departure from true can be tolerated but, as a rough approximation, the following may be taken as maxima:

(a) Variations in half-beam: $\frac{1}{4}$ in per foot of half-breadth
(b) Twist in keel line: $\frac{1}{8}$ in per foot of length
(c) Lack of plumb from centreline to keel: $\frac{1}{8}$ in per foot of depth at point of measurement
(d) Lack of level at sheer: $\frac{1}{4}$ in per foot of half-breadth.

Then a long thin batten, say 15 ft × 2 in × $\frac{3}{16}$ in, should be flexed around the hull to check for surface fairness, with the help of one or two assistants to hold it in place. Particular attention should be paid around the sheer, the flatter areas of the topsides and the bilges. Sheer and topsides will, of course, show up when gloss painted, and it is likely to be extremely difficult to lose all the minor departures from true, which will show up worse in the flat areas. Even in the best glass-fibre boats one will find visible unfairness in large areas, so an objective judgement must be made. Far more of a problem is likely to be the bilges, perhaps by virtue of untrue frame bending, distorted paper patterns, sagging when set up or during mortaring (when the render is wet); certainly the very stiffness of the frames, and of the hull overall, precludes much alteration when rodding is well advanced, so that unfairness then manifest is liable to remain. Ferro hulls seem more prone to this fault than any other type of hull, and it is something of a problem to advise on how much distortion to accept. Perhaps only experience of ferro and the degree of aesthetic injury presented can provide the basis for judgement.

Shell Thickness and Strength

Efforts to assess hull thickness are liable to be frustrating, even in the limited areas which show possibilities, i.e. in which accurate measurements of inside and outside beams can be made. The surveyor who tends to specialize in ferro might well devise for himself a large wooden or alloy caliper, which would allow for some degree of thickness assessment up to a couple of feet from any available edge. This need to get away from edges, especially at the sheer, must be stressed, for such areas tend to be thickened up–as they should be, of course. Obvious spots for measuring are window apertures, ports and exhaust and skin fitting holes, if any. These may well prove one's only hope in a hull with deck and side decks fitted.

So far as decks are concerned one hopes to find hatches and open areas for deckhouses, cockpit, etc., whose upstands may be a guide to thickness or may permit the use of a caliper gauge.

With so many new construction techniques coming into use, it is difficult to give precise guidance on shell thickness. At present many of these constructions are particular to one factory and scantlings are neither revealed nor readily discernible; if a full survey is being made, the surveyor is advised to seek guidelines from the supplier. A classic example is the hull-building material Elkalite, a glass-reinforced cement. The method evolved for larger shells in this material involves spraying a grc coat some $\frac{3}{16}$ in thick on each side of a lightweight plastic-foam core; while $\frac{1}{2}$ in foam is currently used for boats, up to 3 in has been used for flat panels, so that the surveyor must know the thickness of foam before he can usefully assess the working thickness of the cement.

The development of thinner and lighter steel-reinforced mortar shells also means that departures from any norm will increase. A rough guide to these shells is shown in the graph, Fig. 4.

While it seems as difficult to justify the use of frames in a ferro hull as it is in grp or cold-moulded shells (other homogenous structures in which the shell is the strength, not merely a watertight membrane on a space frame) many hulls with web frames will be found. When these have been properly calculated, as is common with New Zealand designs, a reduction by $12\frac{1}{2}$ per cent can be allowed in skin thickness; when they have been added later–say at the behest of a classification society–then their contribution to weight excess must be assessed and noted.

The faithful friend of the surveyor of wooden boats is his little hammer, which bounces off sound timber and rings clear, but whose muffled note so often shows up areas of decay or softness. It is no less help to the surveyor of a ferro hull, for it will ring clear and bounce elastically from a good shell, and will show up a number of faults in a bad one. For instance, where the render is too lean and adhesion poor it will cause the mortar to flake or powder away from the mesh.

Where there is inadequate or damaged meshing the hammer may go right through the hull; such an occurrence seems impossible, but it has indeed happened, and to a new vessel. A yacht, completed from a

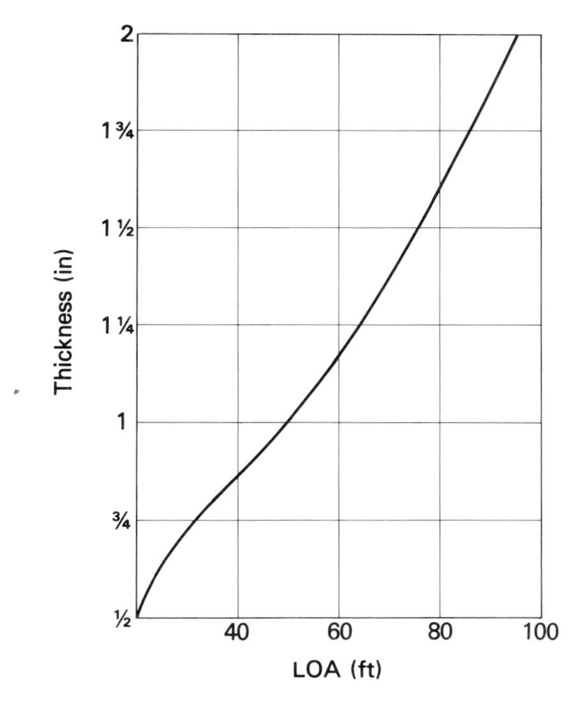

Fig. 4 Approximate correlation between shell thickness and length in normal ferro cruisers.

bought-in hull, sank when launched, after being dropped 2–3 ft and cracking internally; on inspection the surveyor easily penetrated the hull with light blows of his hammer, indicating both inadequate meshing (even a small ice-pick should not penetrate the normal dense mesh structure) and a very low cement content in the mortar.

Where there is a bare shell it may be considered feasible to chip away the mortar down to the longeron core and re-render with a resin-rich mix–this being the only hope for any two-shot method of rendering. The use of grc suggests itself, especially if the interior meshing proves inadequate, but it is as yet an expensive solution. In the example cited, the vessel was completed; however, it is probable that the only valid answer would be to strip out the interior and rig, scrap the hull and build again, using the correct structural methods.

Surface Cover

Experience to date–and this covers more than a century–strongly supports the concept that the mortar cover over the meshes should not exceed $\frac{1}{8}$ in. It can justifiably be argued that a much greater cover is found in reinforced concrete, where it adds to the compression strength; but since it detracts from the flexural and tensile strengths which are so much more important than compression in a boat hull, the greater advantage of a thinner cover must be accepted. In some cases the pattern of the mesh may be just visible, suggesting almost too thin a cover which will require really adequate sealants and epoxy finishes. But the normal problem is overcover, especially on underhung surfaces and reverse curves, such as the deadrise and the garboard areas. It is patently obvious that a surveyor can only pit his luck against natural odds and take scrapings at, say, six locations, with a preference for the topsides where weight is most critical. A further four or so should be taken from the decks if these are in ferro. It is necessary only to chip out a strip $\frac{1}{8}$–$\frac{1}{4}$ in wide and $1\frac{1}{2}$–2 in long, clearing the render down to the mesh and cutting with as sharp an edge to the pit as can be achieved. This will then allow the cover thickness to be measured; the professional could well develop his own gauge for the job, perhaps along the lines suggested in Fig. 5. The pit can be resealed with a resin-rich repair pack after the edges have been brushed with sealer or resin to bind in the repair.

Test Cores

The surveyor will seldom be able to take test cores or bores but it sometimes happens when large skin fittings need to be moved, windows or hatches cut, or similar alterations made. These are diffi-

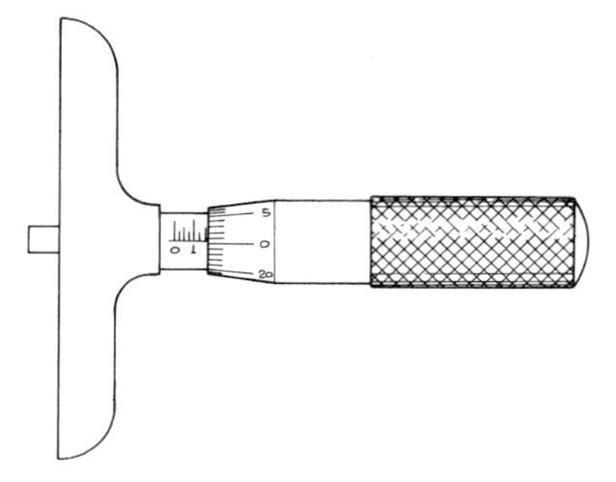

Fig. 5 Micrometer gauge for determining depth of cover over mesh.

cult, although not impossible. In one case, on taking a core from a large foredeck to make a new feed hole for the chain navel a render cover of about $\frac{3}{8}$ in on both sides of the meshwork was revealed. The overall thickness was almost 2 in in contrast to the manufacturer's specification of $1\frac{1}{4}$ in. If this excess cover pertained throughout the vessel it would account for more than three of her ten tons overweight at launch. Although a good proportion of the rest was in the bottom, which was about 4 in thick in the engine room, the vessel no longer fulfills her design criteria, has reduced freeboard and so a reduced steaming range and range of stability plus, by virtue of the added bottom weight, a jerkier roll. This latter has sometimes been claimed to have been engendered by the demands of a classification society.

Inside the Hull

Close inspection of the interior has been covered in Chapter 1, with some emphasis on the depth of render over the mesh. The surveyor should also look very closely at the cusps of the mortar around the frames, especially pipe frames, and use his hammer or ice pick to ensure that they are solid cusps and not merely skins over voids; in time these skins will puncture, allowing the voids to fill with wet air, so rusting the steel beneath and leading to deterioration of the structure. The most difficult joint to make is a right angle, especially in a confined space; such a joint is common where ferro floors and bulkheads are used so there is ample scope for close inspection here, especially since floor areas will normally be inaccessible once the hull is fitted out.

Superstructures and Fittings

The complexity of superstructures, the pros and cons of ferro, steel and timber, are such that a whole chapter must be devoted to them. At this stage one must simply contemplate the effect of ferro work, its strength and execution, rather than its suitability.

If ferro decks are fitted–and this is usually advisable when the design displacement will accept the weight, since they tie the shell together–provision must normally be made for wood or steel deckhouses. The surveyor should look into this carefully. Some designers use ferro upstands as the basis of deckhouse supports; others use timber carlins above and below, through-bolted. The purchaser must be advised of the method of attachment and of finishing the deck edge, with clear expositions of the problems posed and solutions possible.

It has already been noted that larger apertures in the ferro should have been built into the mesh structure, with correctly designed upstands for hatches and coamings and stress-collection rings around window or port apertures. Smaller holes, such as those for skin fittings, may well be drilled using a masonry bit with a tungsten-carbide tip.

If skin fittings have been placed, they need much the same attention and thought as in a steel hull, for it is wise to treat a ferro hull as a steel one with regard to electrolysis. Thus all fittings should be well bedded with neoprene or rubber gaskets between flanges and hull, inside and out. Concrete demands this kind of care anyway, by virtue of its tendency to powder at edges; ferro demands it doubly, insofar as most skin fittings currently available are of bronze. Some smaller ones are available in Maranyl, a non-hygroscopic derivative of nylon, and these are to be recommended.

Ferro is a useful material for engine bearers, provided that they are designed and built into the structure from the start. The material absorbs vibration well, but the rodding should be well-blended into the hull and the joints thoroughly meshed. This can be difficult where the bearer meets the hull at an acute angle, and it is preferable to fill this area with solid ferro, as shown in Fig. 6, despite the weight.

The surveyor should check for truth of alignment, for it may be impossible to correct for error in the lateral plane, though error in the vertical plane may be overcome by tapered tops to the beds. It is wise to ascertain the type and size of engine planned, in view of the difficulty of making changes at a later stage.

Classification and Registration Societies

The growth of ferro construction has led to the active interest of official bodies concerned with building standards. One of the first to promulgate definite standards was the New South Wales Maritime Services Board; these apply only to new construction and predicate that the builder has produced or can produce a test piece of his hull lay-up; sections of this are cut and measured for compression, tension and flexural strengths. It may not be possible for a surveyor to have a

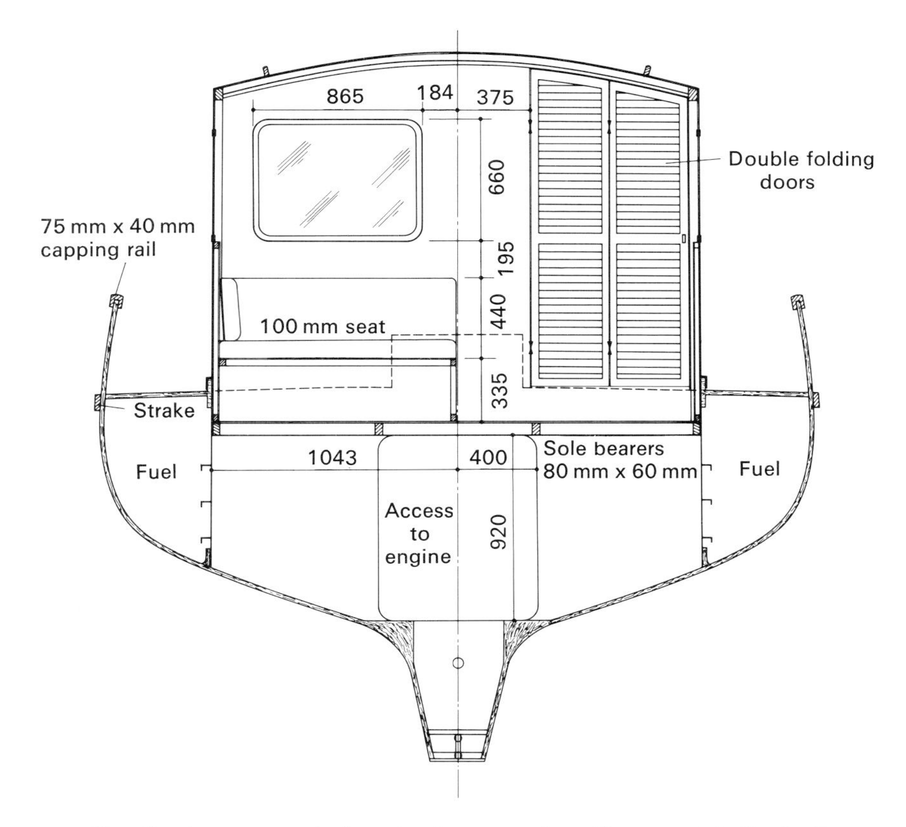

Fig. 6 Arrangement of engine bearers where they run into the hull.

test section and so achieve measured strengths, but the standard will certainly be a guide.

Ferro construction has also advanced well in South Africa, with helpful interest from many bodies including the University of Cape Town, the Cape Portland Cement Company and Lloyds of South Africa. In the UK, Lloyds Register of Shipping has produced Notes for the Guidance of Ferrocement Boatbuilders.

At this stage it will be noted that concentration has been on new hulls offered for sale or purchase, and that the notes have attempted to cover the basic construction concepts without going more deeply into the building techniques, which are covered adequately elsewhere (see Chapter 1). Most of what has been said applies to completed boats, and these will require survey as and when they change hands. The survey must therefore take into account the attachment of superstructures and interior fitments, as well as engine installation, plumbing and rig; these will be discussed in subsequent chapters.

Equally, as the number of ferro boats increases, the surveyor must become increasingly concerned with damage reports. Since the estimate of damage must necessarily be closely linked with the difficulty or simplicity of repair, it is felt that this aspect must be borne in mind when reading the early chapters of this book.

Chapter Three **Decks and Deckhouses**

Decks and superstructures must be a major concern on ferro hulls, the more so in comparison with other hull materials in view of the choice offered. Except where quite unviable by reason of weight, ferro decks are an advantage, especially in transferring what must be a high-stress joint from the sheer to the carlin, i.e. from an area where stresses are always high to one where they are markedly lower.

The concept of torsion-box design was first adopted successfully in timber boats such as some of the popular ply craft of the early 1950s–and to quite a serious extent by the Coastal Motor Boats designed circa 1915. It is already showing itself as a natural development in ferro where the size and displacement will allow of it, for the ferro-deck/ferro-hull joint, tightly meshed together, becomes less of a joint than a shape change in direction, with no loss of strength anywhere. A good example is clearly shown in Plate 4 where the long foredeck blends with a short low deckhouse and thence to a flush poop. The decks have a strong camber, giving the tremendous natural strength of an arch; the deckhouse is small, short and low, with heavy blend radii, and certainly presents the maximum strength of structure *per se* if not always the wisest choice where the weight of tophamper is of concern. Now being built in Cape Town, this yacht (to the CR42 design of the author) will be used for cruising southward and racing offshore in seas notorious for their size and power.

This concept has been developed farther, embodying a flush poop and a longer, but still narrow, coachroof. In this case, however, the construction material was grc sandwich, with an all-up weight of only 7 lb per sq ft–considerably lighter than the 10–12½ lb per sq ft normal in ferro-based structures. However, care must be exercised in interpreting these statements, since the technology of lightweight ferro has already led to shells weighing 4½–5 lb per sq ft and having

Plate 4 The low, short coachroof of CR42 blends well with the long foredeck and is a good example of a ferro deckhouse.

adequate strength. As these techniques become more widely used at the design stage, leading to the concepts of low, all-ferro superstructures, the great torsional rigidity possible within the material will be realized.

If the purchaser is offered a hull in mesh form, before rendering, then there is every possibility of opting for the superstructure to be in these grc sandwich lightweight formats, provided that the design can be so modified, especially in regard to deckhouse height. The structural design will call for individual attention, but a basis of $\frac{1}{4}$ in rod frames at 12 in intervals, standing proud of the inside mesh, longerons at 2 in centres and five layers of $\frac{1}{2}$ in $\times$ 22 gauge welded mesh (three outside and two inside) will prove acceptable.

If the hull and decks are already mortared it is inadvisable to attempt a ferro deckhouse, as it is if the design makes it impossible to achieve adequate headroom with a low structure; as a reasonable guide here it may be accepted that a deckhouse in ferro should not be higher than $1\frac{1}{4}$ in per foot of beam if lightweight ferros are used, or $\frac{3}{4}$ in per foot in conventional matrixes.

The conventional system combines ferro decks and timber superstructures; it is hoped that the combination may soon embrace grc deckhouses, especially in the sandwich form, giving inherent rigidity and thermal insulation. It is not within the scope of this book to detail the construction of decks, which is dealt with elsewhere, only to deal with building upon existing structures. In the widest terms, then, the systems may be presented as follows:

(a) Lightweight vessels with timber decks and superstructures
(b) Medium vessels with ferro decks and timber superstructures
(c) Heavy vessels with ferro decks and timber superstructures
(d) Heavy vessels with ferro decks and steel superstructures.

Each of these will be considered in turn later, but first attention must be given to the basic techniques of effecting the joint between dissimilar materials.

Timber Decks

Once the sheer batten is in place, timber decking will proceed in the manner normal in wooden vessels, but the sheer batten, sometimes called gunwale, beam shelf or inwale, needs to be very strong and well fastened to the hull. In an ideal situation the sheer itself is determined by a steel flat-bar, say $2\frac{1}{2} \times \frac{1}{4}$ in, running clear round the hull inside the rods and above the heads of the pipe frames, but meshed and mortared outside (see Fig. 7). If studs are not welded on to take the timber, holes can be drilled as required, with galvanized-steel screws holding the timber to the steel, aided by a really first-class multipurpose adhesive such as Ralli-bond, Bostik or Gripfill. In a 25 ft hull the timber shelf needs to be some $2\frac{1}{2}$ in deep and $1\frac{1}{2}$ in thick, and is best achieved by laminating three $2\frac{1}{2} \times \frac{1}{2}$ in strips *in situ*.

Less sure though simpler is the termination of the hull in a rectangular hollow section of steel pipe known as rhs (see Fig. 8). If it is not possible to laminate in a timber shelf, the ply deck may fit direct to the steel. This is fine so long as (a) the watertightness of the joint can be guaranteed, and (b) the camber of the deck matches the angle of the steel. Usually this condition cannot safely be met, so a timber wedge is interposed between the ply deck and the steel; the curve of the sheer in the plan form means that this wedge must be cut from a number of pieces, each fastened to the rhs with adhesive and self-tapping screws, but the final joint is strong and watertight. Attention is drawn to the seal of the deck edge with glass-fibre tape, now well-accepted practice in timber boats.

Ferro decks

The distinction, although drawn earlier between lighter and heavier craft, is primarily that between decks with and without upstands. Decks without upstands, which finish either in the raw ferro or a steel

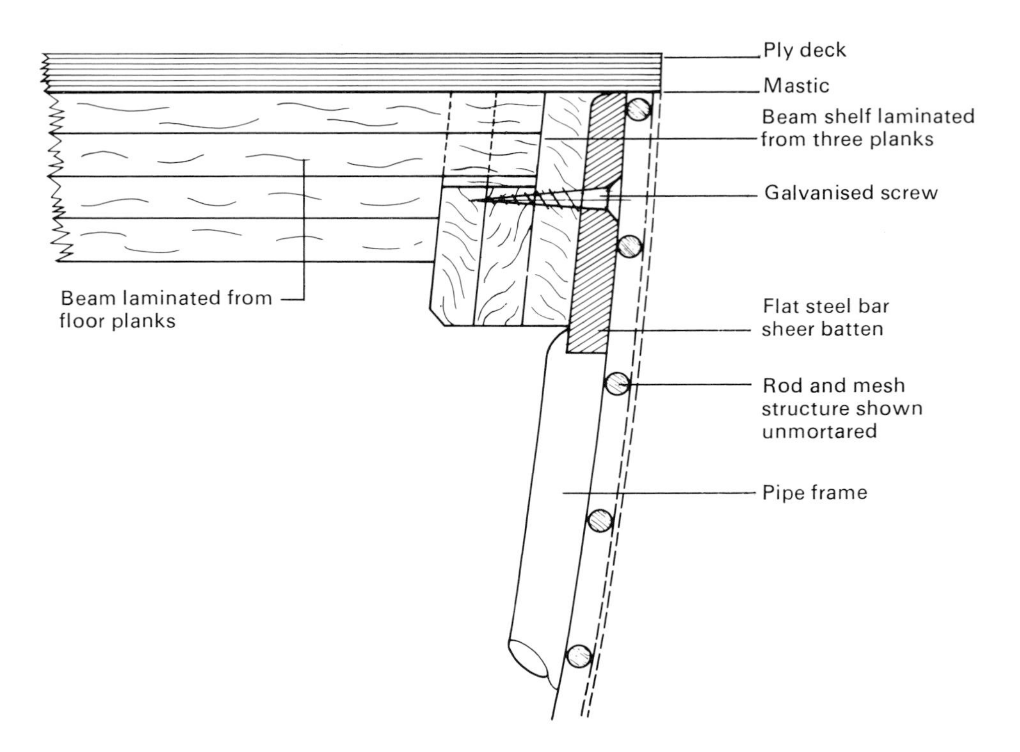

Fig. 7 Sheer-batten system at deck edge with flat bar gunwale reinforcement.

carlin band, are popular in Australasian designs and have much to commend them in smaller craft. The technique is to bend into place a pair of timber carlins, one above and one below the ferro; they are then bedded in mastic, such as Sylglass tape, Sealastic, etc., and bolted firmly together. This means drilling through the ferro deck close to its edge; the mortar tends to break away from the holes, hence the predeliction for a boundary bar and the demand for upper and lower timbers. The bolt holes should be well filled with resin-mortar or mastic as the job is assembled. Figure 9 shows a section through the completed carlin, with a timber lining hiding the raw ferro and the plywood deckhouse side in place.

In larger vessels, or whenever a larger (higher) deckhouse is to be supported, the upstand carlin is preferable; here the ferro deck terminates in ferro upstands–as the name suggests–which may be simple angles, as in Fig. 10 (a) or–especially for larger houses–in a tee format, as in (b); both configurations add enormously to the strength of the deck around the opening, so that there is an increase, not a decrease, in the rigidity of the deck. The deckhouse may be attached

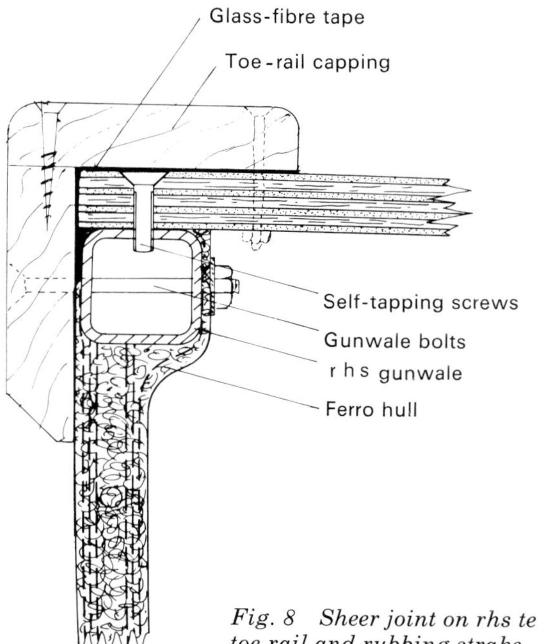

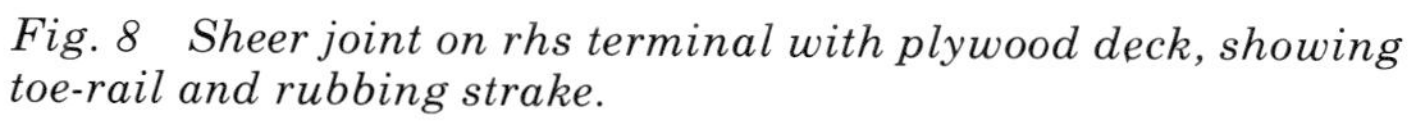
Fig. 8 Sheer joint on rhs terminal with plywood deck, showing toe-rail and rubbing strake.

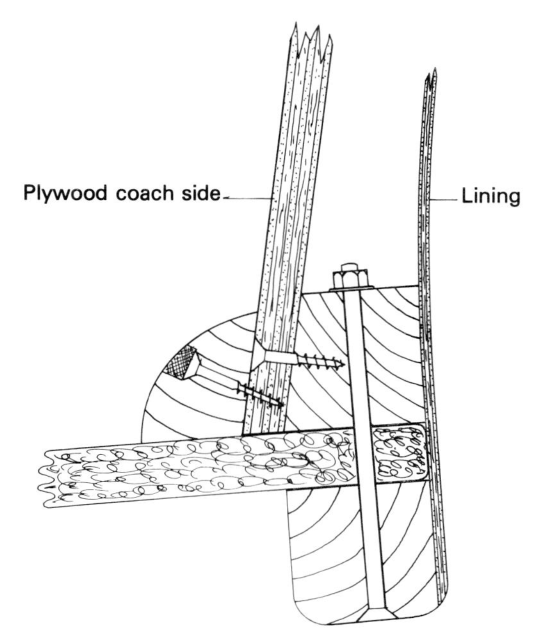

Fig. 9 The combination of ferro deck and timber coachroof when no ferro upstand is provided.

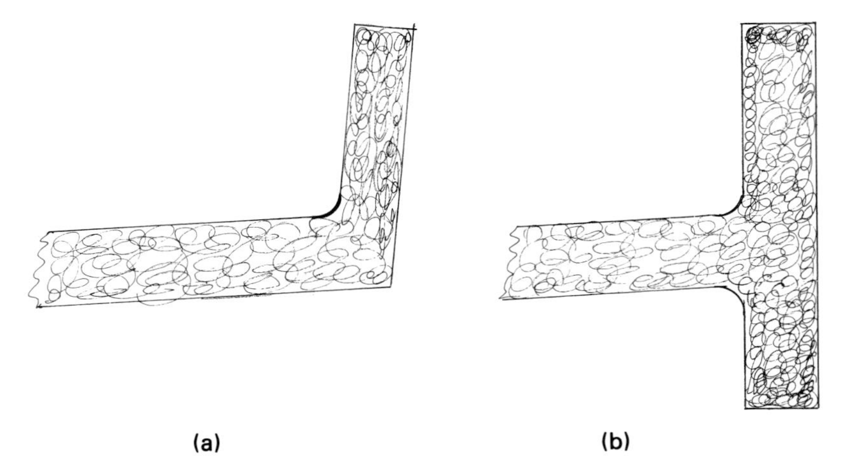

Fig. 10 Ferro upstands for deckhouse carlins: (a) angle, (b) tee.

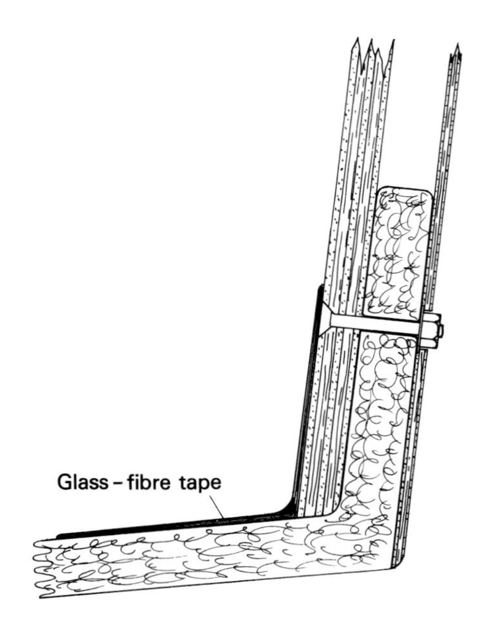

Fig. 11 Combination of plywood deckhouse and ferro angle upstand.

in a number of ways, largely according to size: Fig. 11 shows a simple structure with the upstand sandwiched between the deckhouse side and lining, the whole bedded in mastic and sealed on the outside with glass-fibre tape. It will be clearly obvious that the radius between deck and upstand must be as small as possible, so that everything can be truly bedded down; when this is achieved the joint has infinitely more chance of remaining watertight than that shown in Fig. 9.

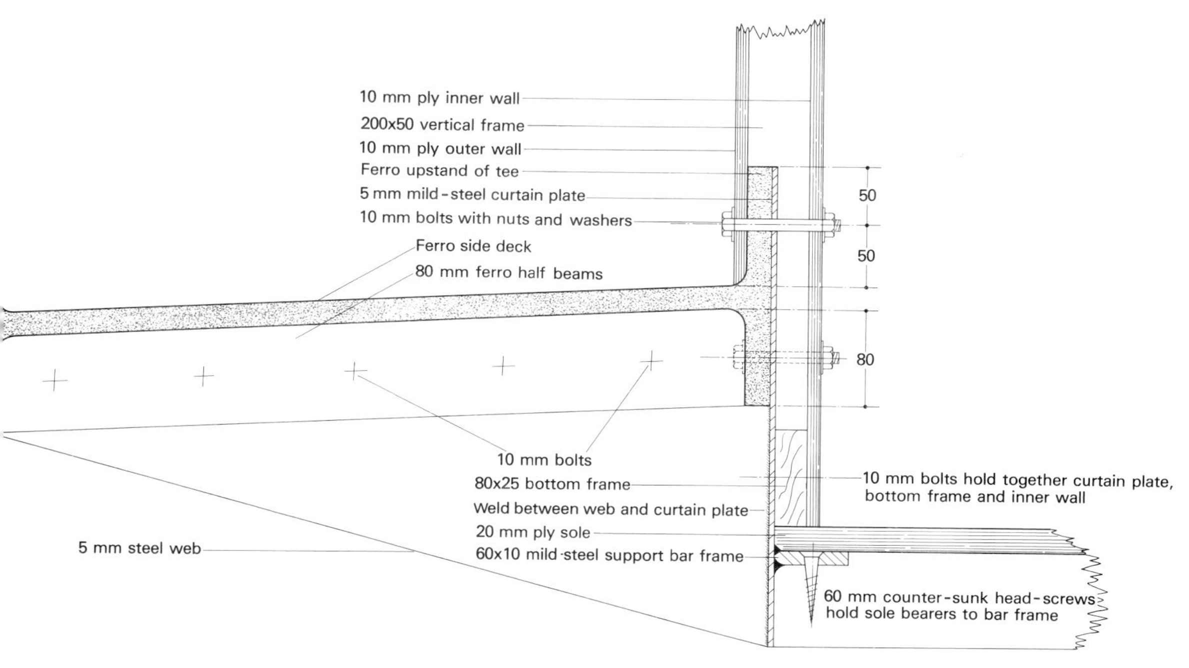

Fig. 12 Combination of duplex plywood deckhouse with ferro tee upstand; this feature is from a large deck saloon and the steel curtain plate, supported by webs, carries the sole at a constant level against the sheer.

Figure 12 shows the tee carlin associated with a complete double skin deckhouse; this is a really superb job and well suited to large superstructures, such as 'semi-sunk' deck saloons, but care must be exercised during the building phase to ensure that the tee arm is either truly vertical or given the designed tumble-home.

Similar attention must be paid to hatches; again, on small craft these may simply be square holes in the deck, to be fitted with through-bolted carlin systems as in Fig. 9. Better results are more likely from the upstand system, as in Fig. 10 (a); and to meet the requirements of classification bodies these upstands may need to be quite high. On a 65 ft MFV yacht to Lloyds, the ferro upstands were 16 in high, clad in timber and capped with watertight hatches. This concept presents a problem insofar that the corners of the ferro need to be generously rounded, while the timberwork is far easier if squared off; ideally the resultant gaps are filled with inverse quadrants, but for practical usage a resin-rich mortar can be grouted in to fill. The gaps should not be left, for they would then trap oxygen-rich moisture, or even salt water, leading to rotting of the woodwork.

Finally, the problem of toe-rails must be considered. The rails themselves are simple enough in ferro, and may vary from 2–3 in to 2 ft in depth (i.e. deep bulwarks). The problem is that of scuppers for the drainage of deck water. The technique of fitting deckside drains, taking the water inside via plastic tubing to skin fittings at or just below the waterline, certainly makes for beauty of line; but the amount of water these devices can clear in reasonable time is so little that, unless associated with very shallow rails (i.e. up to 2 in), they should not be used on a seagoing vessel. In craft where shallow–say 2–3 in–rails are used, the best solution is the complete omission of sections, the whole finally neatened by a timber capping. Where proper bulwarks are fitted, scuppers should be cast into the structure and surrounded by a steel ring.

It is realized that most of the points covered in this chapter are more germane to a treatise on ferro construction than on fitting-out, but it is felt that the way in which the deck structure is organized must have so important an influence on what can or cannot be done with a ferro hull, once purchased, that full consideration of all basic facets is essential both to the prospective purchaser and to his advising surveyor. It is very difficult to change these structures once they have been rendered.

Chapter Four **Small Deckhouses**

From here on it will be assumed that the reader, having considered all that has gone before, is the owner of a ferrocement hull and is going to turn it into a complete, seagoing vessel. Since the most important structure to be sorted out is the deckhouse, to which we gave so much consideration in Chapter 3, we shall now develop this train of thought to include working detail.

Ferro Deckhouses

As stated, the simplest deckhouse is the ferro one, but it is dangerous unless it is very small or very light; Plate 4 shows an excellent example of this type of house. In contrast, Plate 5 shows another that is too long, too square and badly finished, with trowel marks visible from quite some distance away, even though they do not show up in the photo. In completing the vessel there are essentially three considerations, namely windows, painting and lining; the last two items will be covered when these subjects are dealt with for the hull.

It is to be hoped that apertures for windows or ports will have been made at the time of meshing, and if this has been done it is wise not to alter them. If not, however, they must be cut. The outline of the shape should be marked by $\frac{1}{4}$ in drillings at close spacings, using a masonry bit tipped with tungsten-carbide. These holes can be connected by sawing through, using a powered hand-saw and the short 'carbide' blades used for cutting window apertures in glass fibre. This stage having been achieved, the edges of the resulting aperture can be ground back to a reasonable finish; since the only valid form of window support is a metal or timber framing sandwiching the ferro, a fine finish to the edge is unnecessary, for it will be hidden.

Plate 5 A ferro deckhouse which is ugly and overweight; moreover, closer inspection showed a low standard of construction.

The frames, which are likely to be bought in, will need to be bolted through the ferro, and care is needed in ordering to ensure that the bolt holes are well away from the edge of the ferro to prevent break-through. Figures 13 and 14 show standard systems with alloy frames, using the deep timber inside pad as landing for a ply lining. This system was, in fact, approved by Lloyds for hull use, so it may be adopted with full confidence in a deckhouse. It should be noted that fixed ports with deadlights are specified in preference to opening ones; clearly necessary in a hull window, this precaution could well be adopted in the deckhouses of oceangoing sailboats.

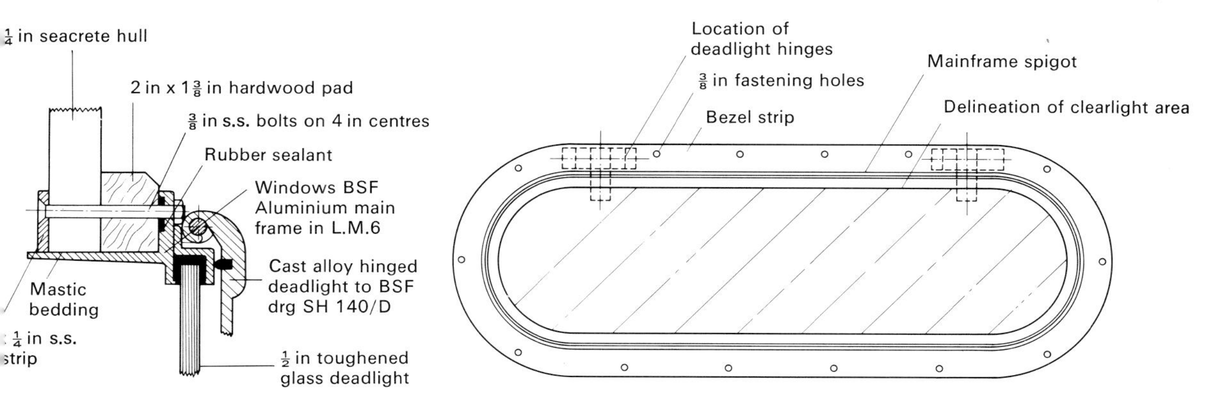

Fig. 13 Lloyds-approved portlight for a ferro hull; it is normal to fit an alloy deadlight inside the glass.

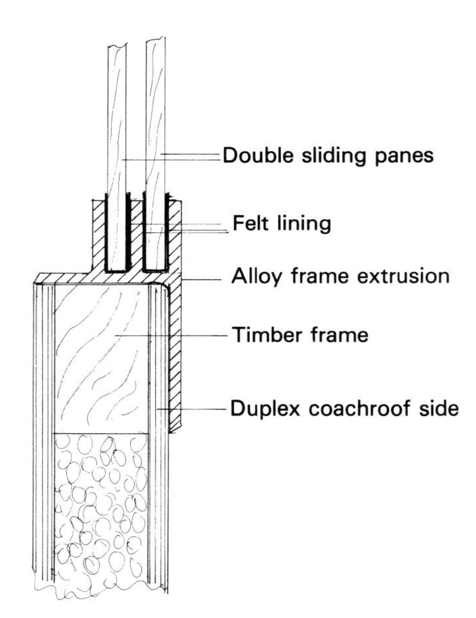

Fig. 14 The type of window fitted into the deck saloon of a power yacht built under Lloyds' supervision.

The choice between glass and clear plastic (Perspex, Lucite or whatever) is perennial. If the house incorporates curves the use of glass can be very expensive or impossible, leaving only plastic. But where glass can be used, its resistance to scratching, its cleanability and its resistance to temperature change and ultra-violet degradation –the ills to which plastic may be subject–make it preferable in most locations. Standard domestic window glass, however, is not strong enough for deckhouses unless it is very thick and small in area; plate glass is usual, toughened is an improvement, while armour glass is

Plate 6   An Ayriel *class yacht, 25 ft overall, running hard.*

Plate 7 Ayriel *showing combination of ferro hull, timber decks and superstructure.*

normally too expensive to be considered except in very special circumstances.

When the deck and deckhouse are of Elkalite or a similar form of glass-reinforced cement, it is normal (at the time of writing) to cut the window apertures after casting is completed. Such a material uses two thin skins of grc over a foam core, so that cutting apertures is far easier than in ferro-reinforced mortars. Once the apertures are cut, however, the methods described above apply.

Timber Decks and Deckhouses

Plates 6 and 7 show a 25 ft ocean-racing type of yacht, adapted for ferro from a design previously built only in cold-moulded timber. A very low hull density was achieved but, even so, it was decided to complete the vessel with timber decks and deckhouse.

In this example the ferro topsides terminated in a square-section steel tube; on this a timber wedge was fastened with self-tapping screws, upon which the plywood deck was mounted, as shown in Fig. 8, Chapter 3. In this hull we have a large aperture, with both coachroof and doghouse, so that half-beams are needed to support the structure; to accommodate these a timber beam shelf is required, together with a laminated timber carlin, which replaces that shown for the ferro-deck method (Fig. 9 in Chapter 3); but now the ply of the coachroof side comes on the inside of the carlin and the watertightness of the joint is provided by the outer beading. It will immediately be appreciated that, good though this construction is, it is unlikely to have the same long-term water resistance that is found with a ferro upstand.

A rather larger vessel using timber decks is the *Endurance 35*, designed by Peter Ibold (Plate 8).

From this point on, construction of the deckhouse follows modern timber-vessel practice. The plywood side of the coachroof terminates in an upper carlin, while the roof itself is laminated from two or three thin sheets of ply, glued together under pressure. Such a technique allows much greater curvature than is feasible with carved or bent deck beams and a roof of a single sheet of heavier ply, and adds markedly both to strength of the deck (by virtue of its curvature) and to headroom below (by the absence of deck beams). Let it here be recalled that this system of laminated, beamless decks and deckhouses (believed first promulgated by the author in 1953) is not so much a beamless deck as a continuous, deckless beam; it provides immense strength for minimal weight, but does demand glued joints in excess of 99 per cent effectiveness over a large area–a feat not always easy to achieve. This coachroof structure is shown in Fig. 15, together with such added niceties as beadings to seal the sawn edges of the ply (a combination of glass-fibre tape and external beading) and a small handrail.

It will be relatively obvious that the foredeck will follow much the same pattern as shown in Fig. 3, Chapter 1, depending largely on its length. At the aft end the cockpit will be adapted from the coachroof technique, with the proviso that the tumble-home provided for the coachroof must now become a splay-out, since to sit against a tumble-home coaming is acutely uncomfortable. It is normal to achieve these angles by planing the timber carlin to suit. However, to twist the ply of the coachroof side from one angle to the other (it is normal to have some 5 degrees of tumble-home and 5 degrees of coaming splay, so giving a 10 degree change) is rather difficult; moreover it presupposes very long lengths of ply. Thus it is normal to break the sheer at the doghouse/coaming juncture, and provide a carefully shaped wedge here. Figure 16 shows the section at the cockpit of a 25–30 ft sailboat, giving specimen scantlings appropriate to a yacht of this size and

Plate 8 Endurance 35 *is a large yacht to have timber decks, which are of marine ply sheathed with teak.*

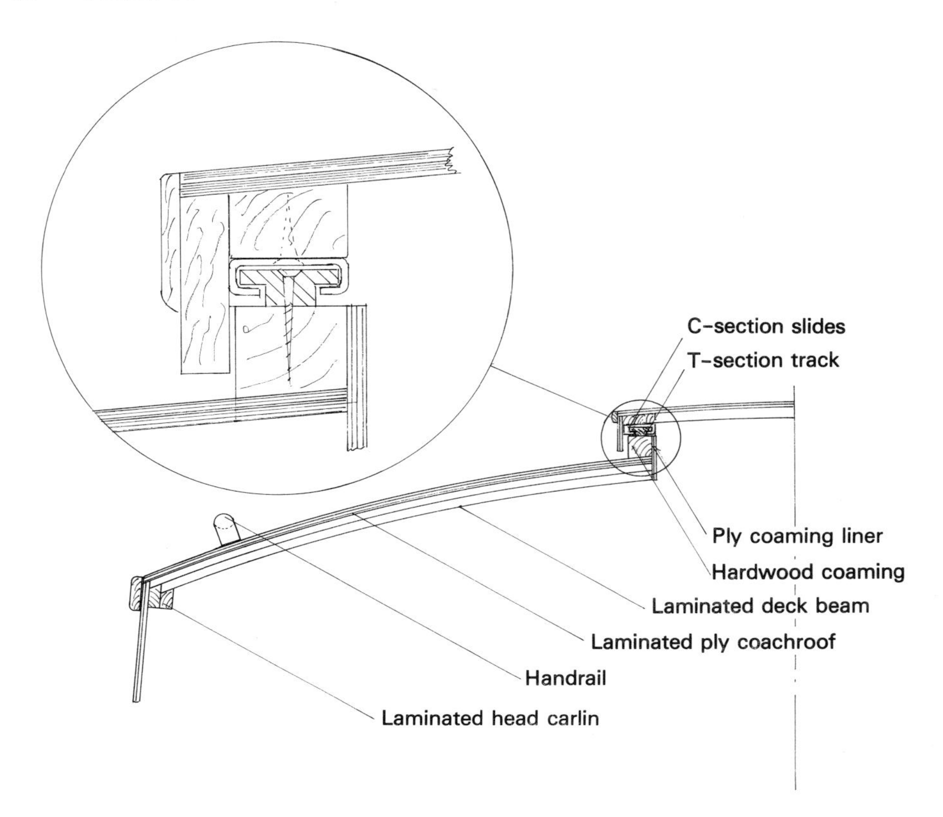

Fig. 15 Section through the timber coachroof of a sailing yacht, showing toe-rails, beams and hatch carlins.

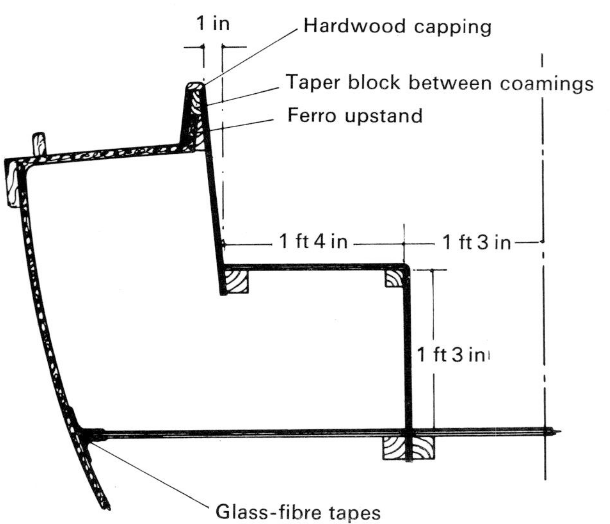

Fig. 16 Section through an all-timber cockpit based on a ferro upstand.

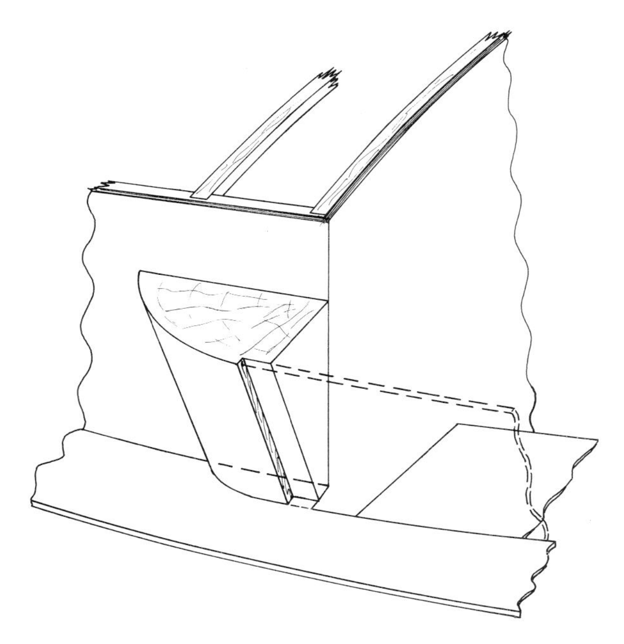

Fig. 17 A shaped wedge provides the transition from the tumble-home of the coachroof side to the splay of the cockpit coamings.

type, while Fig. 17 shows the doghouse/coaming wedge–a feature far more common on the older timber yachts than the modern grp one which is often regarded as the prototype.

Ferro Decks and Timber Deckhouses

This combination falls into three categories dependent upon the type of carlin arrangement used, namely:

(a) Timber/timber with raw ferro deck-edge
(b) Angle upstand in ferro to form carlin
(c) Tee termination forming carlin.

All three are clearly illustrated in the previous chapter, and the basic method of attachment of the deckhouse is discussed and shown.

Method (a) is really suitable only for smaller, lower superstructures on yachts up to about 35 ft overall with deckhouses whose average height does not exceed $1\frac{1}{4}$ in per foot of beam. The general construction pattern closely follows that drawn for the all-timber completion. Such a structure is clearly shown in Plate 7.

Method (b) is strong enough to carry a much higher deckhouse and thus finds favour in power cruisers and small fishing vessels; where the upstand is sufficient it may act as a cockpit coaming in such craft.

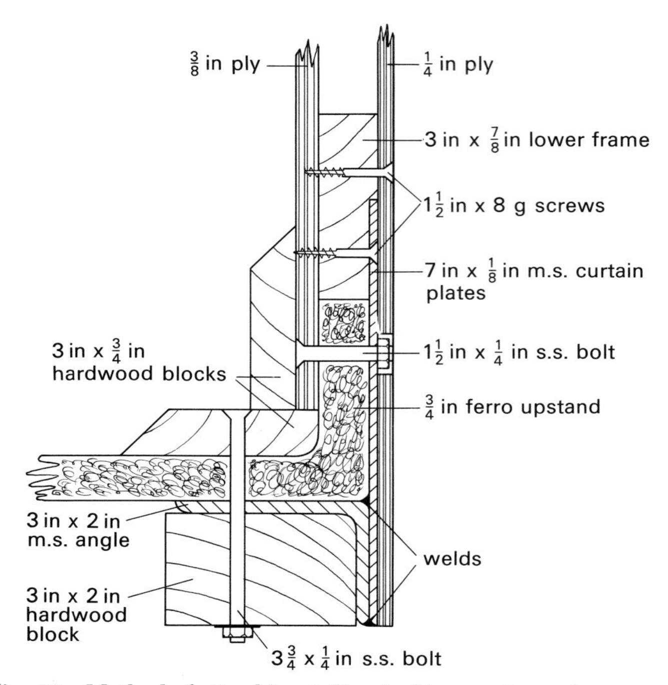

Fig. 18 Method of attaching taller deckhouses to angle upstands.

Care is needed to ensure that the upstand will provide adequate support for the height of the structure envisaged, with 1 in per foot of superstructure height as a reasonable guide on a 3 in minimum. Figure 11 in Chapter 3 shows a simple system appropriate to the 3 ft high wheelhouse on a small raised-foredeck job, while Fig. 18 shows another method, more appropriate to taller structures, with the side frames carried down to the wheelhouse sole bearers. If such a scheme is to be used for houses more than about 8 ft square, the tee carlin is advisable. Figure 19 illustrates a simple and convenient method of termination for a cockpit coaming which has not been finished in a rectangular section or similar device permitting a capping rail to be bolted on.

In planning the installation of such a wheelhouse, especially in a fishing boat where the modern tendency is to steer from forward and fish over the stern, the effect of a considerable sheer to the deck must not be overlooked.

A further area which needs consideration is the front of the deckhouse, which is seldom vertical, even in fishing craft: in yachts the front is likely to be well raked aft, which demands the most painstaking joinery; in modern workboats the trend is towards a forward rake, which certainly simplifies the timberwork but–equally–complicates the bolting. Figures 20 (a) and (b) illustrate ways of providing raked fronts from a vertical upstand.

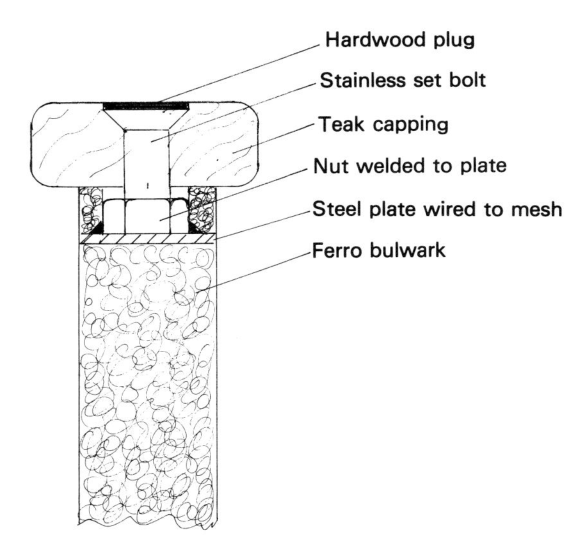

Fig. 19 Capping a ferrocement coaming or bulwark in teak or similar hardwood.

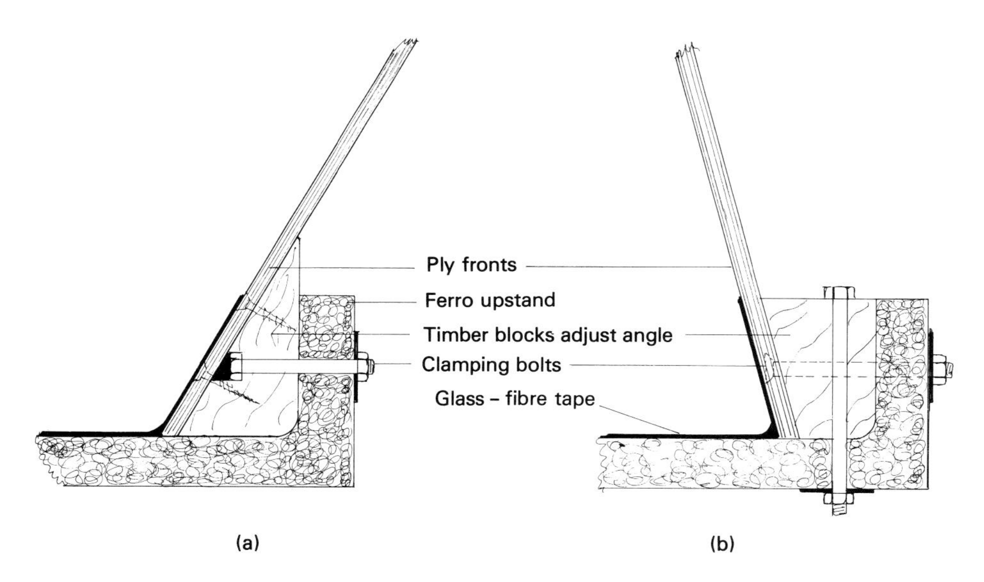

Fig. 20 Achieving raked coachroof fronts on vertical ferro upstands: (a) aft rake, (b) forward rake.

Small Metal Deckhouses

So far, all consideration has presupposed timber, especially plywood, superstructures; however, the potential of metal structures must not be overlooked. Light alloys will be mentioned, presupposing one of the seawater resistant alloys that are covered by such specifications as NP8 and DS54. Such structures have many advantages, including comparative ease of working, fair ease of sealing joints, whether welded or riveted, cold riveting rather than hot, and a high strength/weight ratio; their prime disadvantages are expense and supply, for it is sometimes difficult to get seawater grades in any but ton-lot quantities. This is a pity, for such alloys would be more commonly used if they were more widely available; it is to be hoped that the situation will improve and that later writings can give these materials the attention their mechanical properties deserve.

Meanwhile it is perhaps appropriate to note, for those who are fortunate enough to find supplies of the right materials, that the marine grades need shielded arcs for electric welding and real expertise if gas welding is used. Therefore it is better to use rivets than to risk joints for which the correct technology is not available. It is advisable to lute the joint with mastic or one of the heavy epoxy sealants, since such riveting is normally a cold process, and so the chemical properties of the luting are unaffected. The superstructure itself should be bolted to the ferro decks/upstands (it is to be clearly understood that metal deckhouses are not really suitable for mating with timber carlins) in the same way as ply or steel ones, except that stainless steel or Monel bolts should be used to reduce the potential for corrosive interaction between the alloy and the steel matrix. For like reasons, both surfaces should be de-greased (most makers of marine paints supply de-greasing agents for aluminium), given thorough coats of bituminous paint, and separated by a good layer of mastic; as ever, this should be of the kind which never really hardens. A final point to note is that the edge of the aluminium at the upstand joint will need to be stiffened with a doubler to provide enough metal to prevent distortion by the bolts; if this is riveted on, care must be taken to use countersunk-head rivets, otherwise there will be bumps between the metal and the ferro, making sealing more than slightly difficult. There is much to commend timber here; a typical ferro-alloy-timber structure is shown in Fig. 21.

Small Steel Deckhouses

Without doubt the most logical material for larger structures on a ferro hull is sheet steel: there are no corrosion problems arising from dissimilar metals; the material is stiff in its own right and thus well-suited to flat panels–and these are an essential part of larger deckhouses; it can be welded with ease, on and off the job; and, with reasonable safeguards against rust, it has longevity. The basic method follows that set out above for sheet alloy insofar as the structure is bolted to the upstand with the need for careful barrier

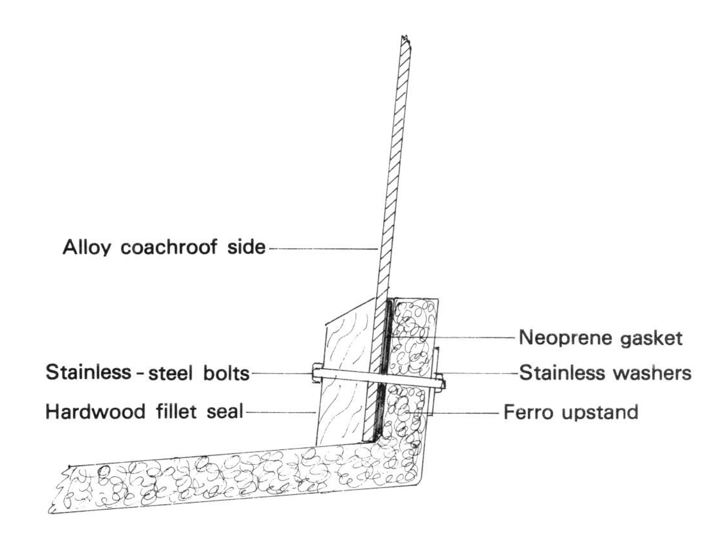

Fig. 21 Combining a low alloy coachroof and ferro angle upstand.

coatings and mastics. This is not so much because of metallurgical electrolysis as to avoid crevice corrosion, that insidious degradation which arises when two metals are separated by a very thin layer which tends to break the air down into an oxygen-enriched form and so attack the metal virulently. Not a great deal is published on these chemical processes, and that which is available presupposes a depth of academic knowledge inappropriate to a book such as this; but they do exist, they must be accepted, taken note of and guarded against.

However, the ease with which steel can be welded permits the fabrication of strong and watertight joints at the carlin with greater certainty, perhaps, than with any other material. In Fig. 22 the steel sheet is firmly through-bolted as before, but now there is an outside reverse channel welded to the main panel, so that the ferro upstand is sandwiched between the sheets. In this way, not only is the joint completely sealed against the ingress of moisture from above, but the weight of the whole structure is shared between the flange of this reverse channel and the through bolts, thus adding greatly to the strength overall. A word of caution must be sounded in the interpretation of this illustration, which shows a pressed flange welded on–a nice simple format: this works well if the deckhouse sides are quite straight or have only a small degree of curvature to which the angle can be bent during welding, but will not work if the curvature is too great. One solution here is to make the top of the flange from rectangular hollow section, for this will bend with more readiness than open angle.

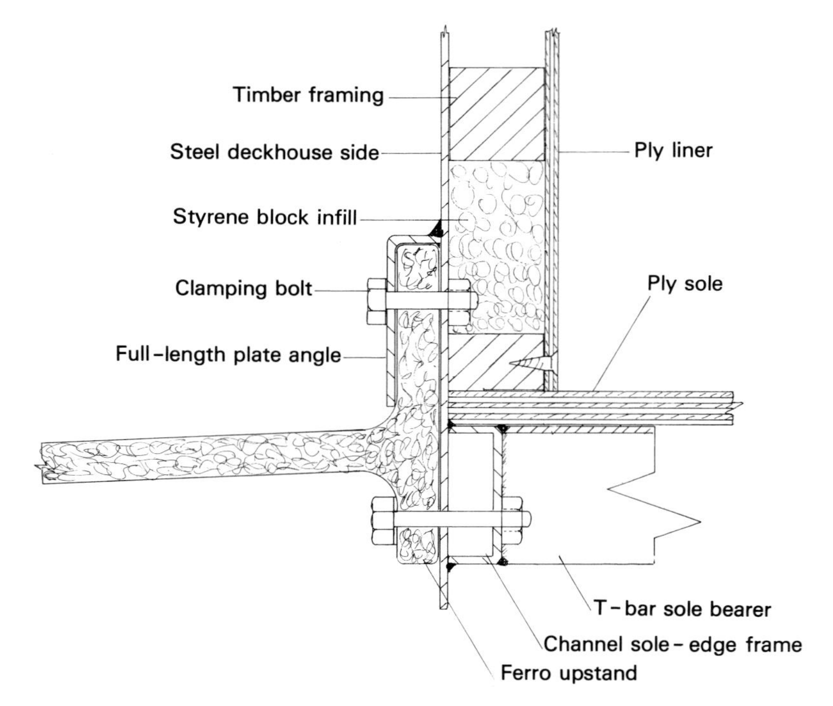

Fig. 22 A larger steel deckhouse based on a ferro tee upstand.

As ever, the sequence of operations is important if the best results are to be achieved, especially where curvature is involved. If the whole structure is square throughout, then the channel can be fully welded on and all the holes drilled before the house is brought to the hull. But where this technique cannot be adopted with certainty, a method of cut and try is inevitable, as follows:

(a) Make a hardboard template of the profile of the upstand.
(b) Mark on it the positions of the bulkheads, stiffening frames, etc., and in the light of these determine the positions of the through-bolt holes.
(c) From the template mark out the carlin edge of the steel plate and drill the bolt holes.
(d) From the template drill the bolt holes in the upstand; core and seal if necessary.
(e) Bolt the sides of the house to the upstand, using alternate bolt holes, with the nuts on the upstand side, to permit later removal.
(f) Tack-weld any butts needed in the panels.
(g) Again using the bolting template (a), mark off and drill the holes in the vertical web of the flange.
(h) With the aid of such levers, fids, etc., as are needed, bolt the flange through upstand and steel plate, using the empty alternate holes

left when the sheet was bolted in. To do this it follows that the nuts already holding the panel must be removed and the bolt ends tapped back flush with the ferro, to permit the outer flange to lie equally flush. It follows that care is needed to achieve the proper sequence of bolt insertion and removal. (*Note.* When the upstand is of the tee format or the coachroof sides are very low, the sheets can most conveniently be held in place by G-clamps and the flange bolted on without previous fixing.)

(i) When the flange is firmly held to the contours required by the upstand, tack weld it to the coachroof side, using 2 in tacks on 8 in centres.
(j) Remove the whole structure from the hull, reverse it and tack weld the underside of the flange, placing the tacks between those on the upper face.
(k) Complete the fillet welds on the exposed face of the joint.
(l) Complete any butt welds in the sides and add any stiffeners needed.
(m) If possible, complete the superstructure of the boat.
(n) Replace either the whole superstructure or the sides and front, first painting the mating surfaces with epoxy tar and luting the joint with mastic or bedding compound. Remember that both sides of the upstand (and its top face) are classed as joints and need luting. All the bolts will be inserted, probably in a skip sequence to provide an even distribution of pull-down strain.

There are two schools of thought on this item, both valid, namely whether to build the deckhouse *in situ* or off the boat. Certainly the latter course demands confidence in one's measurements and checks for distortion, for it may prove impossible to make the bolt holes realign if the flange/side system has distorted during fabrication of the structure as a whole; moreover, a fairly large structure is apt to need a fair size of crane to lift it on to a large vessel. However, it does more readily permit the use of heat sinks to reduce welding distortion, and allows work to proceed in the hull while the deckhouse is under construction, which can save considerable time if the house is fairly large or complex: in a smallish vessel it may be useful to do much of the interior work before adding the deckhouse, and here an *in situ* job can produce a fire hazard from welding sparks. In passing it might be commented that fabrication on a rough jig of either timber or steel angle can greatly reduce the chances of error or distortion.

A steel deckhouse will require lining to prevent condensation, and this is reflected in the construction for, unless the house is very small and low, it will be stiffened, the usual form being angles or tees, toe-welded to the sheet. In general terms the scantlings of these stiffeners are chosen to give a metal thickness up to 50 per cent greater than that of the sheet and areas of 12 times the sheet gauge; thus a $\frac{1}{8}$ in sheet would be stiffened with $1\frac{1}{2} \times 1\frac{1}{2} \times \frac{3}{16}$ in tee or angle; the same would hold a $\frac{5}{32}$ in sheet and a $\frac{3}{16}$ in one would use $2 \times 2 \times \frac{1}{4}$ in maximally. These figures must be taken as wide approximations, for the scantlings are determined more by the volume of the house to be supported. But with such framing the builder can line his steel with styrene blocks, either glued to the steel or jammed between the frames, and panel out with pegboard, hardboard or ply, held to the frame webs with self-tapping screws. Prior to the placement of such insulation all the steel-work should be heavily wire-brushed to remove loose millscale and surface rust and given a good coat of epoxy tar.

When the structure is small enough or curved enough to stand without frames it is preferable to insulate with a flexible foam such as polyurethane, totally glued to the steel by one of the proprietary adhesives developed for this work, such as Clam or Bostik. A sheet thickness of $\frac{3}{4}$ in should suffice for most applications. Domestic styrene tiles are sometimes used, and can be adequate for yachts normally used under temperate maritime conditions, but the fixing instructions supplied therewith–'a dab at each corner and one in the middle'–must be ignored, for the entire surface of the tile must be coated with glue.

Framing of the deckhead itself will depend on the amount of curvature involved and on the facilities available; angle or tee sections are markedly less tractable than rectangular hollow sections, and this will either mean restriction to curvatures of under about 14 ft radius equivalent or will require rolling to shape; rhs will bend more easily cold, and a fair degree of curve (say to 10 ft radius equivalent) can be achieved by hand, using a simple pipe-bending tool or even the wooden beam with a hole in it known colloquially as a 'plumber's mate'. When the curvature is comparatively slight it can often be induced simply by jacking up the beam centre, with a vertical bar and wedges, to the requisite crop and expecting the deckhead to hold it when the plates are welded into place, which it usually does.

As with the sides, insulation is needed and is carried out as outlined above, except that the deckhead curvature is likely to call for flexible foams. Total-area glueing is necessary. It is useful to organize the system to leave a gap of $\frac{1}{2}$ in or so between the foam and the lining, be it board or stretched fabric, to allow the easier running of cables for cabin lighting. Incidentally, these cable runs should be planned

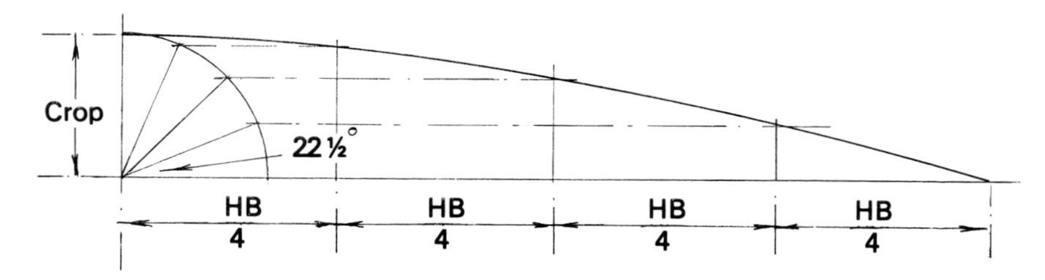

Fig. 23 Traditional method of determining deck camber.

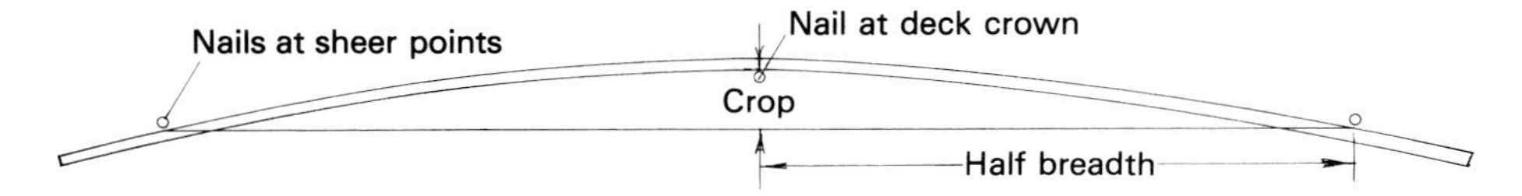

Fig. 24 Camber drawn by the sprung-batten method.

before the foam is placed, for they will almost certainly demand drilling of the deck beams.

In passing, a note should be added on deck crop and camber, which are germane to all constructions. Two terms are here used and may be defined:

Crop is the height of the deck centre above a straight line from sheer to sheer.

Camber is the upward curve of the deck from one side to the other. There are three ways of calculating camber:

(a) The traditional deck curve in which evenly spaced crop ordinates equal the vertical intercepts on the main crop circle produced by basic angle lines, as shown in Fig. 23.

(b) The jack-curve method in which the curve is that taken up by a batten held only at three points, namely sheer, crop centre and sheer, as in Fig. 24.

(c) The true-arc method, in which the camber is the arc of a circle; here the extremities are more heavily curved than in methods (a) and (b) which were devised to overcome this. But machines are usually happier rolling a true arc; moreover, if each beam has the same radius, or if their radii change uniformly, and if the centre line is straight, then the deckhead plates will form part of a cylinder or a cone and so lie smoothly without distortion. For guidance, if a change to arc-form is contemplated, the rolling radius is given by

$$R = (b^2 + h^2)/2h$$

where b = half the beam or width of deckhouse
h = crop at centre of curvature.

It is doubtful whether conversion to this form pays once the curvature radius exceeds 15 ft.

Chapter Five **Large Deckhouses**

By a large deckhouse we imply in essence a two-deck vessel, even if this is merely a deck-level wheelhouse above a low-headroom engine compartment. Structurally the essential features are weight and windage, coupled with the presupposition that the house sole is at or about main deck level. For such a structure a full ferro upstand is mandatory, and a tee edge is better than a simple angle. The upstand has two jobs: it must support the deckhouse, and it must carry the sole and sole bearers.

Ply Deckhouses

Trixie is a 65 ft MFV-type yacht, a heavy displacement craft with a timber deckhouse; this structure contains a very large saloon (21 ft by 13 ft 6 in), a galley and, right forward, a pilot house combined with chart room. Designed primarily for tropical living, *Trixie* has relatively narrow side decks at main deck level, but her boat deck extends the full width of the ship, overhanging the deckhouse and so providing shade to the windows from a sun high overhead, and protection from heavy rain; moreover, streamlined support arms add greatly to the lateral rigidity, giving the house a 4-point support structure instead of the more normal two. Plate 9 shows how the structure finally looked when afloat; Fig. 25 shows a longitudinal section and Fig. 26 a transverse section.

From Fig. 25 we see the problem posed by the rising sheer: a single-level sole would have stood well above the deck aft if at an acceptable level forward, or been far too low forward if acceptable aft. The obvious solution was a step (or rather, steps) for:

Plate 9 This photograph of Trixie *clearly shows the forward-raking deckhouse with overhung boat deck.*

(a) There is a step up of 1 ft in the main deck level (largely to bring up the cabin sole levels where the forebody begins to fine down).
(b) There is a 9 in step up just aft of this inside the deckhouse, used to divide the saloon from the galley and pilot house.
(c) There is a similar step in the boat deck immediately above this, to maintain headroom.

Steps (a) and (b) meant some complexity in the tee edge of the upstand, while (c) posed difficulties only of appearance, for it was considered desirable to give the impression that both decks flowed with the sheer. However, since it was earlier agreed that the upper control station would be an open bridge (for a full wheelhouse would have looked very high), we designed a clover-leaf structure in light alloy which embraced the bridge in the centre, occupying only half the beam, with forward facing breakwaters outboard of this, sweeping back to the rear of the funnel and completely hiding the upper-deck step. Later, however, it was decided to replace these with an open steel rail giving access around the front of the flying bridge; the step thus became visible, but the valance and toe-rail system blends it smoothly. The low, streamlined, funnel/mast complex grows naturally out of the step (it carries the heat-extraction system from the ventilation rather than the engine exhausts). The aesthetics of the design of funnels and masts, and even more of the mast/funnel combination, are

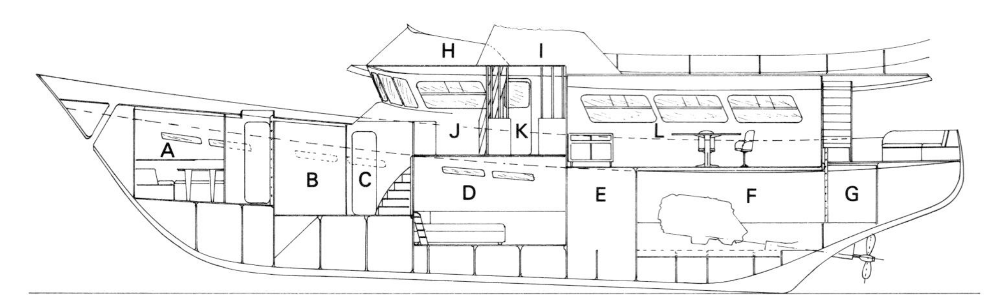

Fig. 25 Longitudinal section of Trixie *showing the stepped-saloon solution to the problem of matching superstructure sole to rising sheer.*

A Crew's quarters	*G Lazarette*
B Toilet shared by two guest cabins	*H Flying bridge*
C Lobby leading to two guest cabins	*I Funnel/mast*
D Owner's suite	*J Pilot house*
E 10-ton fuel bunker	*K Galley*
F Engine room	*L Deck saloon*

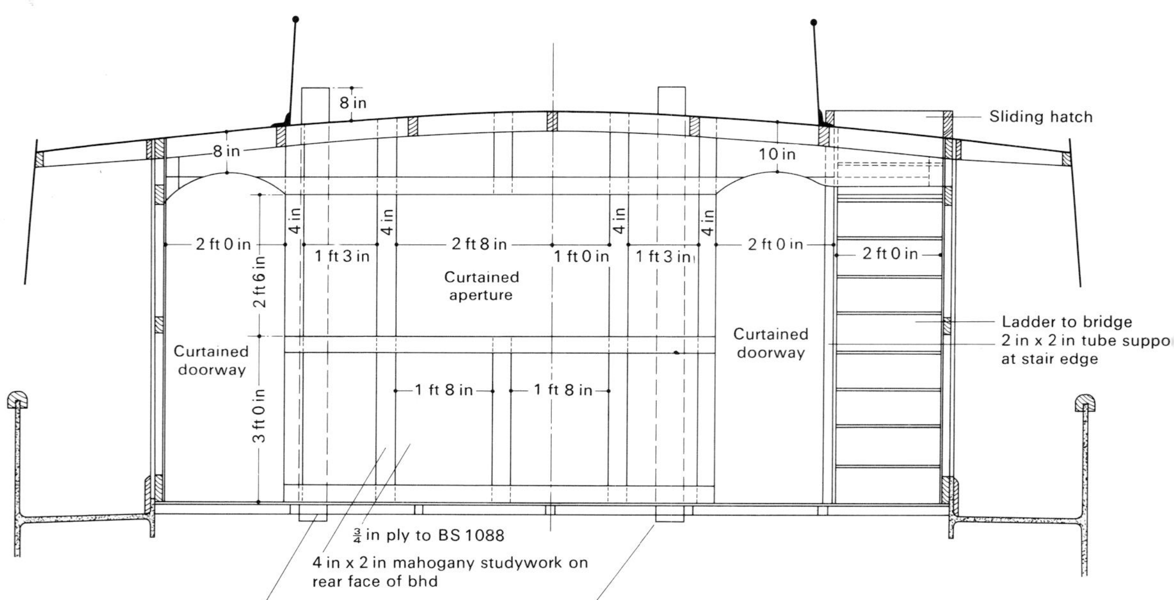

Fig. 26 Transverse section of deckhouse at step (Station 11).

definitely thorny and beyond the scope of this book; all we can say is that it is easy to make mistakes, to produce structures which are just too high or too large, or to design them small and neat on paper and find them dwarfed by people in practice.

Because this yacht will spend its life in tropical waters, great attention was paid to the flow of air through the deckhouse, since most of her owner's living time will be spent here rather than below. Moreover, she is intended as a home, with the owner's wife rather than a paid hand in the galley, which is one reason for putting the galley in the deckhouse and not below. In consideration of these factors it was decided to erect a strong support system at the steps, based on a wall of polished metal tubes of square section doubly clad in ply to the height of the cooking equipment; this was teamed with a similar division wall between galley and pilot house, so allowing unobstructed flow of air from end to end of an open-vista, light and airy house. Moreover, the cook would not be confined between four walls, but would be part of the company when preparing meals; equally, the feeling of space, plus the airflow, would be invaluable in very hot weather. Regretfully it must be reported that the classification society supervising construction could not conceive of a deckhouse which was not redolent with solid bulkheads, so the outcome was a pair of small cabins forward, as Plate 10 shows.

Had this deckhouse, measuring 34 ft by 13 ft 6 in, been all at one level its support would have been a considerable problem; but, as Fig. 25 shows, there is a deep step and an all-ferro fuel bunker, so that the largest unsupported area is only 13 ft by 13 ft 6 in over the engine room. With the sole at two levels and effectively in three sections it was decided to fit curtain plates of $\frac{1}{4}$ in mild steel to the ferro upstands, bolted at frequent intervals, and to weld to these sole bearers of 4×2 in rectangular hollow section (rhs) steel tubes. It is true that tee or angle bar might have been lighter, but the rhs allows both the deck itself and the lining below it to be fastened simply by self-tapping screws. Intercostals of the same section increased the overall rigidity, and were spaced so as to carry portable plates (as distinct from true hatches, which are by implication opened more often and more easily) over the engines and over the master stateroom, the latter to pass the double bed below. But a span of 13 ft 6 in requires intermediate supports, even if not demanded for classification; in the engine room these are provided by steel pillars welded to the deckhead framework and bolted to the engine bearers; in the master stateroom they carry the bathroom/bedroom interwall which, although well off-centre, reduces the unsupported span to an acceptable 9 ft. It will here be seen that the need to support such a large sole must affect the layout in the hull beneath it, and this must be catered for in the design-planning stage; it cannot be met as an afterthought. Methods and spacings vary with both classification rules and the stiffness modules of the beams, but a reasonable first guide might be that the unsupported length in feet should not significantly exceed 1·25 times the cross-section of the beam envelope in square inches; thus a 4×2 in rhs structure needs pillars about 10 ft apart, though this would not hold good if the deeper section of the beam were horizontal rather than vertical. Another way of putting it might be to limit the span to $2\frac{1}{2}$ times the beam depth but this, too, needs care insofar that the

Plate 10 Looking forward in Trixie's *deckhouse, it can be seen how the partial bulkheads demanded by Lloyds cut off the galley and wheelhouse; the step in levels is also clearly seen.*

cross-arm width contributes to the beam's resistance to distortion. The use of bending modules is safest, of course, but these are not normally available outside design offices. Finally it should be noted that these approximations are for straight beams: putting a camber of $\frac{1}{2}$ in per foot in the upper deck enabled 4 × 2 in beams to span 13 ft 6 in without support, for the curve–even one so slight–adds sufficient to the beam strength.

This method of building the deckhouse sole bearers led to a useful by-product. When the whole system had been welded to the curtain plates and all these plates had been welded together and bolted to the ferro upstand, the entire structure was unbolted from the hull, craned off and moved away from the building slip into the woodwork shop. Re-erected, blocked up and trued for level, it became the base on which the whole deckhouse was built, away from the hull, thus allowing interior engineering to proceed in the hull without the complications of joiners working overhead and of a deckhead in place to restrict light, access and movement. As it happens, the restricted headroom in the building shop would have precluded erection before launching and, indeed, the road-bridge clearances between the yard and the sea eventually led to the completed deck-house being fitted well away from the yard after a road journey.

In a yacht–or even a modern working boat–it is not really acceptable to show the framework supporting the sides of a deckhouse, and some cladding is normal. In this large yacht it was decided to take this concept to the obvious stage of using a heavy cladding and so produce cabin sides with an I-beam structure of really enormous strength; the final scantlings called for $\frac{3}{4}$ in outer and $\frac{3}{8}$ in inner plies, glued and screwed to 4 × 2 in framing, closely spaced as shown in Fig. 27. The interframe spaces were filled with tailored styrene blocks 2 in thick, for otherwise they would have filled with damp air which would have rotted the timber in short order; again, even so fragile a material as styrene adds greatly to the strength of the structure when glued to both enclosing sheets. Such a structure is not cheap; but it passes the requirements of a classification society and hence has more than a fighting chance–indeed, as near a guarantee as can be given–of withstanding the worst that the sea and wind can throw at it.

Figure 28 shows how this timberwork is attached at the deck and Fig. 29 the arrangement of the deck beam and edge valance adopted. It should be noted that this edge valance, being a sheet on edge and thus constituting a tee-beam at the edge of the upper deck, greatly stiffens this deck and virtually eliminates any chance of its flexing.

It was earlier noted that the overhung deck edge is supported by two arms, raked and blended in the manner normal on large liners. Again, a box structure with styrene filling was used, with careful blending of the upper-end structure into the valance to ensure good stress distribution. The lower ends of the arms are bolted to the ferro bulwark; Fig. 30 shows the method. Care in workmanship is vital here, for any gapping between ply and ferro will attract water and so lead to rot. Mastic is needed on both mating faces, and it is to be hoped that a really effective gap-filling sealant/adhesive will soon be available.

When finally sheathed in glass fibre and epoxy resin, and fitted with opening windows in light-alloy frames, plus access doors with deep storm sills and with a well-constructed ladder between decks, such a deckhouse is expensive, whether built by professional or amateur: indeed, if one adds mast, funnel and guardrails, its cost from a professional builder may equal that of the hull and decks it surmounts. But its strength can match theirs and it will endure as long as they do.

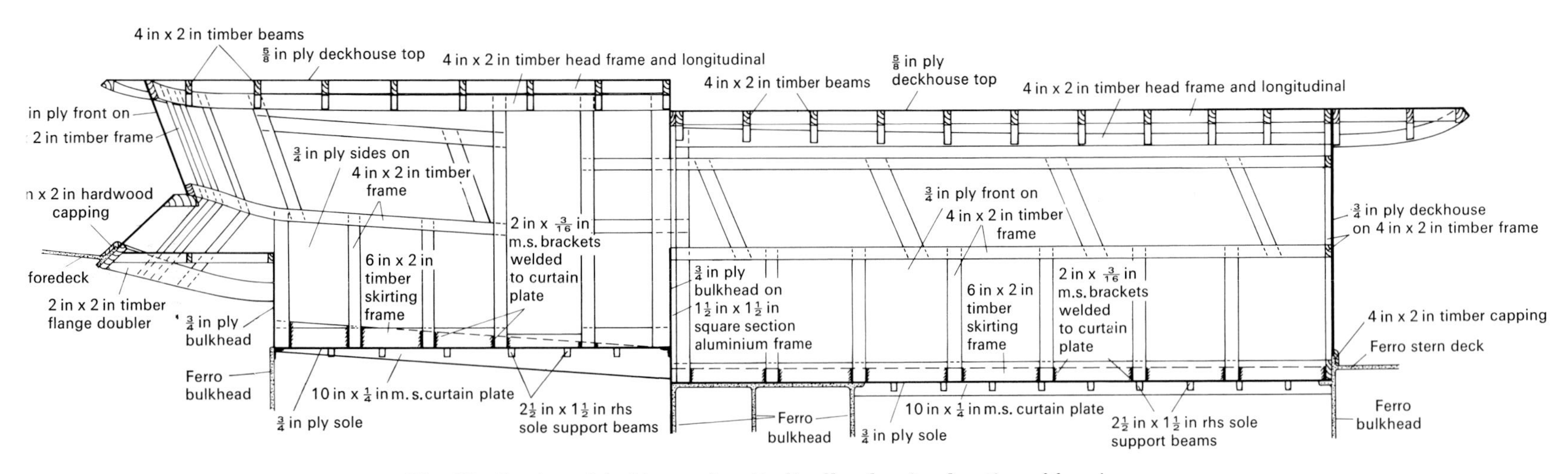

Fig. 27 Section of deckhouse, longitudinally, showing location of framing.

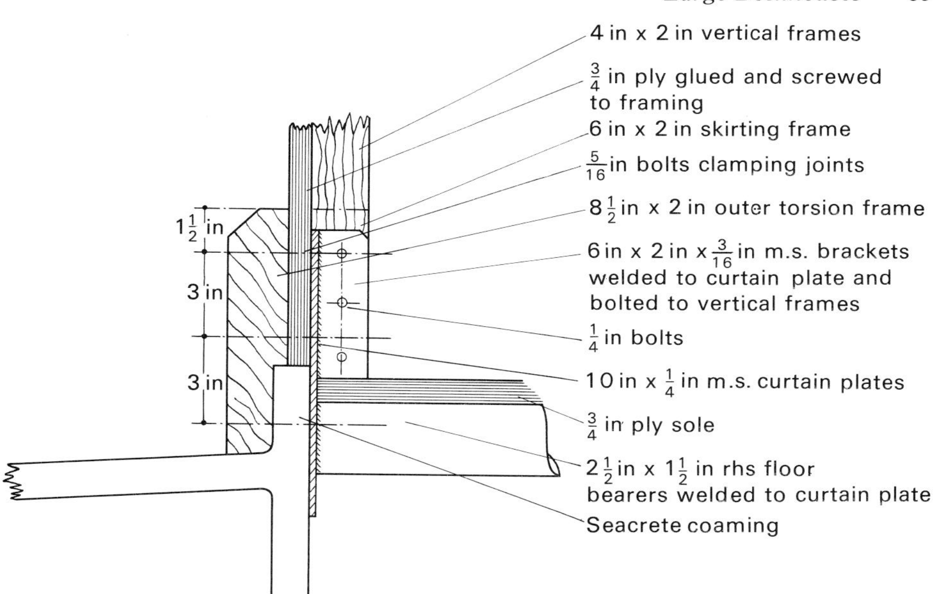

Fig. 28 Section through deck carlin of a very large deckhouse.

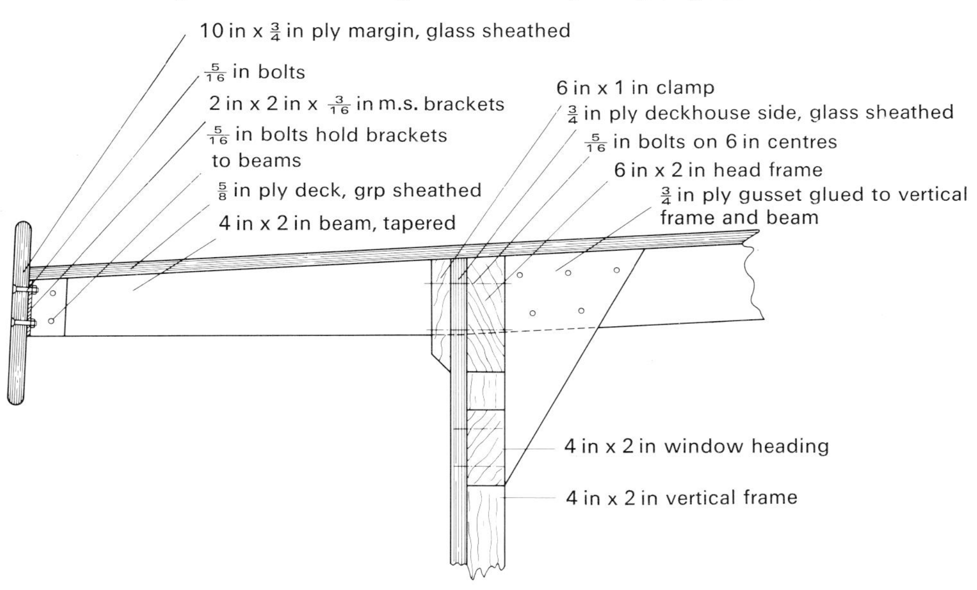

Fig. 29 Section at head carlin of the deckhouse in Fig. 28.

Steel Deckhouses

Rovonne illustrates the other approach on similar lines, the essential difference being in the use of steel instead of ply for the deckhouse. Her hull form is similar in being an MFV type, with heavy displacement, high ferro bulwarks and an upswept sheer. Again the layout

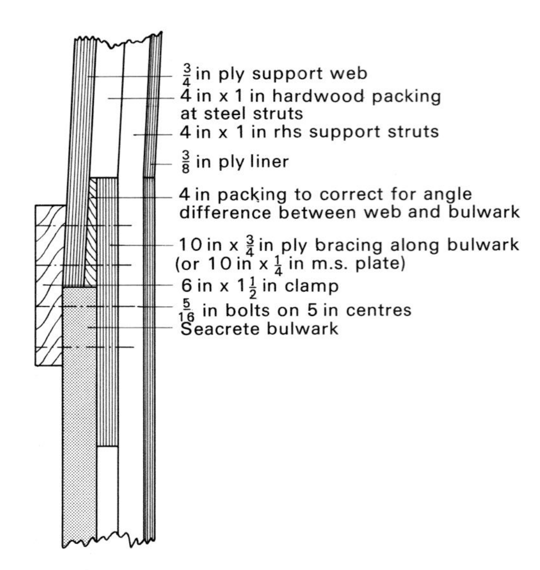

Fig. 30 Joint between the ferro bulwark and the wooden arms supporting the boat deck.

chosen placed a deck saloon over the engines and again her use as a mobile home in tropical waters led to the siting of the galley in the deckhouse. The 15 ft reduction in length is, of course, accompanied by a reduction in depth, so that the *Trixie* concept of three levels–stateroom, pilot house and galley, flying bridge–was not feasible and a two-level system was really the only one. This means that much of the navigation and handling will be done from the wheelhouse, so that the helmsman must necessarily be relatively higher than in the larger yacht. Thus a clear-cut change of level is unavoidable, but it is now blended with the funnel to make a design feature. Within the deckhouse itself this step of 2 ft makes it very difficult to open the saloon and wheelhouse into a single unit, and the decision to go for complete separation is a wise one. Of course, provided the wheelhouse is not overburdened with navigation equipment it will be an excellent spot in which to sit when the sun is not too hot.

Again, the boat deck overlaps the deckhouse to give protected side decks and shade the windows from tropical sun. There is, of course, a substantial step in the side decks, allowing higher soles in the accommodation, but careful use of styling features allows the single-level aspect to be maintained, as shown in Fig. 31. The feature which makes *Rovonne* stems from this, for the line of the boat-deck valance is continued forward to provide a substantial steel bulwark alongside the wheelhouse; continuation of this around the front of the house provides an open bridge of easy access, and a second control station here permits the yacht to be handled from outside. The steelwork also forms a useful breakwater to protect the deckhouse proper should

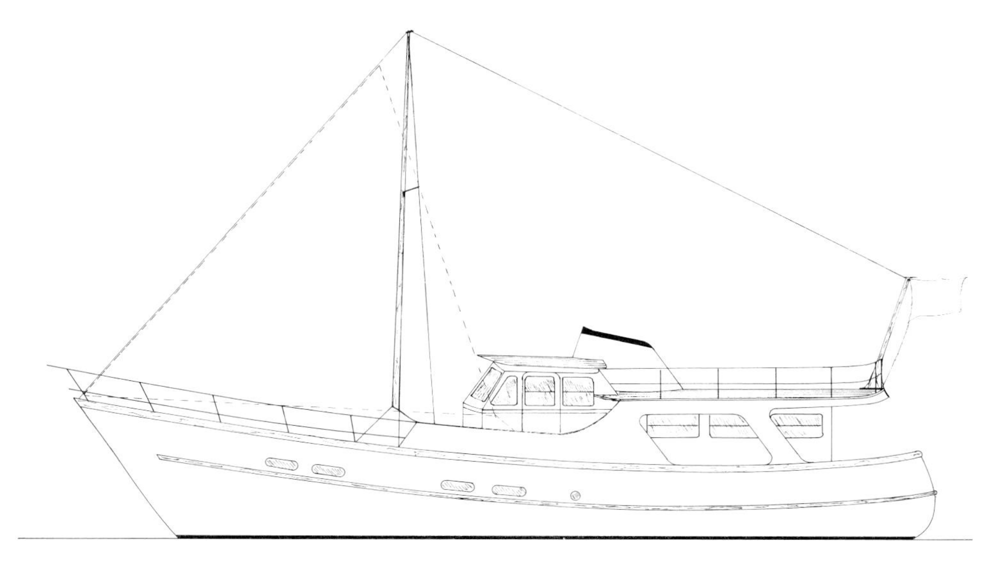

Fig. 31 Profile of 50 ft ocean cruiser Rovonne.

she encounter conditions so bad as to cause her to pitch her head right into green water. Substantial guardrails go forward and around the bows, providing protection on the large foredeck; there is room here to carry a good-sized launch, leaving the boat deck itself to an inflatable and life raft.

Whereas *Trixie* was designed to achieve her range by tankage alone, and could theoretically steam over 7000 miles on her bunkers by using each engine alternately, *Rovonne* has no such capacity and achieves her 3500 miles by supplementing her propellers with sails. While these are not large, and require Trade winds for efficacy, their presence calls for two masts, which have a profound effect on styling. *Trixie's* funnel/mast is out, as is the twin funnel idea popular with working versions of the hull: early sketches indicate a feel for rather a tall funnel and only one mast, braced from the breakwater and carrying a square sail, but the final option was for a low, long funnel and fore-and-aft sails on one mast. A further alternative would be to use a flying bridge here, in place of a funnel, but, while there could be adequate protection when seated at the helm, there could be a great feeling of insecurity when standing, especially in a seaway. In this respect the difference in size between the 50- and the 65-footers shows very clearly. In passing, and especially as an aid to those planning such layouts, it should be noted that one strong reason for the reduced funnel height was the decision to mount the radar scanner atop the wheelhouse: this device is fairly heavy (around 200 lb) and sweeps a circle of 5 ft diameter. Cantilever mounting off the front of the mast is not a good engineering concept–it was difficult enough on *Trixie*, where the mast is very broad-based.

So much for the aesthetics and layout. The structure is based on the same techniques as on the larger boat, with 4 × 2 in sole supports welded to a curtain plate of mild steel, bolted to the tee-section upstand at the carlin. Areas spanned are much smaller, the aperture over the engine room being only 11 ft by 11 ft: despite this, pillars fall to the engine bearers, more because they are easy to fit and do a good job than because they are really vital. A ferro bulkhead divides the engine room and accommodation up to main deck level aft, and is continued above this in a ply sandwich, as on *Trixie*. The wheelhouse is 11 ft by 7 ft 6 in and is carried in the same way, but the presence of a corridor 3 ft wide beneath it reduces the unsupported span enormously by virtue of the longitudinal bulkheads, again of ply sandwich on 2 × 2 in rhs verticals.

The sides, back and front of this deckhouse are fabricated in $\frac{3}{16}$ in mild-steel plate framed in 2 × 2 × $\frac{3}{16}$ in tee bar toe-welded to the sheet; this reduces the ply lining to a lining as such rather than an integral part of a sandwich, so that $\frac{1}{4}$ in ply is adequate especially when the styrene infill panels are glued to it. The deep step makes it far more difficult to build this house away from the hull, for the sheet-steel sides must perforce contribute to the holding together of the curtain-plate system; despite the possibility of crevice corrosion in the long term, it is felt that lapping the sides over the outside of the curtain plates produces the strongest job.

The boat deck itself could with advantage be of $\frac{3}{16}$ in treadplate, for this deck will not often be used by large numbers; however, the attraction remains of teak planking bolted down on $\frac{1}{4}$ in studs welded to the plates, and contributing enough to the strength of the deck to permit a reduction of steel plate thickness to $\frac{1}{8}$ in, with $\frac{1}{2}$ × 4 in teak planks. A number of adhesives are available to glue teak to steel which, of course, much strengthens the structure; care should be taken to read the instructions, for with some adhesives the teak must be wiped with a detergent before glueing to remove its natural surface oil. Again, be sure to leave adequate gaps (half the plank thickness) between planks, filling these with a non-hardening mastic, to allow for expansion when wet. The deck itself is carried on 3 × 2 in tee bar, toe-welded to the steel and lined with $\frac{1}{4}$ in ply held in place by self-tapping screws. As before, styrene infill panels are glued to both ply and steel, but these might be planned to allow fully recessed fluorescent-light panels, and should certainly be arranged to permit easy running of all wiring leads.

The beams terminate in a $\frac{3}{16}$ in steel valance, which in turn links with the support arms in the same material. It is reckoned good practice to bring these arms flush with the outside of the ferro bulwark, so a joggle must be pressed or welded in to carry the steel down inside the bulwark for bolting. Figure 32 sections this joint and shows how the joggle is hidden by a plywood lining; once more the liner and foam infill is used as a sandwich to increase strength.

In the working version of this craft, where cost and simplicity assume greater importance, the arms can be taken straight down inside the bulwark without the joggle; in this event the fore and aft edges should be supported by 2 × 2 in angle bar, toe-welded, to protect the edges otherwise exposed. Great care is needed to seal the joint between steel and ferro to prevent ingress of water, and it may be advisable to grind away the inside angle at the top of the bulwark and fill this with an epoxy sealant.

Finally when the overhung deck is short and lightly stressed, as in *Lake Fisher*, a tropical side trawler, it may be sufficient to terminate the arm support in a simple angle structure, with bolts alternately horizontal and vertical. While it lacks the ultimate strength of the larger systems discussed in detail above, it is adequate over a wide range of usages and should be given serious consideration before being rejected in favour of greater complexity. It cannot have the same resistance to torsional or cantilever loadings, but where it is felt that these are not high, the method is viable; such a situation might have been brought about in *Trixie*, for example, had there been three support arms instead of two.

Full-width Deckhouses

There is a strong temptation towards the concept discussed above in which an upper deck overhangs side decks, for it provides protection

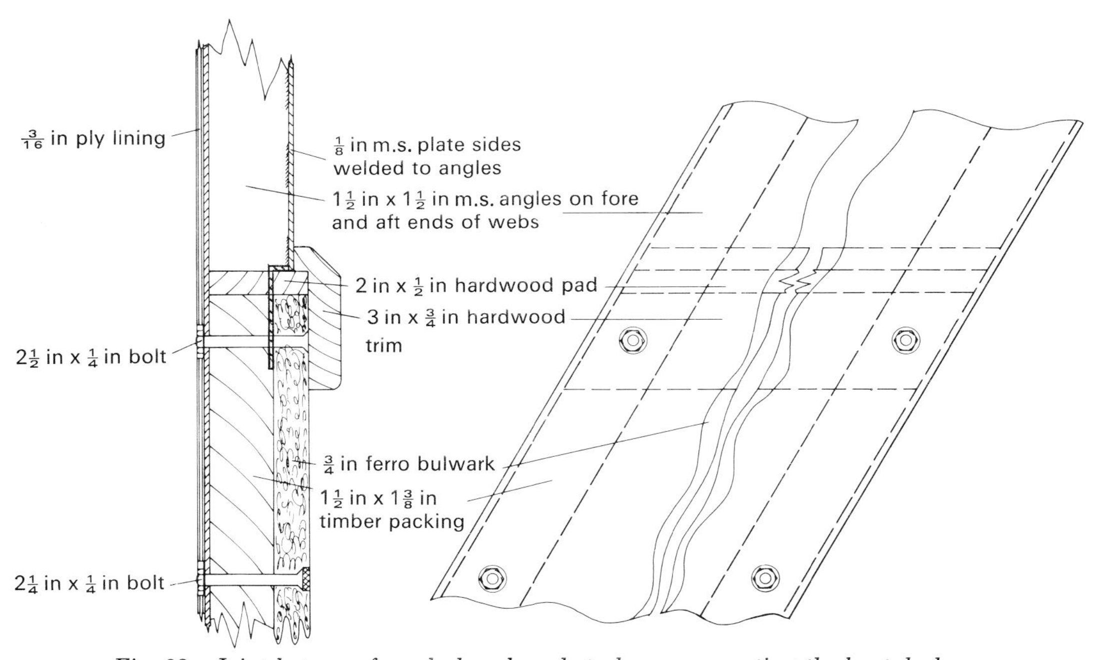

Fig. 32 Joint between ferro bulwark and steel arm supporting the boat deck.

from the sun or rain and rapid access from foredeck to stern. Earlier this century, however, there was a vogue for the full-width house, which could prove most useful when the requirement calls for sleeping cabins on deck as well as below, obviously at the expense of saloon space.

There could be difficulties in applying this to either of the hulls discussed above, because of the need for steps in the decks, and *Rovonne* will react markedly better than *Trixie*. In Fig. 33 we see the effect of this on the smaller boat. To go aft, one must enter the wheel-house and pass through the saloon, but the structure is strong and the distance to be traversed is not great. The length of the full-width superstructure is, in fact, only 11 ft, and it is probable that practice with a boathook or similar aid could much ease the problems of handling fend-offs when mooring. Figure 34 compares the layouts in block form, and the significant gain in saloon space shows clearly. But it must be noted that a significant degree of tumble-home needs to be built in, to reduce the chance of damage to the windows when rolling alongside a quay or jetty; in some tidal ports with passing commercial traffic this could be a real threat.

Structurally there are two problems:

(a) Two joints must do the work of the four previously discussed.
(b) These joints must remain watertight when exposed to the full force of the sea.

It seems likely that the most promising solution is the inverted channel, using an all-steel structure; the main sides of the house come down to some 6 in below the bulwark on the inside with a welded channel on the outside; through bolts clamp the arms of the channel

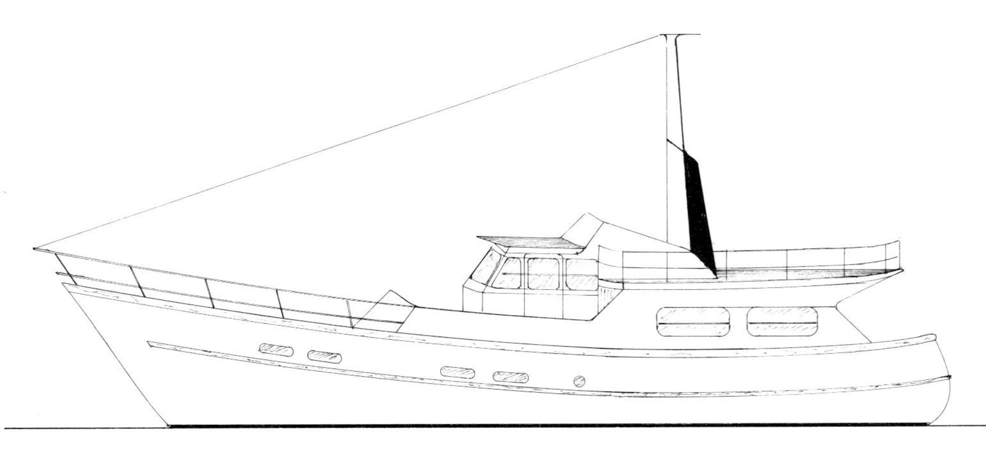

Fig. 33 Rovonne *as modified to incorporate a full-width deckhouse; the owner opted for an upper flying bridge, so moving the funnel/mast aft and leading to a complete change of styling.*

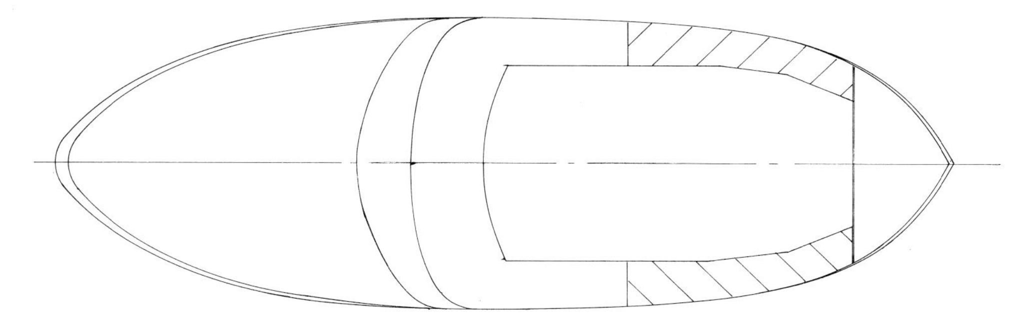

Fig. 34 Comparison of the deckhouses in the two Rovonnes*; the saloon areas are 215 and 275 sq ft so that the side decks, shown hatched, occupy 22 per cent of the available area.*

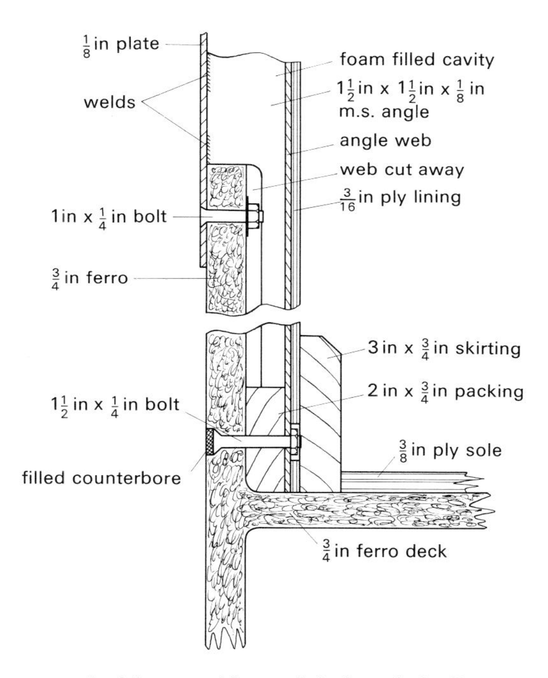

Fig. 35 Joint between deckhouse side and bulwark in Rovonne *with full-width deckhouse.*

so formed, and a Neoprene gasket between the outer steel and the ferro bulwark reduces crushing loads on the ferro and adds to the water resistance. The steel structure needs to be carried on frames, which in turn must go down the full depth of the ferro bulwark and there be bolted, a situation which calls for channel-section frames rather than tees. (See Fig. 35.)

It can truly be argued that it would be easier to secure a watertight joint by bringing the main sheet outside the bulwark and having the support channel inside. However, this then means a joggle in the vertical framing or a most expertly welded joint at a broken frame, with channel up the ferro joined to a tee on the steel: dangerous if one is not perfectly certain of welding.

It follows, of course, that this type of deckhouse is not feasible if ferro side-decks and upstands are already in place, unless one is prepared for the drastic step of cutting away the up-facing part of the carlin edge and leaving only the down-facing lower half.

If the full-width aperture does exist, the normal sole bearers can be put in; for such a short length as on the *Rovonne* example it is likely that the through-bolted curtain-plate system will work, though it must be noted that the hull will have a plethora of bolt holes, which is not good. Again, with confidence in the welds, the sole bearers can be welded to the vertical frames carrying the superstructure, though the possible sheer load on the bolting system must be calculated beforehand. The use of support pillars below the sole bearers now becomes vital, and great care must be exercised in the design stage to ensure adequate bracing from below, to minimize the loadings on the side fastenings. Of course, if it is possible to add a ferrocement ring shelf to carry the outboard edge of the sole, then the sole structure itself will contribute to its own support.

In consideration of these structural problems one must conclude that the decision to erect a full-width house should not be undertaken without the closest co-operation of a qualified naval architect specializing in ferrocement.

Chapter Six The Rig

Because of the low materials cost of the hull, and even the low cost of a professionally-built hull, many a builder in ferro has spoilt his ship at the rig stage, for the combined cost of spars, sails, standing and running rigging can frighten even the experienced. He who fits out his own interior can use ingenuity and craftsmanship to produce first-class results at low cost; while he who is determined and knowledgeable, with a mechanical bent, may save much by marinizing an automotive power unit or by rebuilding a secondhand marine engine. But on rig the savings are few and problematical. True, anyone capable of building a large yacht and fitting it out below should be artful enough to build his own wooden spars, but it is difficult to buy all the requisite fittings for these and recourse to a blacksmith may be needed. Prime spruce or Oregon pine in really long planks is not easily obtained today, so that careful selection of timber and practice in long scarphing is essential, for the price of failure in a mast may be the loss of the vessel and her crew.

A few brave souls tackle the making of their own sails, and the expert should not discourage the amateur sailmaker, just so long as he is content with small or light sails. A good seamstress with a heavy-duty sewing machine (which normally has as standard a foot for zig-zag stitching) can certainly make sails up to 150 sq ft in cloths up to 7 oz per sq yd, but beyond this the machine is operating at the limit of its capacity, for the four-fold cloth thickness at simple seams, which becomes six-fold in storm canvas, places a great strain on anything but specialized machinery. Moreover, few amateurs can find enough floor space to lay off, cut out and tack a sail much bigger than 150 sq ft. Mainsails, i.e. any sail set on two or more spars and so requiring seam doubling at the edges, trebling at the corners, grommeting and roping, are even more a professional's task, though the true ocean voyager ought to be quite familiar with finishing techniques –what the sailmaker terms 'bench work'–for he will need such techniques to carry out repairs at sea. The man who is really determined should still avoid anything but small, lightweight mainsails (remember that the mizzen of a yawl may be of the heaviest cloth despite its small size); he could well begin with light baggy sails such as balloon jibs before progressing to genoas, spinnakers and working headsails.

Standing rigging calls for little comment in this context, being standard steel wire with spliced ends to mate with spars or deck attachments, normally in the form of eyes but occasionally as swages. These will be discussed later. Happily, the days of the hand-turned wire splice are numbered, for, apart from being a murderous operation, the result has only 80 per cent of the load capacity of the wire from which it is formed. The mechanical splice, in which hydraulic pressure causes soft metal to flow between the strands of adjacent wires and so link them, needs a special press and so tends to be a professional job. Swaged terminals, especially in the smaller sizes, can be made by the amateur provided he is most accurate in size matching and doesn't attempt to fit a metric terminal to imperial size wire. Rod rigging seems rather out of place over a ferro hull.

Running rigging, of Dacron, Terylene, nylon or polyester rope should be bought in from professionals only if the builder wishes to save time and effort, for splicing and whipping rope is basic seamanship calling for little specialist knowledge and no specific gear, beyond a decent pair of fids or marlinspikes (one large and one small). Most modern yachts use ropes from man-made fibres rather than those of hemp, manilla and cotton, which are now likely to be expensive, difficult to obtain and of relatively short life.

The majority of hardware and chandlery is best bought in, and only those items which are difficult to get should be made. It is almost impossible to get standard fittings for masthead, hounds and spreader roots to fit the larger wooden masts, so these must be designed and made; likewise, items such as runner levers (except in stainless steel) and deadeyes are on such extended deliveries, despite appearing in retailers' catalogues, that the toil of fabrication may be less trying than the misery of trying to get one's order filled.

Choice of Rig

In general terms it is reasonable to expect that the designer of the hull purchased for fitting out will have provided drawings for the correct rig; and the builder wishing to alter this should consult the designer, who should be fully cognisant of the variations possible and non-permissible, with reasons. If there are no plans for a rig, and no designer to query, the amateur is well advised to seek professional advice, again from a qualified yacht architect rather than a seaman, no matter how experienced. Let it here be interjected, however, that some designers are so blinded by their virtuosity within Rules of Rating and the like that they may lose sight of the specific problems of the deep-sea cruising yacht; then the seaman, often working more by eye and intuition than by mathematics, will be the better man. Having said all this, there may still be those who seek guidance on the subject, so brief notes are now provided on the various aspects of rig. However, it must be stressed that almost every criterion here propounded may need modification in the light of the individual vessel; the rig and scantlings which may suit one vessel may be utterly wrong for another of the same length, and only careful consideration of many other parameters will provide a safe way forward.

There is a wide variety of rigs now available, all long proven at sea, so that individual studies need be but brief. On the whole, ferrocement yachts are large and heavy compared with those in timber or grp (which may also be large and heavy but can equally be small and light). The relatively high hull weight per square foot of ferrocement craft usually leads to relatively low ballast ratios and slack sections (for greater displacement), giving a hull with less power to carry sail than the stiffer sections and higher ballast ratios of grp. However, because the displacement is there, the ferro hull really needs a good spread of sail to drive it, and since it is not advisable to push the area skywards in the current fashion, rigs with long bases are preferable.

Cat or Una Rig

The boat with one mast and one sail has been more popular in North America than in most other areas. Its prime merits are simplicity of gear and ability to sail close to the wind; its demerits are the size of the gear in anything but dinghies and difficulty in running dead before the wind, the imbalance caused by having all one's sail out on one side often being coupled with a tendency to bury the bows by having the mast right forward. It is not a rig to be commended for serious seagoing, though the vessels of the great catboat era in the USA made many voyages well offshore in difficult conditions. Largely a product of New England, the bigger cats were maids of all work, the sailing forerunner of the general purpose launch, because the rig was simple. But as 27 ft boats grew to more than 12 ft beam and spread nearly 1200 sq ft in a single sail, they demanded a very special race of seamen. Basically a heavy centreboarder with limited ballast, achieving stability from great beam–leading to the '2-beam' cat in which the beam approaches half the length–the type would, in fact, be well suited to small ferro boats, and a yacht of, say, 21 ft by 9 ft, spreading

Fig. 36 The Cat-boat or Una rig.

about 300 sq ft in a gunter sail, would be an attractive proposition for estuary cruising. Figure 36 shows a typical American cat.

Bermuda Sloops

The variations possible with this most popular of all rigs have been appearing in the yachting press for half a century, so that little need be said except to reiterate the earlier warning against tall rigs, with their attendant large heeling moment. The tall, very narrow mainsail of high aspect ratio is certainly the most efficient to windward in smooth water, when one can sail close to the wind; but the sail tends to twist badly, so that a kicking strap or boom vang is vital to hold the boom down. The whole rig must be set up tightly, to preserve tight luffs in the large headsails involved, so that the compression loads on the mast and attendant stresses on the hull through mast step and chain plates are very high indeed. The older rig with a broad mainsail and small jib (even when helped by a bowsprit), which was so popular in North America until the adoption there of the International Offshore Rule, would be far better suited to ferro, albeit now much out of fashion. True, from the aspect of the standing rigging a broadly-based masthead rig is good; Fig. 37 shows such a rig set on a 40 ft hull with a reasonably generous area of 700 sq ft. But the price of simplicity is high, for the headsails are large with 320 sq ft in the working jib and 550 sq ft in the genoa, so that powerful multi-speed winches are essential.

Dividing the foretriangle produces the cutter, Fig. 38, which adds the support of an inner forestay to the advantage of smaller sails. If the inner jib, more properly called the forestaysail, is set on a boom or

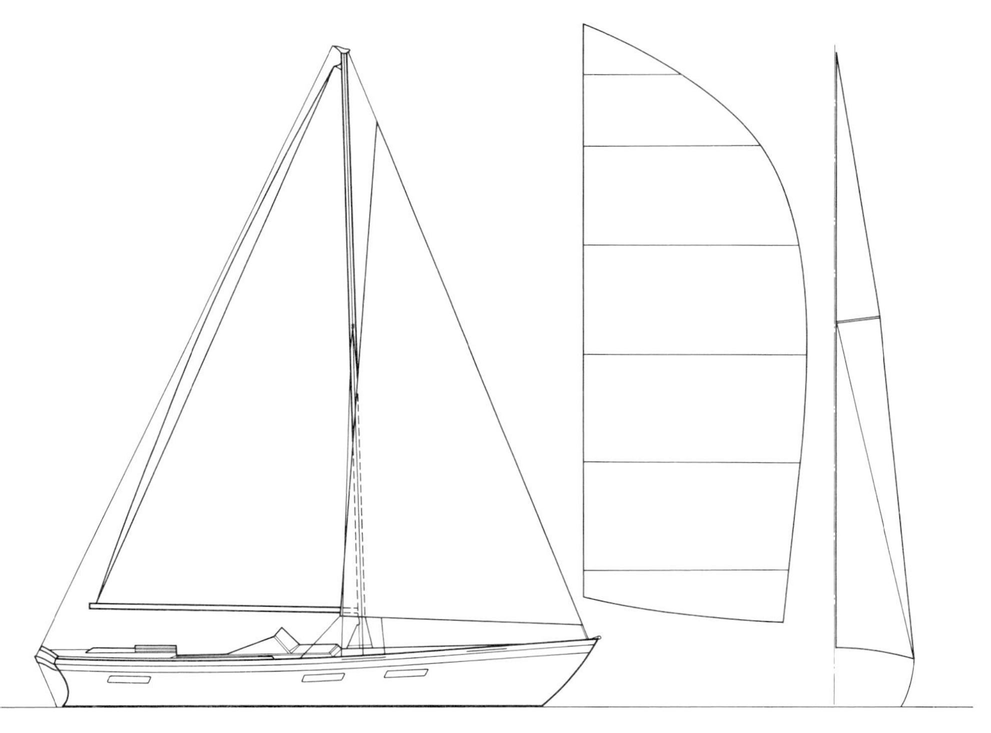

Fig. 37 A 40 ft sloop setting 700 sq ft in two sails.

club, so as to be self-tacking, the rig is easier to handle than the sloop, despite the long jib sheet which needs more power in the winch than the same area set in staysail form. It must be conceded that getting the two headsails working together to full efficiency is not simple, and also that the club-foot staysail needs great study to get it working well; in this respect the loose-footed sail is better, and though this then means two sheets to tend, they need less muscle than the single sheet of the comparable sloop.

Gaff Rig

Long out of fashion, the gaff rig is slowly making a comeback, especially among those dyed-in-the-wool cruising enthusiasts for whom rating, rules and racing are anathema. Its basic attraction, especially for the impecunious, is that it has a large working area, with little provision for the profusion of genoas and their attendant hardware which impoverish the racing man with his 'efficient' machine. In

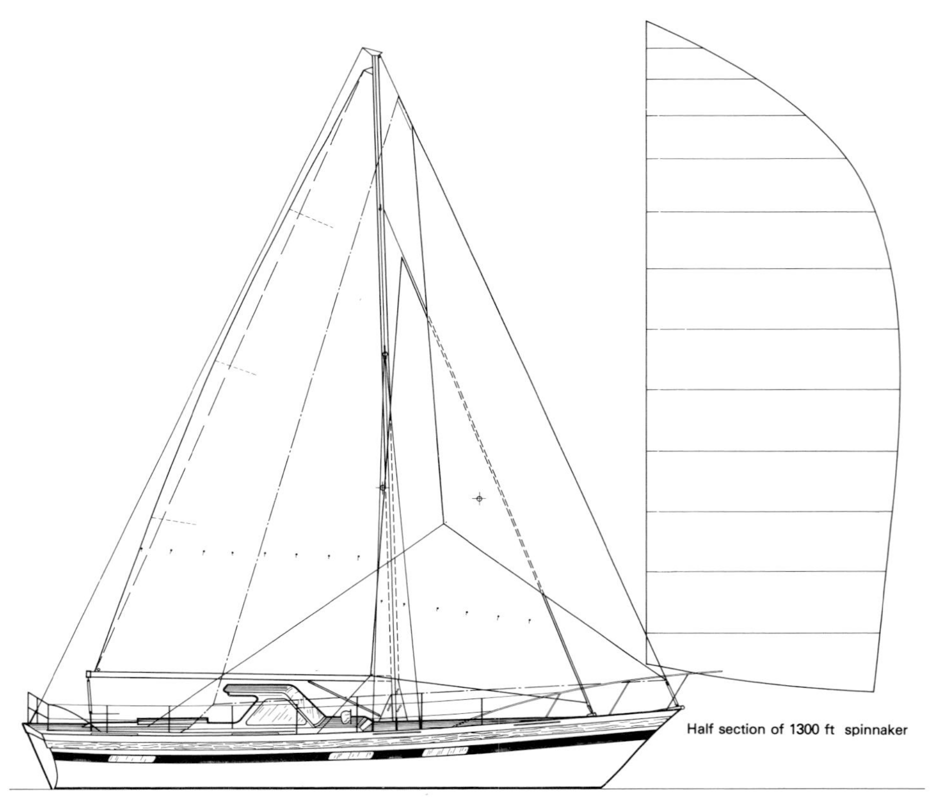

Fig. 38 The hull in Fig. 37 provided with a short clipper bow and cutter rig setting 745 sq ft in three sails.

this respect it makes for good light-weather cruising, for it has the necessary area right from the start. True, the gaff-rig sailor must be wise to his reefing techniques, for he must reef rather than change headsails; but since his sail area will be spread out along a much greater base than in the Bermuda counterpart, the centre of effort will be lower and so the heeling moment will be less. The rig will not stand being driven as close to the wind as a good Bermuda rig, whose greater windward efficiency and–ultimately–easier staying caused it to oust the gaff.

Nonetheless, because this rig demands more flexibility, and thus slacker rigging and hence together less strain on the vessel, and because it is a very powerful rig just off the wind, driving a yacht through a seaway with decision, it is one which should be well considered for the small ferrocement yacht. Plate 11 shows the combination of gaff main and club-foot staysail which was so popular in single-handed workboats around the turn of the century together with jib and topsail. This 26-footer sets almost 100 sq ft more working area than her Bermuda counterparts, yet requires attention to only one set of sheets when tacking and has an inbuilt whisker pole when running.

Plate 11 The classic format of yesteryear–a jackyard cutter built in 1974.

As gaff cutters get larger the sizes of the spars increase, and a solid Oregon pine gaff 20 ft long is a heavy object to hoist and lower: this was another good reason to abandon the rig. Yet if it were replaced with an alloy spar, of perhaps one-quarter the weight, with a winch on the throat halliard if needed, these difficulties would disappear.

Yawls and Ketches

By definition, yawls and ketches have two masts of unequal size, the smaller being aft. It has always been difficult to tell t'other from which: many years ago one argued than the mizzenmast of a yawl lay abaft the rudder post, while that of a ketch lay ahead of it: there are all sorts of anomalies hereby created, perhaps the most widely known being the sailing barge, whose miniscule mizzen was set on the forward face of the transom while the rudder (to whose blade it was sheeted) was hung on the aft face. For the most part such anomalies mattered only to the purists; but when those handicapping cruisers for racing gave the ketch a rating advantage over the yawl the anomalies proliferated until the RORC pontificated that a vessel with less than 9 per cent of its total measured working area in its mizzen was a yawl, while one with more than 9 per cent was a ketch. Even with these two criteria to help, a seaman will swear a yacht be a yawl when she is technically a ketch, so the problem is still with us.

Both rigs achieved popularity by division of the sail plan and shortening of the main boom. When both masts were gaff rigged the yawl would heave-to to under headsail and mizzen, one backed against the other, and might also make some sort of weathering under these sails in gale conditions. But with the greater popularity of racing the main joy of the mizzen was its ability to set a staysail whose area was not measured for rating. Nonetheless, provided the area of the mizzen is not too small, either as a fraction of the total area or in relation to the spars (one has seen sails of less than 10 sq ft on yachts really far too small to have split rigs), the rig has proved effective in many waters: Plate 12 shows a yawl with the mizzen as 9 per cent of the working area, and the mast steps about the middle of the raking rudder post.

For a long light hull there is nothing to beat the ketch, especially if the spars are just all-inboard; the individual sails are small, handling is easy, and helm balance can be achieved under all conditions by sheet tension; moreover, jib and mizzen balance well, giving a useful hard-weather rig. But when the displacement is heavy and the hull short and fat, the rig base is reduced; the designer must then go for tall, narrow sails, which are all wrong on such a hull, and he will almost certainly be shy on his working area, leaving an undercanvassed boat. Unfortunately, a combination of smaller spars and a touch of romance, backed by some truly great voyages in ketches, has

Plate 12 The yawl has the mizzen mast (technically) aft of the rudder post.

made this rig popular with builders of ferro hulls, frequently with unhappy results. Plate 13 shows a 40 ft ferro ketch of a well-known class.

Wishbone Ketch

The great problem of the ketch–inadequate area–arises from the large empty space between the mizzen and the leach of the mainsail. An attempt to overcome this was attributed to the American, Frederick Fenger, who teamed the mizzen staysail of the schooner with an upside-down jib set abaft the mainmast, with its clew held out by a split gaff or wishbone, sheeted to the mizzen head. The effect is shown in Fig. 39 (b) which compares the wishbone ketch with a conventional ketch on the same hull. The problem of this rig is essentially that the wishbone imposes considerable strain on the mizzen head, and the rig may have begun its fall from grace when the flogging of this spar in a gale led to the complete dismasting of Alan Colman's almost new 83-footer *Wishbone* in the mid-1930s. It is quite possible that alloy spars would have withstood the strains.

Schooners

When the unequal masts are reversed, with the smaller forward, the result is a schooner. And when the wishbone ketch is reversed into

Plate 13 The Endurance 40 *is a fine example of a ferro ketch.*

the wishbone schooner the stresses of the wishbone are taken at the hounds of the mainmast, a double triatic stays the two mastheads at kind angles, and we have a very tight rig indeed, complicated only by running backstays from the mainmast hounds. Figure 40 (b) shows this rig set on a 40 ft hull, producing an adequately canvassed sailboat of comfortable size yet easily handled by two. This rig seems most suited to the larger ferro yacht, for it spreads an adequate area over a long base, with a low centre of effort and thus a reduced heeling moment: the sails are individually small, and only the jib needs tending when going about. In heavier weather the drive is much reduced by handing the wishbone, and in extreme conditions the yacht will still handle well under her boomed staysail alone. Adding sail for light airs is not easy, but a vast quadrilateral wishbone, overlapping the main, will be valuable for reaching and running on a rig which is basically best adapted to beating.

This is a comparatively new and still somewhat rare development of the much older staysail schooner, so popular among the really large yachts of the late 1920s and 1930s. It is a good seagoing rig in that both masts are stayed independently, and its multiplicity of small sails makes it well suited to family cruising, with 'a lot of small hands to pull on a lot of little strings'. Again, it is at its best beating and reaching, at its worst running; its power on a close reach may be typified by the 40 ft *Vamos II*, Fig. 40 (a), which logged a genuine 30 nautical miles in 3 hours and 157 nautical miles in 21 hours, the former along the Irish coast, the latter across the Bay of Biscay. In the 1930s the rig developed a reputation for being hard on its racing crews, and as subsequent repetition led to the elimination of the word racing it achieved an undeservedly bad reputation. The fact that the 35 ft staysail schooner *Magellan Cloud* has won races when sailed single-handed against fully crewed sloops may give the lie to this idea. Again, the big area is spread well along the hull, providing a better drive/heel ratio than a sloop, and so the rig is well suited to ferro.

In the limit–at least at the time of writing–perhaps the ultimate in schooners is seen in *Pallas Athene* (Plate 14), which combines staysail and wishbone rigs over her three masts: 74 ft overall, with 22 ft 6 in beam, she was, at her launch in 1973, the largest ferrocement sailboat in Europe and the largest bilge keeler in the world. The quadrilateral sail between the masts is known variously as a Fisherman and a Jumbo; the largest size carried is then a King-size Jumbo or a Jumbo squared, according to taste.

The gaff schooner is the true breed, and few sailboats have ever approached the great Grand Banks schooners of the 1910–1930 period for beauty, speed and seaworthiness. This rig can be hard work to handle, especially in the larger sizes–and it seems quite out of place in small boats. It is the rig chosen for a new fleet of 70 ft ferro-hulled charter yachts, for it has a romance that no other rig can match in

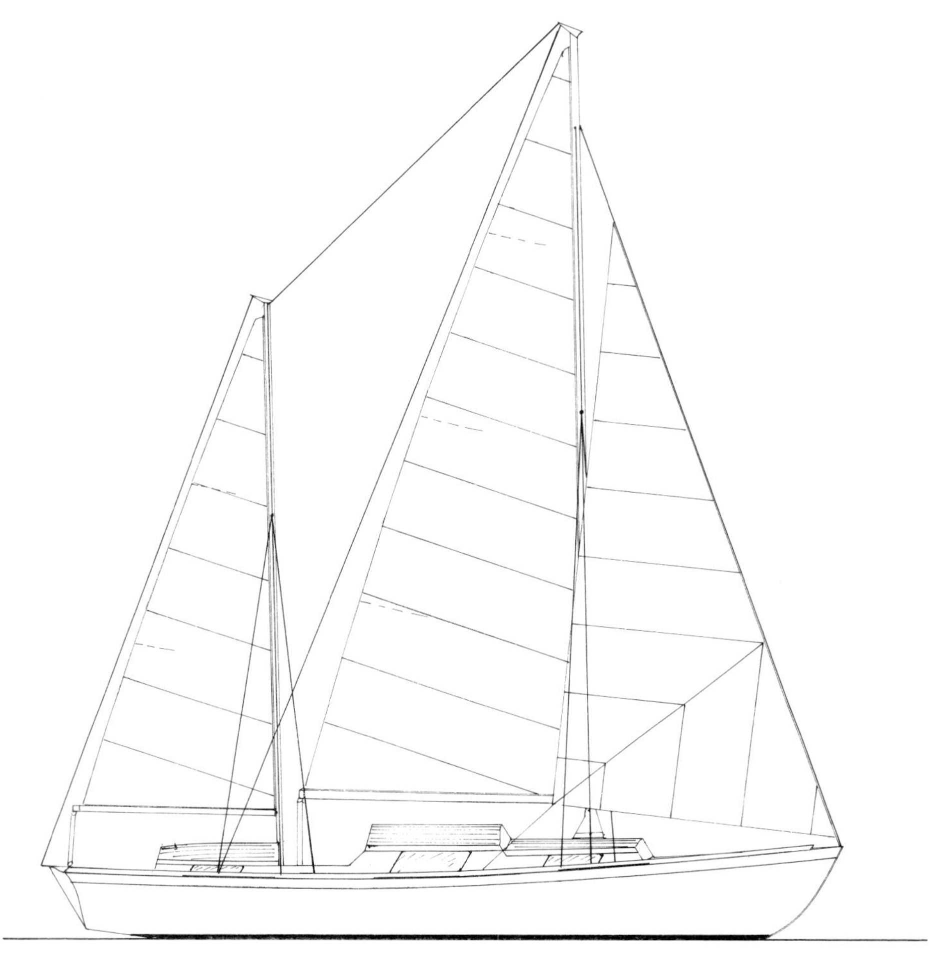

Fig. 39 Comparison between ketch rigs on the Rhodesia *hull.*
(a) As a conventional ketch she sets a working area of 470 sq ft.

vessels too small to cross square yards. Because ease of handling with a small crew is of paramount importance, it was considered advisable to step the mainmast farther aft than became normal after 1918, so reducing the size of the mainsail. As it happened, the client had a great fondness for the classic trading schooners of the Baltic, with their steady motion and great stability, so this became the type model, the only real departure from traditional being in the use of pole masts instead of separate topmasts. With a working area of 2155 sq ft in the lowers, and another 600 sq ft available if topsails are set, these vessels are adequately canvassed for all but really light airs, yet the largest sail is only 800 sq ft, well within the capacity of a pair of reasonable seamen under all conditions, and of one man up to force 5. It is true

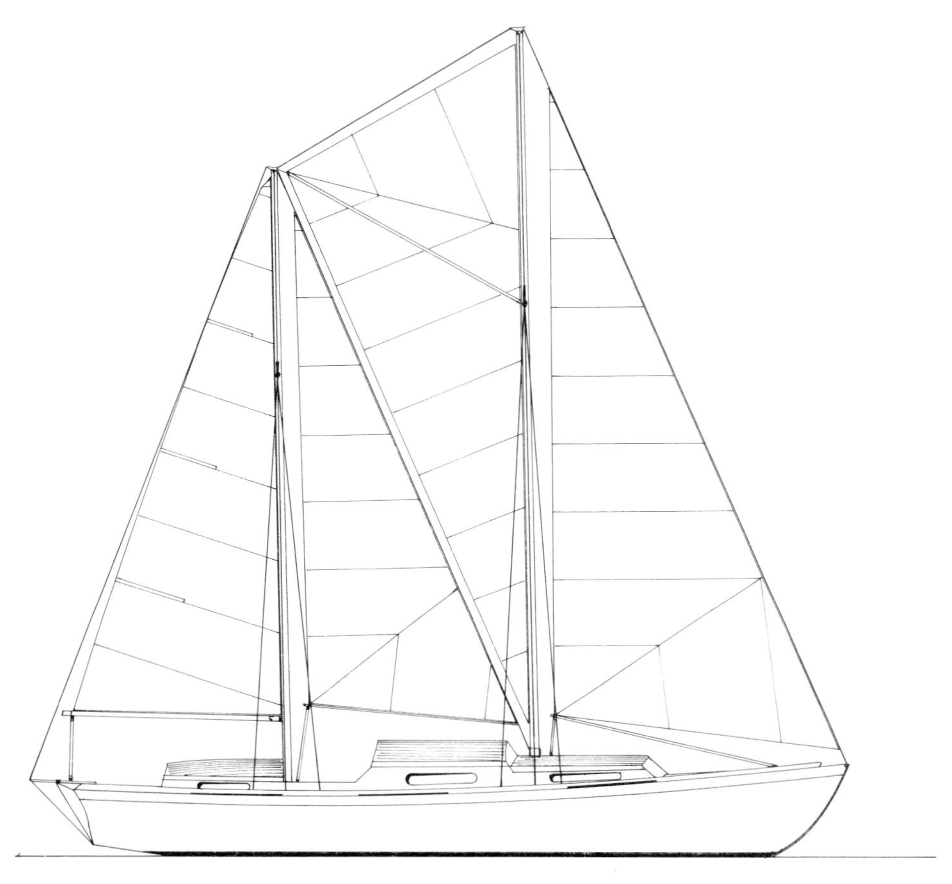

(b) As a wishbone ketch her working area becomes 510 sq ft.

that this rig lacks the windward ability of the racing schooners, such as those of the New York Pilot Service or the Grand Banks fisherman around the turn of the century; twin diesels overcome this deficiency rather better, especially for long distance charter, leaving trade wind work–reaching and running for long periods in blue waters–as the most efficient and most comfortable sailing.

Square Rigs

From the early part of the seventeenth century until the tail of the nineteenth, the brig and brigantine developed and grew in popularity for almost every class and type of working vessel between 60 and 120 ft overall. The definitive separation of the terms is that, while both have two masts, the brig has square sails on both, while the brigantine has square on the foremast and fore-and-aft sails on the mainmast. Begun

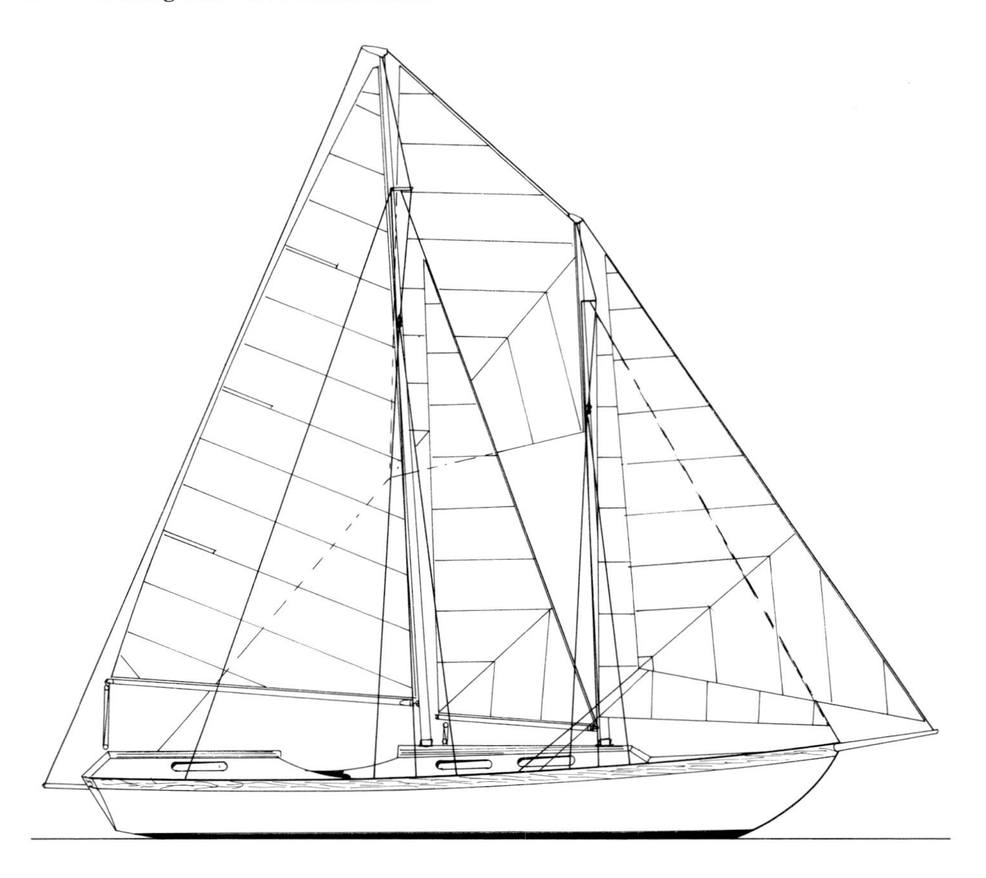

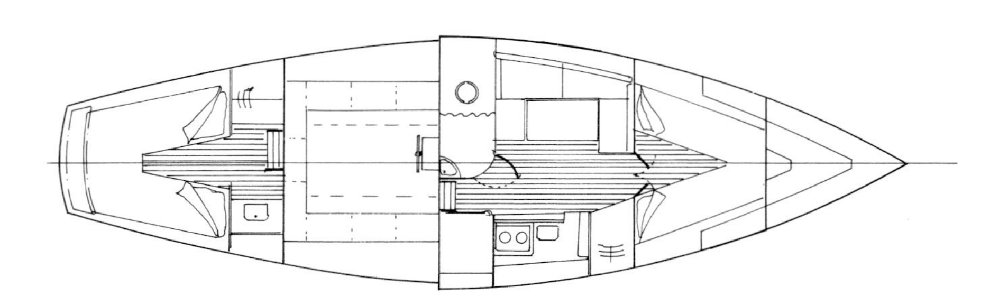

Fig. 40 Comparison between schooner rigs on the Vamos *hull.*
(a) The conventional staysail schooner sets 690 sq ft in the five sails, but the quadrilateral fisherman topsail is difficult to handle.

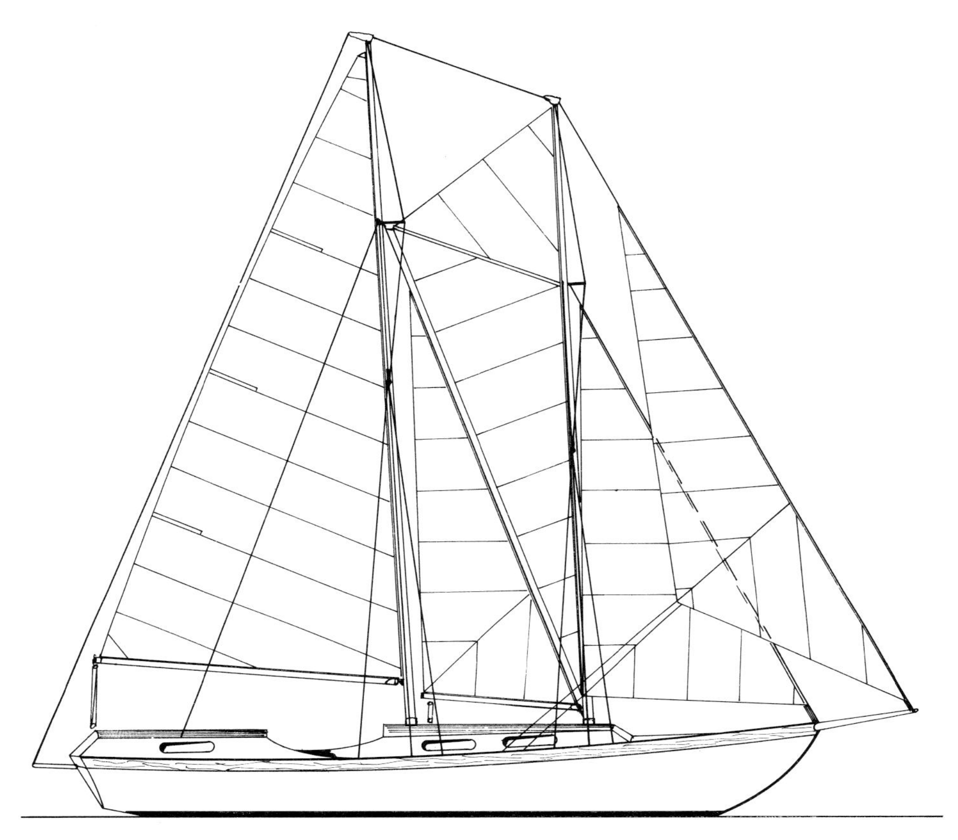

(b) The wishbone rig sets 745 sq ft and handling is greatly simplified.

in humble coasters, these rigs peaked in the small, very fast, gunboats of the world's navies, and in the packet boats which carried mails and passengers on shorter voyages. It is generally true that these rigs were preferred to schooners by owners and masters, because of their flexibility, but they still demand crews who can go aloft in all conditions to handle sail, and on this score alone, if on no other, were bound to lose out to the now more conventional fore-and-aft schooner.

However, since 1970 there has been a revival of interest in square rigs, after almost a century of neglect, one of the most notable being the British training ship *Royalist* to a Colin Mudie design. These rigs have captured the imagination of a number of builders in ferrocement, who may well be the prime group to rekindle the 'square' torch. In fact, square rigs do allow a large spread of sail to be dispersed over a long base, so leading to a much reduced heeling moment in comparison with, say, the Bermuda rigs; in this respect they are particularly applicable to ferrocement, especially when the original design produces slack bilges, heavy displacement and a low ballast ratio–all features which have been common in ferro hulls and which lead to reduced stability and sail-carrying power. Moreover, many larger ferro yachts are built by groups of amateurs, which form the nucleus of the largish crews required. The comment must be added that these rigs are not suited to vessels under 45 ft, and for those which must operate short-handed.

Determination of Area

The determination of a viable sail area to be set over a hull is bound to be trying, and becomes increasingly difficult as the volume of data on the hull characteristics diminishes. Comparisons with similar vessels are useful, but must be handled with knowledgeable caution. Sailing recognizes two basic situations characterized by (a) skin-friction resistance and (b) wave-making resistance; the former is largely determined by the area of wetted surface and is of importance at low speeds and in light airs, while the latter is a function of displacement and its distribution along the hull and forms the major holdback force which the drive of the sails must overcome. Insomuch that light-weather performance can, and normally is, augmented by light-weather canvas, the ratio between sail area and wetted-surface is seldom considered. Thus most of the aids to the calculation of area

Plate 14 Pallas Athene *combines both the schooner rigs of Fig. 40. Nearly 75 ft long and 22 ft 6 in beam, this 3-masted schooner was probably the largest ferro yacht afloat when this book was written.*

are based entirely on displacement, on the power/weight ratio concept.

In the simplest terms we can find a ratio by dividing the sail area, A, by the displacement to the power $\frac{2}{3}$, $\Delta^{2/3}$, (the conversion being necessary to eliminate the concept of unit or dimension from the result). So a small ferro yacht of, say, 30 ft overall could well have a displacement of 8 tons, from which $\Delta^{2/3} = 8^{2/3} = 4$. Comparison of a large number of yachts shows that this ratio, $A/\Delta^{2/3}$, should lie between 120 for yachts of heavy displacement and 180 for those of light displacement; hence our divisor, $\Delta^{2/3} = 4$, gives a sail-area range of 480–720 sq ft. But 8 tons is heavy for a 30-footer, so we may take the lowest figure and aim for 480 sq ft, which is in fact high for a 30 ft hull. In comparison, a 30 ft cruiser of very light displacement, say $2\frac{3}{4}$ tons, will produce an area range of 240–360 sq ft, and experience shows that we must aim for the top end of this range for adequate performance in light to moderate conditions.

This comparative method does no more than advise on the order of area probably needed to drive a given displacement, and since it is derived from experience alone, i.e. it is based on amassed data, it can be interpreted only in the light of experience.

More useful, perhaps, is that originally proposed by Admiral Turner: ballast-moment/drive-moment = 16–20, i.e. a range of 25 per cent. Here the ballast moment is defined as the weight of ballast multiplied by the distance of its centre of gravity below the metacentre, while the drive moment is the sail area times the distance between its centre of gravity and the metacentre. Hence both terms are related to the transverse metacentre, a point whose position is almost certainly not known. For practical purposes it may be regarded as that point about which the vessel heels, at least initially. It lies above the waterline by an amount which, in practice, varies with the stiffness of the sections, being lowest in slack sections and highest in stiff ones. For a first approximation in a well-designed hull of normal proportions it may be reckoned to be about half the beam above the waterline, i.e. 5 ft in a 10 ft beam.

So if we return to our 30-footer and suppose a beam of 10 ft and a draught of 5 ft, we may calculate a metacentre 5 ft above the waterline and a ballast of 6500 lb with a centre of gravity 4 ft below the waterline. This gives a ballast, or righting, moment of $9 \times 6500 = 58{,}500$ lb-ft. To achieve 480 sq ft over this hull will call for a mast about 36 ft above water, with a centre of effort likely about 15 ft up, i.e. 10 ft above the metacentre, giving a drive, or heeling, moment of 4800 sq ft-ft. Our ratio is $58{,}500/4800 = 12{\cdot}2$, which suggests a tender ship. So we must either reduce our sail area, reduce its heeling moment (by using a sail plan with a broader base and less height) or increase either the weight of ballast or its leverage.

For the more technically minded. Professor Skene's famous textbook on yacht design, in its early edition, equates heeling and righting moments; here the heeling moment is taken as the area of the sails, multiplied by the wind force and by the vertical separation of the centre of effort and the centre of gravity, while the righting moment is the weight of the ballast times the horizontal displacement of its centre of gravity. This, of course, is zero when the yacht is upright, and increases as the yacht heels. So, if we consider that our vessel should be in neutral equilibrium at 30 degrees of heel at the bottom of wind force 5, we have these data:

Let us consider a vessel sailing steadily at 30 degrees angle of heel at the lower end of wind force 5, or 20 m.p.h. We know that such a wind exerts a pressure of 1·4 lb per sq ft and, if we assume that the centre of effort is 15 ft above water level and the centre of gravity is 4 ft below it, the sail area A in square feet will exert a total force of $1{\cdot}4A \times 19$ ft (the separation) $\times \cos 30° = 26{\cdot}2A \times 0{\cdot}86 = 23A$ lb per ft.

Assuming a ballast of 6500 lb, whose c.g. has moved out 2 ft at 30 degrees heel, the righting moment is 13,000 lb per ft. As the vessel is in a state of equilibrium, we must balance force and righting moment so we can write $23A = 13{,}000$, or $A = 13{,}000/23 = 565$ sq ft.

This area is on the high side for today's standards, which tend to be conditioned by the Bermuda sloop, but is, in fact, almost exactly that used on a 1972 design of a gaff cutter of the presumed proportions, albeit of slightly less displacement. In general terms it may therefore be reasonable for the ferrocement yacht builder to begin his area estimate on this basis, provided he knows the weight of his ballast and can estimate within reason the depth of its centre of gravity below the estimated flotation line.

Spars: Sizes and Problems

The detail of sizes of spars, weights of sailcloth and scantlings of standing and running rigging is really beyond the scope of this book, and the builder with an established desire to sort out his own salvation rather than leave such specifications to the respective experts will find few reference works to help him; the original–not revised–version of Skene's *Elements of Yacht Design*[1] gives useful examples of calculations for round spars by the classic Euler formula

$$P = \pi^2 EI/L^2$$

where P = breaking load (lb)
I = moment of inertia of section (in^4)
E = modulus of elasticity
L = length of unsupported section (in)

Of these parameters, I will vary widely with the section chosen for each spar and must be calculated from basic formulae, E will be lifted from standard tables and L will be a design feature of the rig. It will immediately be seen that a given compression load (and the bulk of sailing strains in a rigged mast can be translated back to compression) can be carried in a variety of ways: long sections need either stronger (i.e. large E) materials or large cross-sections (i.e. large I). On the whole, experience is the best guide to the balance between these parameters. And if the builder opts to buy alloy spars from a reputable maker he will almost certainly also receive gratuitous advice on his rigging plan.

Calculations by Euler, of course, presupposes a knowledge of the forces on the sails, which is easier said than done. In his *Rigs and Rigging of Yachts*,[2] Philips-Birt shows a standard graph relating the scantlings of hollow spruce spars to more easily determined parameters. He determines a scantling criterion which takes the stiffness of the hull and the staying of the spar into account.

$$\text{Criterion} = B + M + H + 2 \cos 4A$$

where B = ballast ratio
M = metacentric height as fraction of waterline beam
H = height of foretriangle as fraction of mast height
A = average shroud angle

Thus in a modern masthead sloop of 35 ft overall, in ferro, B would be about 0·3, M about 0·3, $H = 1{\cdot}0$ and A about 15 degrees, giving $2 \text{ cost } 4A = 2 \cos 60 = 2 \times \frac{1}{2} = 1$; hence our criterion is $0{\cdot}3 + 0{\cdot}3 + 1{\cdot}0 + 1{\cdot}0 = 2{\cdot}6$.

The graph, Fig 41, relates directly the displacement in tons and the longitudinal dimension of the mast in inches, with two curves for criteria 1 and 3; thus our criterion of 2·6 would be fairly close to 3, and with a displacement of 11 tons (which would be average for this size) we see the need for a D measurement of 9·5 in. Experience of spruce masts shows that the mast width, d, should be $0{\cdot}8D$ while the thickness of the side staves is conveniently $0{\cdot}18D$, although in practice one uses thinner side staves and thicker ends. So our mast will be $9\frac{1}{2} \times 7\frac{1}{2}$ in at its largest section, with $1\frac{3}{4}$ in walls; in practice one would use 2 in end walls and $1\frac{1}{2}$ in sides. Now the experienced yachtsman will immediately realize that this is a large mast; indeed it presupposes a masthead sloop rig, essentially with single spreaders, and considerably lighter scantlings would be used for a ketch or yawl. It should be noted that D and d should not be tapered by more than 20 per cent in a masthead sloop, whereas in older vessels using $\frac{5}{8}$ or $\frac{3}{4}$ triangles it was normal to halve both D and d at the masthead, with an accompanying reduction of weight aloft and thus of heeling moment. It should be considered that such a spar, devoid of all fittings, will weigh some 350 lb in spruce and 420 lb in pine, against 200 lb in alloy; giving heeling moments of 7000, 8400 and 4000 lb-ft respectively.

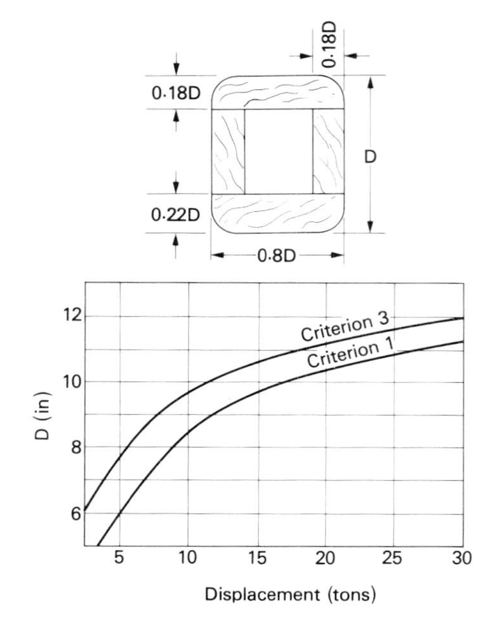

Fig. 41 The correlation between sizes of wooden spars and displacement in sailing yachts; the criterion is given by

$$C = B + M + H + 2 \cos 4A$$

where B = *ballast ratio*
M = *metacentric height as fraction of waterline beam*
H = *foretriangle fraction (=1 for masthead rig)*
A = *shroud angle.*

In this example the difference between the pine and alloy moments is equivalent to the heeling force of more than 160 sq ft of sail in a fresh breeze.

Such considerations take on greatest significance in smallish ferrocement yachts, more so than in yachts of lighter materials because the material's density leads to hull sections with slack bilges and thus of small form stability, while the tendency to over-build and under-cost leads to reduced ballast ratios or over-high centres of gravity, especially when concrete and punchings form the ballast; at the same time, a professionally made timber mast with solid galvanized fittings is often half the price of the alloy/stainless steel combination, and even cheaper when made at home (no great task). The normal outcome then is a combination of tender hull and heavy rig, leading to instability–either lack of power to carry sail or, in the limit, a low angle of recovery and thus a tendency to capsize. Indeed, the author recalls sailing a 40 ft cutter which clearly suggested that it would capsize once the lee deck went awash: most unnerving.

The remedy is obvious, if painful by virtue of its cost: either use lead ballast or alloy spars or both, or reduce the rig height. Some designs, especially those from coasts having much light weather, do tend to carry excessively tall rigs, especially as Bermuda ketches, where one must go up to obtain adequate area. One otherwise excellent design called for masts 60 ft and 40 ft above deck on a 48 ft hull: fine if they are of alloy and balanced by lead ballast and a good ratio (e.g. greater than 35 per cent), but in Oregon pine set over ballast of cement and punchings they could be suicidal in a fresh gale.

Yet because there is much to be said for wooden spars, in terms of appearance, reparability and cost, it is a pleasure to see them return once more to the offshore scene. In ferro yachts the solution to the weight problem lies in spreading the rig along the hull instead of soaring skywards, of using the gaff mainsail, and the ketch or schooner rig to achieve area low down, drive without heel. The Tahiti ketch, combining gaff main and Bermuda mizzen with a moderate bowsprit, is deservedly popular among blue-water sailors.

In designing booms and gaffs, experience again is a better guide than mathematics, although we can use as a basis the standard formula

$$d = \sqrt[3]{(16PL/\pi f)}$$

where d = diameter (inches)
P = total pressure on sail (area × wind pressure)
L = length of spar (inches)
f = maximum fibre stress (5000 lb for spruce).

In the example above we assume a 40 ft mast; with a mainsail luff/foot ratio of 2:1 we carry 325 sq ft on a boom about 18·5 ft long; if we wish to carry full sail in the middle of force 5, where the wind pressure is around 2 lb per sq ft, the formula gives a boom diameter of $5\frac{1}{4}$ in which experience indicates to be a trifle large, since 5 in would be the normal maximum for a circular spar, or 6 × 4 in rectangular.

Skene's book gives the simple formula $d = 0{\cdot}015L$, but this produces a diameter of only $3\frac{1}{2}$ in, which is really too small; his gaff proportions are better at $d = 0{\cdot}020L$, giving $d \simeq 4{\cdot}7$ in. It must be remembered that the shock loadings of gybing a long boom are very considerable; the modern ocean racer, with her tall narrow mainsail, puts her stresses into the mast, and the short boom is rather more lightly loaded.

The question of shape and taper is allied to the method of reefing selected. Roller reefing is easiest on a circular boom, less easy on an oval one and most difficult on a plank-on-edge boom. A sharp taper in the foot nearest the gooseneck helps stow the luff rope, and a collar stops it from pulling a riding turn down onto the gooseneck and so jamming the mechanism. A tightly rolled deep reef on a straight boom will result in clew droop, which on a small cruiser can be so pronounced that the boom end sweeps the cockpit: the tapered boom, which is so satisfying aesthetically, defeats roller reefing. There are many solutions to the clew-droop problem, the best three being:

(a) Fit tapered battens along the outboard 10 per cent of the boom, thus effectively increasing its diameter.
(b) Fit a reef cringle 6–12 in (according to size) above the main clew and pull the two together before reefing; this takes out a triangle of sail along the foot, thus raising the clew.
(c) Fit a deep row of reef points, running upwards from luff to leach; use normal roller reefing for, say, 2–4 rolls, but tie in the deep reef if close reefing seems necessary, and roll on from there.

Finally, a brief word on bowsprits, which are often given inadequate consideration since there is little documentation to guide one. The load on a forestay carrying a large yankee jib or a genoa may well be close to the displacement of the yacht itself. This upward pull on the end of the bowsprit is resisted by the tension in the bobstay, and the outcome is a compression load on the bowsprit which is the vector sum of the two stay loadings. Such a large compression is really best taken by a steel tube, welded firmly to a wedged base plate, or at least between a pair of substantial angles, which are in turn multiply bolted through a strengthened area of the foredeck.

Standing and Running Rigging

Calculations of the loading pattern of spars and rigging are a basic part of mechanics, but fall down because the loads are subject to sudden fluctuations; it is not so much the magnitude of the forces applied as the rapidity of application which leads to gear failure. So it is normal to resort to a rough rule-of-thumb determination of standing rigging sizes rather than detailed calculation; experience, as ever, weights the final judgement. A first approximation is that any major group of stays should just be able to carry the weight of the vessel. Thus, a sloop's single forestay must have a breaking load equal to the two forestays of a cutter, and the normal breakdown here would show break-loads of Δ for the sloop and $0{\cdot}6\Delta + 0{\cdot}4\Delta$ for the outer and inner forestays of the cutter, where Δ is the displacement. In a similar way, the three shrouds on each side of the mast must total Δ, with an average breakdown of $0{\cdot}4\Delta$ for the main shrouds and $0{\cdot}3\Delta$ for each of the lowers. Between this rough gauging and painstaking computations there is virtually nothing, and the amateur is strongly urged to seek the aid of an experienced rigger or a naval architect.

Two factors which influence the chosen stay sizes and which are easy to grasp are the construction of wire rope itself and the method of termination. The classic hand-turned eye-splice finished off by being wormed, parcelled and served, looks fine, especially on older vessels, but in truth has but 80 per cent of the strength of the rope itself, while the finishing coverings hold water and so lead to corrosive breakdown of the wire. Far better results are achieved by mechanical splices, in which a soft metal ferrule is made to flow into the individual wires of the rope by hydraulic pressure. The more modern alternative is to insert an olive into the lay and screw a terminal on the ends; this has the advantage that it can be done with hand tools *in situ* and the disadvantage of having been developed for stainless-steel wire; it can be used on galvanized wire, of course, but one should keep a weather eye lifting for incipient corrosion.

The choice between galvanized and stainless-steel wire for standing rigging is often made on grounds which are more emotional than mechanical. The essential pros and cons are roughly the following:

(a) Stainless corrodes from the inside outwards, and thus hides its weakness until it fails.
(b) Galvanized fails in its outer wires, hence showing its deficiency; but such failures, small though they be, can tear hands and sails.
(c) Accidents and errors apart, stainless should have a useful life 2–3 times that of galvanized, and require rather less maintenance.
(d) Galvanized is easier to work by hand should the need arise.
(e) Stainless is about four times the price of galvanized, size for size, and may require a more expensive size or lay.
(f) Stainless turnbuckles are stronger, diameter for diameter, than their galvanized counterparts but, for a given strength, are 3–4 times the price. They may, however, last twice as long without care.

In selecting turnbuckles and shroud plates the possibility of galvanic corrosion between stainless steel and the mild steel of the hull reinforcement should not be overlooked, for it is the hull which will suffer, not the shroud plates or turnbuckles.

Wire rope comes in a variety of lays, but for standing rigging on yachts the two most commonly used are 1 × 19 and 7 × 7, i.e. in the first the rope is laid from 19 separate wires spun together, while in the second 49 wires are spun, first into ropes of seven strands and then into the final rope made from seven-strand groups. Although 1 × 19 is easier to galvanize, this lay is most often used for stainless; 7 × 7 is the most common galvanized rope and is certainly far easier to use than 1 × 19, especially in the larger sizes. It is noticeably more flexible although not significantly weaker. (See Table 1.)

Turnbuckles should naturally be of a size to match the breaking strain of the wire they tension, and the data needed to determine this are seldom available. In Table 1 an effort has been made to provide a broad correlation as a guide to the builder who has no access to more professional advice, but this should be sought whenever it is available.

Table 1 Approximate breaking-loads (lb) of steel-wire ropes

Diameter	Circumference	Rigid					Flexible	
		Galvanized		Stainless			Galvanized	Stainless
(mm)	(in)	7 × 7	7 × 19	7 × 7	7 × 19	1 × 19	6 × 19	6 × 19
3	$\frac{3}{8}$	1,388	1,277	1,200	1,120	1,590	1,098	941
4	$\frac{1}{2}$	2,464	2,284	2,130	2,000	2,820	1,950	1,680
5	$\frac{5}{8}$	3,852	3,584	3,330	3,130	4,410	3,040	2,643
6	$\frac{3}{4}$	5,555	5,174	4,810	4,500	6,350	4,390	3,808
7	$\frac{7}{8}$	7,571	7,056	6,550	6,130	8,640	5,980	5,174
8	1	9,117	8,422	8,530	8,000	10,200	7,795	6,765
9	$1\frac{1}{8}$	11,514	10,662	10,752	9,946	12,900	9,878	8,893
10	$1\frac{1}{4}$	14,246	13,147	13,300	12,500	15,910	12,186	10,976
11	$1\frac{3}{8}$	17,248	15,904	16,106	14,784	19,244	14,739	13,260
12	$1\frac{1}{2}$	20,496	18,950	19,200	18,000	22,930	17,562	15,814
13	$1\frac{5}{8}$	24,058	22,266	21,616	20,675	26,942	20,608	18,547

The failure of a strainer could lead to the loss of a mast (it has happened more than once, and this at best is expensive and at worst leads to the loss of the vessel. As a general rule the lower end of the rigging should be flexible, so that the fork-and-fork strainer should be shackled to the shroud plate rather than connected by the fork itself. The upper fork should embrace a solid heart thimble around which the eye is made. Such a system is patently impossible when the stay ends in a swaged terminal which is directly screwed into the body of the turnbuckle. Then the need for the lowest-end flexibility conferred by a shackle or toggle becomes more urgent.

Tuning and adjustment of the stays is certainly too complex to be entered into here, except to remind the builder that it must be done. And once it has been done all turnbuckles should be locked, for they will otherwise most assuredly undo themselves. Many stainless turnbuckles are fitted with locknuts, and if these are correctly and firmly locked with a spanner they will almost always be safe. Locking by contrabanding with soft-iron wire may be belt and braces, but...On galvanized turnbuckles without locknuts it is, of course, essential. It is worth recalling that it is far easier to tune and lock diamonds and jumpers while the mast is on deck than when it is stepped and they are a good many feet aloft. This may seem obvious but it is surprising how many people forget.

Among the staunch traditionalists there is a return to the lanyard in place of the screw. Hemp, normally tarred, was traditional; but it rotted. It stretched when dry and shrank when wet. Nelson kept his seamen more than busy dealing with hemp lanyards, especially when he needed maximum performance. Synthetic lanyards are a great deal less trouble, but even they cannot really hold the tension against the pull of a big headsail, and we have had to revert to metal strainers on at least one gaffer to prevent the yankee jib bagging out horribly as it stretched the main shrouds. Tuning is obviously going to be a problem, and it is definitely wise to use a six-part lay-up between two harp shackles than the three- or four-part system offered by the classical deadeye, which should be avoided unless really demanded by authenticity.

Running rigging falls into two main classes– halliards and sheets. Halliards of flexible wire, i.e. that laid up around a rope core and of 6 × 19 construction (see Table 1), have much to commend them, especially the ability to be wound onto a winch drum and so stowed tidily; wire halliards with rope tails, which need cleating and coiling, can only be described as a menace. Wire normally stretches less than cordage, which is an advantage for headsails, especially those with long luffs. But a combination of prestretched 3-strand polyester halliard and a good tack tackle will produce better results with less strain on the hands. On larger vessels a halliard is often lead round a conventional sheet winch set horizontally on the mast to reduce the labour of 'swigging up' to get a tight line; again, a tack tackle takes the pain out of this. In general, then, the preferred material for halliards is prestretched polyester (Terylene or its equivalent, e.g. Dacron). For sheets which are normally winched or which take a great deal of strain 3-strand Terylene rope has much to commend it, but it tends to become hard and somewhat unyielding when wet, so that it can be brutal to salt-softened hands. For mainsheets and sometimes for headsail sheets, a plaited polyester rope is used as being kinder to handle. In the smaller yacht strength is normally not important, in that ropes of adequate diameter would really be too small to handle, so that those selected are over-strong for their task. Halliards of hemp and sheets of cotton have generally departed, except for a few diehards: they were the best of their time, and their time was long, but synthetic fibres last longer with greater reliability.

Ropes of nylon, polypropylene and other fibres have a place on board, often associated with ground tackle, but seldom as part of standing rigging. Of these, nylon is tremendously strong, and has much elasticity–too much for most sheets and halliards, though it has been used happily for sheets on small cruisers: we have one length of soft plait still able to carry loads after close on 20 years– and it was bought as government surplus! Again, more for general guidance, Table 2 shows breaking strains for a few common cordages.

Finally, one must mention briefly splices, knots and blocks, and simply ignore winches, leads and other deck gear, all of which become so much a matter of personal taste that the builder who asks advice from six friends will get six different answers. Splices, knots, hitches, bends–the whole gamut of marlinspike seamanship *is* seamanship, not

Table 2 Approximate breaking-loads (lb) of cordages

Circumference (in)	Natural fibres				Synthetic fibres							
	3-Strand lay									Plaited		
	Sisal	Manilla	Hemp	Cotton	Nylon	Terylene	Polythene	Ulstron[1]	Polypropylene[2]	Nylon	Terylene	Ulstron[1]
$\frac{3}{8}$					460	500	360	320			360	300
$\frac{1}{2}$			222		700	650	440	550			650	560
$\frac{5}{8}$			447		1,100	875	630	800			700	670
$\frac{3}{4}$	560	642	559	398	1,650	1,250	880	1,110	1,210	1,160	1,200	1,100
$\frac{7}{8}$	750	880	760	525	2,250	1,700	1,200	1,500	1,630	1,640	1,700	1,400
1	1,056	1,298	893	645	2,980	2,240	1,540	2,000	2,120	2,300	2,240	1,950
$1\frac{1}{8}$	1,235	1,450	1,260	850	3,750	2,800	1,980	2,400	2,500	2,800	2,700	2,450
$1\frac{1}{4}$	1,397	1,738	1,738	1,000	4,590	3,500	2,400	3,000	3,140	3,600	3,470	3,000
$1\frac{1}{2}$	2,090	2,618	2,640	1,696	6,610	5,000	3,400	4,250	4,480	5,900	4,900	4,200
$1\frac{3}{4}$	2,816	3,520	3,520	2,097	9,040	7,000	4,600	5,750	6,150	7,140	6,700	5,700
2	3,916	4,930	5,040	2,570	11,650	8,960	6,160	7,280	7,610	9,500	8,600	7,200
$2\frac{1}{4}$	4,700	5,950	6,160	3,525	14,785	11,200	7,610	9,410	9,860	11,850	10,750	9,400
$2\frac{1}{2}$	6,260	7,950	7,830	4,000	18,150	13,890	9,410	11,650	11,870	14,350	13,350	11,500

[1] Multifilament polypropylene. [2] Monofilament polypropylene.

boatbuilding; it is well covered in a number of books, of which that by Jarman and Beavis[3] can be thoroughly recommended. Blocks come basically into two classes: plastic and wood. Wooden blocks–ash cheeks, bronze bound, with roller bearings in the bronze sheaves, are beautiful reminders of more spacious days, now expensive and hard to come by, and in need of annual maintenance. However, they go so much better with a gaff rig, even when rove with synthetics. On the whole, today's blocks are of Tufnol or nylon, or one of their plastic derivatives, all water lubricated and easy-care. And so long as they are correctly sized for the loads imposed by the sheets or halliards they are an excellent choice, with a wide variety of reputable manufacturers offering proven wares.

And, in general, this is the note on which to end this chapter–it is difficult, and quite unnecessary, to choose rig and rigging which are not well proven; the choice is wide, and there is a host of experience on call for him who would but seek it.

Notes

1. SKENE, Norman L. (1948) *Elements of Yacht Design*. New York, Dodd, Mead & Co.
2. PHILLIPS-BIRT, D. (1954) *Rigs and Rigging of Yachts*. London, Adlard Coles Ltd.
3. JARMAN, C. and BEAVIS, B. (1976) *Modern Rope Seamanship*. London, Adlard Coles Ltd.

Chapter Seven **Power and Drives**

The difficulties, both technical and financial, which beset the builder rigging his sailing cruiser are no less–and indeed may prove rather more–when consideration is given to mechanical propulsion. So great is the overall complexity that it will be impossible to do justice to the task, and all that can be hoped for is a reasonable set of guide-lines.

Although ferrocement hulls as small as 15 ft have been built (by McAllister) and powered by 7 h.p. air-cooled units, for the purpose of this book outboard motors or small inboards are not of serious interest. The development of the small diesel outboard will make its mark in certain fields, especially perhaps in the smaller canal and river cruiser; these are covered briefly. On the whole, however, our main concern is with the conventional multicylinder inboard unit burning petrol or diesel.

Petrol or Diesel?

There are many arguments for and against each of these two fuels and the engines which use them, but overall there is an increasing bias towards diesel, primarily on the ground of its reduced fire hazard (or rather, 'explosion hazard', for diesel fuel burns very merrily–it wouldn't be fuel if it didn't). In many countries there is also a price advantage; for example, marine petrol in the UK is at least five times as expensive as 'offshore' diesel bought in large quantities (e.g. 1–10 tons). For the sailing man who uses his engine solely as an occasional auxiliary, primarily to enter or leave crowded moorings, the lower cost and weight of a petrol engine may well outweight the lower cost of diesel fuel, which is likely to double for the small quantities he will buy. If the difference in engine first cost alone is

£400, as it may well be, the fuel cost differential is 25p per gallon, the sailor must use 1600 gallons more diesel than petrol to equate the unit cost. In more practical terms this can mean that a keen sailor who averages 4 hours motoring each weekend and 30 weekends a year (allowing for holidays, etc.) could spend £30 more on petrol than on diesel; this saving of £30 a year in fuel costs would have to be amortized over 13 years to meet the engine-cost difference.

It is certainly true that the petrol engine has disadvantages, prime among which is a reliance upon electricity for its functioning. Of course the modern yacht, even a 'pure' sailboat, carries a substantial electrical load, so that alternators and batteries are evils associated with both engines. Moreover, only the smallest have any means of hand starting in the event of battery failure; the larger diesels, with cartridge or compressed-air starting, are rather outside the scope of this book and are normally in the charge of experienced and competent engineers. Explosively, petrol is no more dangerous than bottled gas: a properly installed system, with all the right precautions taken when refuelling, should be no trouble; the man who smokes while refuelling really deserves to be burned to death.

Prime advantages of the petrol engine are its quietness of running and its lower weight and volume for a given horsepower in comparison with the diesel. True, the latter is making ground on all these counts, especially in the 30–60 h.p. range, but the differences become formidable around 200 h.p., even in the high-speed range.

The Paraffin Engine

Not so popular today as it was some twenty years ago is the old compromise of the paraffin or kerosene engine: the fuel is better known as TVO–tractor vaporizing oil–and has a lower flashpoint than domestic paraffin, although even this has been used in some units, especially those with low compression ratios. Indeed, in the spark-fired internal combustion engine the cylinder compression is a guiding factor in the choice of fuel: the higher the compression ratio the higher must be the octane rating. Few marine engines run at compression ratios of 10 or more, which would call for octane ratings in excess of 100, though aviation spirit of very high rating has occasionally been used at sea. Most of the units likely to be considered will run quite happily on 92 octane–2-star petrol–with compression ratios of just above 8. But some of the really large, older types of American automobile engine, with capacities up to 7 litres, have compressions as low as 6·5:1 and will run on paraffin. A note of distinction here: the true paraffin unit was close kin to the semi-diesel, the beloved hot-bulb machine of the early years of the twentieth century; in this the fuel was first pumped into a large copper sphere, normally preheated by a blowlamp and subsequently kept hot by exhaust gases. Thus a fuel of low inherent volatility was vaporized before being fed to the carburettor: it was all simple, robust and relatively foolproof, but there is no doubt that preheating the bulb was a thankless task and made starting engines a protracted operation. To avoid this the petrol-paraffin engine was developed, a unit which begins operation on petrol and is then switched to the cheaper fuel when it reaches the full operation temperature. The advantages of the petrol unit in respect of lightness, quietness and low volume are retained, and operation on low-cost fuel is added: the disadvantages are a decided smell of burnt paraffin (unless the exhaust gases are discharged via a tall funnel), some fiddling at the start-up, and up to 10 per cent loss of power.

For the sailing man using a small auxiliary, such complexities are not worth the saving; for the man operating a 60 ft yacht or larger, especially for charter, where regular schedules are needed, the reduced noise and comparative cheapness of both first cost and running can be attractive, since some 200 h.p. can well be needed. For the pure powerboat owner the diesel will normally be first choice, except for racing craft perhaps. Yet it is worth considering that a 1973 build of Conqueror (a 73 ft planing cruiser in ferro) is based on paraffin engines. Here is quite a useful example to consider. This craft, called *Snow Maiden*, was begun to provide a working testbed for new ferrocement construction techniques based on the achievement of a prime surface density of 8 lb per sq ft (40 kg/m^2), which is light. The total weight of the hull, decks and superstructures as a shell was computed at 22·5 tons, and the estimated cost was very low indeed. As an experimental craft it was felt that a simple layout and decor were the order of the day, so that a total weight, ex engines, of 27 tons was suggested as adequate. The owners wanted to reach 20 knots, and the first design study suggested two V12 diesels with an all-up weight of 6¼ tons, giving a displacement of some 36 tons with a small fuel load. The engines cost estimate, excluding sterngear, was of the order of £16,000 and even then it seemed unlikely that 20 knots could be sustained for more than half an hour.

The solution was cheap, light and complex. Four 7-litre automobile engines were secured for a nominal sum, but after the expenditure of considerable time and money in finding them. These were marinized and converted to petrol/paraffin operation and then fitted with simple forward-neutral-reverse gearboxes. They were then mounted in line abreast across the ship and each pair was coupled by toothed belts to a propeller shaft. It was thus possible to have each pair facing in opposite directions and secure handed rotation of the propeller shafts from non-handed engines. Careful tuning of the engines (which yield 700 h.p. each for automobile racing) is expected to yield better than 350 h.p. (continuous) on the shafts with an all-up weight, including fuel, of 30·5 tons, yielding a theoretical maximum of 26 knots. The installed cost was one-fifth that of the twin diesels, with a guarantee of speed and approximately twice the running costs. Of course, such a subterfuge is hardly likely to be possible in a professionally-built luxury yacht, but is certainly acceptable in an experimental craft or in one being built from scratch by its owner. But a note of caution must be sounded: don't try it unless you are a fully experienced mechanic, or have total access to one such; for marinizing, paraffinizing and belt-coupling these monsters is no task for the amateur and needs a large backing of competent resources.

So far little has been said of the marine diesel as such–for no other reason than that this workhorse is the backbone of boating. The petrol engine has its place, especially in high-speed craft, and much space has been devoted to the paraffin engine because in spite of being rather out of fashion it yet has a very useful function. But by 80 per cent of yachtsmen, especially those building from the comparatively heavy ferrocement hull, the diesel will be chosen. Basically we have four considerations, two referring to the craft itself, i.e. whether sailing or power, and two to the engines, i.e. whether basically an automotive unit or a heavy-duty marine or industrial one. There is often a fair degree of interrelation, of course, plus circumstances in which certain solutions are not feasible or possible.

Choice of Power: Sailboats

Under the generic heading of sailing auxiliaries we shall consider the full range, from sailboats in which the power unit is minimal–just enough to make home in a flat calm–to the motor-sailer in which the engine plays as vital a role as the sails, or even takes a greater part. The owner with an eye on racing performance will opt for the smallest possible power unit, usually teamed with a two-blade folding or feathering propeller with the narrowest possible blades to minimize drag. Efficiency under sail takes precedence over power performance, but often to the point where the only use for the auxiliary is in entering or leaving the marina. On the face of things, this is adequate, for the true racing man can always sail. However, for the average weekend sailor, who must be at his desk on time on Monday morning, there are two conditions which call for power of a much higher order, namely the foul tide and the calm which follows the storm; the former, in either a flat calm or a headwind, can prevent return to base with inadequate power; the latter condition is the old fisherman's *bête noir* –a horrible lumpy sea, sails slatting uselessly and all gear chafing like mad. The power required to deal with a seaway is rather greater than that needed for a flat calm. To illustrate: some years ago, in association with the design of standard trawlers, it was found that a 65 ft boat needed 65 h.p. to make 5 knots in a flat calm, but over 130 h.p. to make the same speed in a 5 ft sea. Now the speed is low for such a vessel, and the wavelength is small in comparison with her length and freeboard. But the power requirement doubled.

Another illustration of the problems of underpowering was shown by a 40 ft schooner in which the builder had installed the wrong drive unit, partly on a weight basis, partly to pare costs. With an engine 20 per cent under power and a variable-pitch propeller it proved impossible to achieve full pitch on the screw without overloading the engine, and so much reducing its speed and power. When caught in a gale in Dublin Bay the combination took nearly an hour to force the ship's head through the eye of the wind and might have led to the loss of a new craft had not the sails held.

With such a background it is possible to examine the basic factors determining the installation. Prime calculations relate power requirement to waterline length and displacement. Many sailing men accept the adage that the maximum speed at which a yacht will sail is about $1\frac{1}{3}$ times the square root of the waterline length; for example, a yacht of 36 ft waterline gives

$$V_{\max} = 1\tfrac{1}{3}\sqrt{36} = 1\tfrac{1}{3} \times 6 = 8 \text{ knots}$$

Examination of the speed/power curve, Fig. 42, for this yacht shows that when $V = \sqrt{L}$ the power requirement is really quite low, but that the graph steepens rapidly above $V = 1\frac{1}{3}\sqrt{L}$ and, although the line

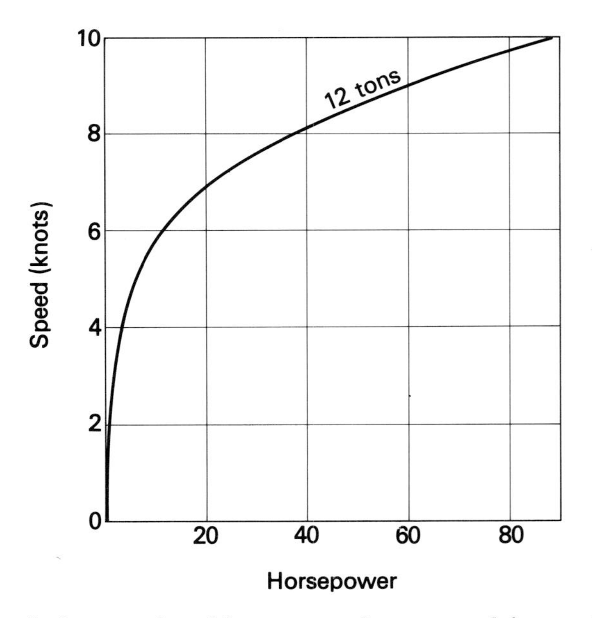

Fig. 42 Curve relating speed and horsepower for a normal ferro sailing cruiser of 36 ft waterline.

continues upward, it is doubtful whether the conventional fine-ended sailboat would be able to absorb the power needed to drive her at such a speed. But it is certainly reasonable to install a motor of 30–35 h.p. and so peak at 8 knots in smooth water, with a reasonable chance of maintaining 4 knots in a seaway, or 5 knots against a 3 knot tide (which is not unusual). It follows that such a combination of seaway and tide could reduce the forward 'over the ground' speed almost to zero.

Moreover, few will want to run an engine at its maximum speed for long, even though it be rated as maximum continuous speed, and the normal loading of an engine by a propeller drastically changes the speed/power curve. Figure 43 shows two curves for a typical diesel; one is for the basic engine on a test bed and shows a gradual change of power with r.p.m.; the other is for the engine driving a correctly matched propeller (called a 'typical propeller-law curve') from which the rapid loss of horsepower with reduced engine r.p.m. is clear. Thus for long journeys under power, i.e. those of more than half an hour, it would be normal to run at about three-quarters of full revs and so–by combining Figs. 42 and 43–at about 7 knots.

A critical point was mentioned earlier in referring to the fine ends of a sailing yacht. Essentially this refers to the stern, and leads to the oft-observed situation of a yacht under power digging a hole and dropping her stern into it, particularly when driven faster than the hull wants to go. The associated phenomenon of a tall stern wave

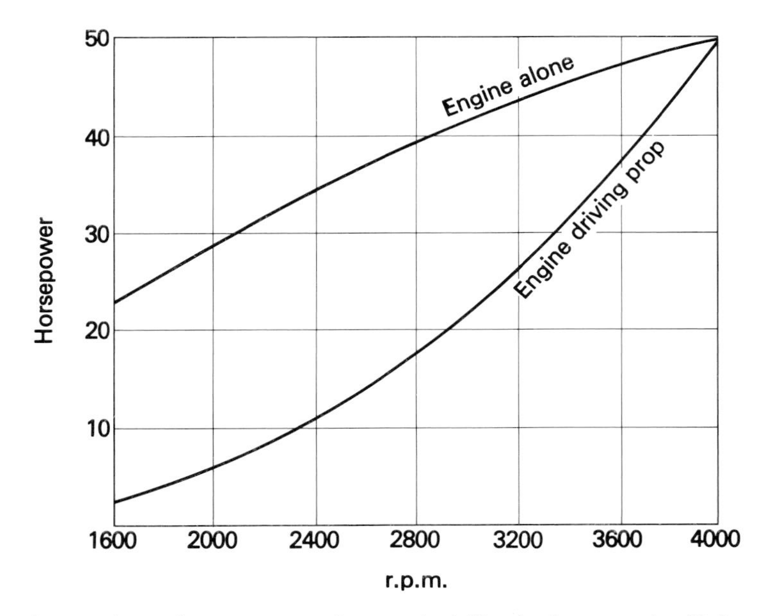

Fig. 43 Comparison of power curves for a typical diesel when running light and when loaded by a propeller.

rises essentially from the steepness of the run-up of the buttocks towards the transom: the flatter the buttocks the faster the boat, which explains why those who make Rating Rules hold boats back by steepening the buttocks and pinching the sterns. Thus the builder with such a hull knows that he can achieve only a limited speed and can select his power unit accordingly.

Thus speeds beyond $V = 1\frac{1}{3}\sqrt{L}$ bring us more truly into the realm of the motor-sailer and a rather different type of stern, with more width and a flatter run. In many ways this hull form is extremely well suited to ferro, for it gives the ability to carry weight without excessive slackness in the bilges. Thus, the 36 ft w.l. of the pure sailing craft can, by virtue of a stern of adequate buoyancy, now absorb up to 100 h.p. and so maintain a cruising speed of 10 knots. Even so, it should not be thought that such a hull cannot sail, though it needs above-average design to effect a real compromise. Shallow draught is

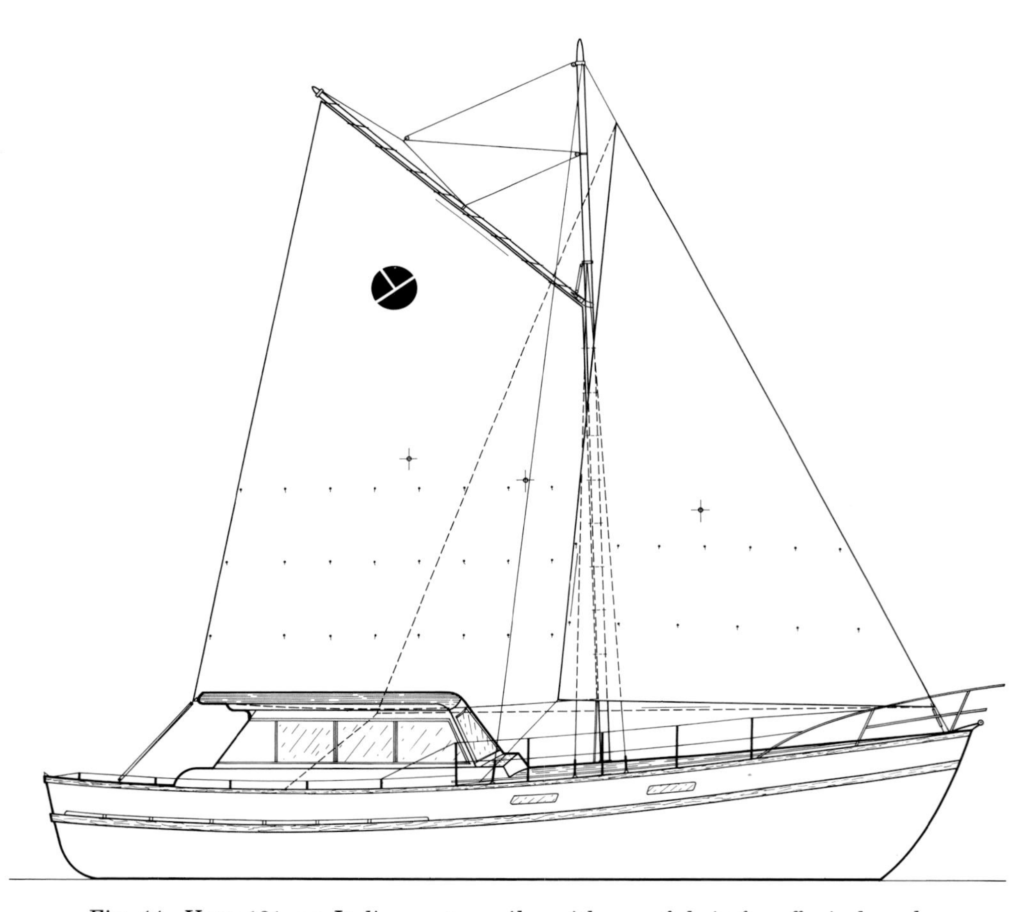

Fig. 44 Yara 121, *an Italian motor-sailer with a useful rig for off-wind work.*

customary with the motor-sailer, which now tends to rely more on power than on draught for windward ability (it was a professional seaman who commented that the best rig for beating to windward is an 8-cylinder diesel); bilge keels can do a great deal to help sailing by reducing leeway, albeit at the cost of some loss of speed under power, and they confer the advantage of roll reduction when motoring. The rig itself should be chosen for its power when reaching; a typical example is the loose-footed, gaff sloop outfit of *Yara 121*, shown in Fig. 44.

Choice of Power: Planing and Displacement Cruisers

From the motor-sailer the logical step now is to the pure powerboat, and here we are dealing with two essential formats, namely planing and displacement hulls. On the whole, planing or semi-displacement hulls in ferrocement are few and far between at the time of writing, and certainly tend to be of the larger variety with a considerable thirst for power. Attention has already been drawn to *Snow Maiden* and the interaction of weight and speed; and Fig. 45 shows the curve relating speed and power for this vessel. In many ways she would be a good choice for the owner seeking a long, light craft, easily driven, for she is a handsome yacht when at rest and can operate quite happily at displacement speeds.

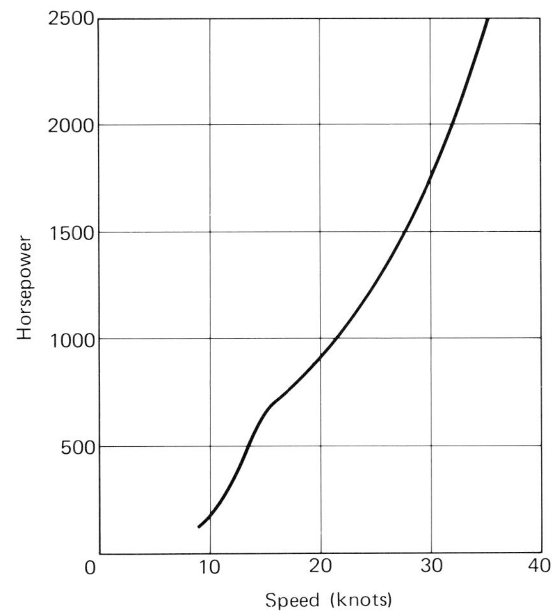

Fig. 45 Power/speed curve for Snow Maiden *with a displacement of 35 tons on a 60 ft waterline; the power hump shows clearly.*

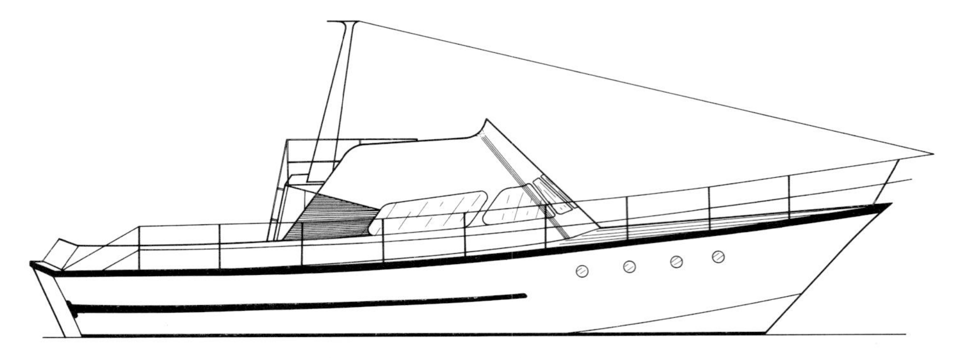

Fig. 46 Libertad *is a 43 ft planing cruiser designed for normal ferro construction.*

At 43 ft overall, *Libertad*, Fig. 46, is a much smaller craft, with half the weight and only 30 per cent of the internal volume of *Snow Maiden*. Figure 47 shows her speed/power curves for direct comparison with those for the larger yacht, and the beneficial effect of the lower displacement/length ratio of the larger craft is clear.

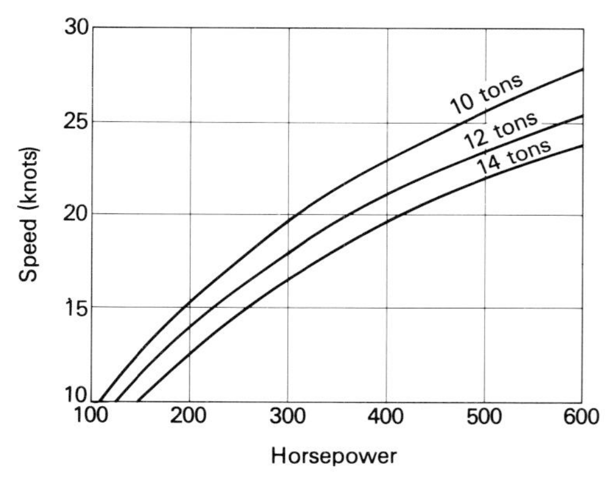

Fig. 47 Correlation between speed and power for Libertad *over a range of probable displacements.*

The displacement hull, i.e. one which is intended to be driven at speeds under $V = 2{\cdot}0\sqrt{L}$, forms the backbone of the ferrocement powerboat fleet. Mention has already been made of the luxurious *Trixie* and even larger craft based on the fishing-boat or MFV hull form, and the use of ferro in the construction of working craft which is spreading steadily throughout the world. Essentially the hull form dictates a limiting speed, with many of the criteria expounded for sailing craft holding good. Within the limiting speed range the builder must opt for the balance between speed and power to suit his needs. Where expense is not spared the installation of maximum power gives the advantage that it is there when needed but need not normally be used; against this is the possibility of a low limit speed engendered by a low safe-tickover of the engine: a yacht with a minimum speed of 3 knots could be a disaster in a crowded port. Such a consideration especially relates to a single-screw craft: a vessel with twin engines has essentially more manoeuvrability and can reduce power greatly by operating on one engine only.

For both the long-distance cruising yachtsman and the commercial operator the most important factor is more likely to be fuel consumption, and its effect on range rather than speed. He will select an economical speed for his hull form and power accordingly, remembering that range means fuel weight, which increases displacement and so the power requisite. So, whereas for *Snow Maiden* we draw a series of speed/power curves for different displacements, for a displacement craft we draw power/weight curves for various speeds. Thus for a simple 50 ft trawler the figures are as shown in Table 3. This, of course, is an alternative presentation of speed/power/weight data, with the advantage of simple presentation but slower interpolation. Clearly evident from the columns is the exponential rise in power with speed ($P \simeq V^{1 \cdot 75}$), and the slower, linear rise of power with displacement. With a reasonable knowledge of his overall parameters the owner can determine a basic engine, and thence his operational characteristics. It is highly unlikely that his displacement will vary outside the 30–55 ton limits and it might be reasonable to think in terms of 250 h.p. in such a vessel. This would permit a 55 ton displacement to be driven at speeds of about $8\frac{3}{4}$ knots, while to attain 10 knots the displacement must be limited to 35 tons–a substantial difference reflecting load capacity.

Allied directly to this, of course, fuel consumption for a modern diesel might be taken as 0·4 lb/h.p./hr; this is more than many modern engines use but it is wise to be generous lest optimism lead one to run out of fuel. So our Table can be re-written in terms of fuel consumption, based either on miles run per ton or tons used per thousand miles. Taking more or less extreme examples of the latter we find that to drive our 55 tons 1000 miles will use 2 tons at 7 knots, 3·1 tons at 8 knots, 5·6 tons at 9 knots and 7·4 tons at 10 knots, all of which must be subtracted from the load capacity of the vessel. Since the light weight,

Table 3 Shaft h.p. shown as a function of speed and displacement

Speed (knots)	Displacement (tons)						
	25	30	35	40	45	50	55
7	32	40	48	56	64	72	80
8	56	70	84	98	112	126	140
9	100	130	160	190	220	250	280
10	170	210	250	290	330	370	410

ex fuel and cargo, of such a trawler is liable to be about 30 tons, these fuel loadings will reduce the cargo capacity by 8, $12\frac{1}{2}$, 22 and $29\frac{1}{2}$ per cent respectively. On these bases, then, should the builder of the ferrocement displacement craft select his power units and his method of operating them, insofar that, while the trawler owner may more appropriately relate speed to loss of cargo space, the long-distance cruising yachtsman may well relate it to range: thus, in our above example, 7·4 tons of fuel will give 1000 miles at 10 knots, 1330 at 9 knots, 2400 at 8 knots and 3650 at 7 knots.

Type of Engine

At the beginning of this chapter the two basic types of diesel were listed as automotive and marine, and subsequent discussion has made no distinction between them. For practical purposes these may really be regarded as high-speed and low-speed units, and the essential basis of their design principles arises from the frequent speed changes and comparatively short operational uses of the high-speed or automotive unit and the days of constant-speed operation which characterize a ship's engines (i.e. a large vessel such as a tanker or liner). Normally, allied characteristics are small capacity and light weight for the high-speed unit and large capacity and great weight for the low-speed one. Thus, from a truly automotive unit such as the Ford 6D, with a capacity of 5·95 litres, one can achieve 250 h.p. at 2450 r.p.m. on a weight of 1300 lb, while the same power will come from 13·75 litres at 2000 r.p.m. on a weight of 2400 lb in an engine designed originally for industrial use; a fully marine engine, hand-made on a line which produces only three a week, will yield a maximum of 200 h.p. at 1500 r.p.m. on a weight of 3 tons. It will therefore be seen that the choice is wide; but examination of the engines available will greatly cloud the question of what is, or was, automotive. Indeed, quite where high-speed becomes low-speed is not very clear, except at the extreme ends, such as the really big units turning at less than 1000 r.p.m. and the small ones exceeding 3000 r.p.m. Moreover, while the dyed-in-the-wool marine-engine adherent may scoff at automotive units, it must be recalled that, by the time these are marketed for marine use by reputable manufacturers, they are truly marine engines. Buyers must seek beyond the name mystique and select the right unit for the job.

The classic heavy-duty, slow-running workboat diesel tends still to be characterized the world over by two names–Kelvin and Gardner; although both companies build high-speed engines, they are best known for the big hand-built jobs, usually of 6 or 8 cylinders in line with capacities in excess of 2 litres per cylinder. For many years these engines were available only in normally aspirated form, producing comparatively low indicated horsepowers at 1000 or 800 r.p.m., but coupling with massive torques. Yachtsmen often used a simple straight through drive, while fishermen seldom needed more than 2:1 reduction. In the last decade they have acquired turbochargers and speeds up to 1500 r.p.m., but have retained their essential virtues of immense strength, apparently indefinite life and very low fuel consumption (0·3 lb/b.h.p./hr). Equally, they retain their disadvantages of weight and volume; Fig. 48 compares a 6-cylinder unit with a high-speed (2000 r.p.m.) American engine based on an industrial prime-mover. These big engines are seldom able to find a place in sailboats or cruisers under 50 ft, but they have both great utility and great appeal in larger cruisers and in working craft.

There are, of course, other large units with equally revered names, but these are generally too large for the class of owner/builder for which this book is written.

Although the most important factor in the entire drive system is the thrust produced by the propeller, a high-speed unit can be geared down to drive a big propeller slowly (as in a steam turbine); but these engines are less suited to the grind of, say, workboats or ocean-crossers than the heavier ones.

The sailing man will most certainly select an automotive-based unit, and may indeed marinize one himself. The motor-sailer may have more of a choice, though his automotive unit will come from a heavy lorry. The power man will probably use a unit based on either an engine developed for a heavy lorry or an industrial engine. Since the latter term now embraces mobile civil-engineering machinery, with engine outputs up to 700 h.p., there can be little doubt about their reliability. However, automotive and industrial duties tend to be intermittent, whereas marine usage tends to be continuous; hence much care should be taken in interpreting the manufacturer's literature when selecting a unit. For example, many makers classify

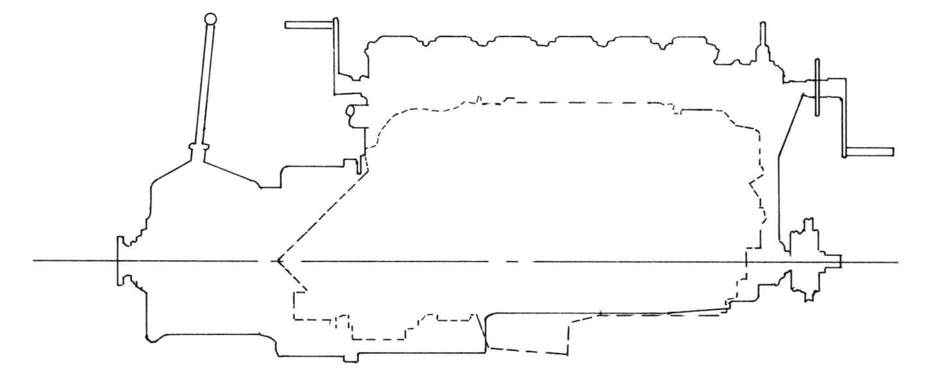

Fig. 48 Comparison between the hand-built marine diesel and one of the same output based on a higher-speed but heavy duty automotive diesel. The solid line shows a Gardner 6L3B, the broken line a Caterpillar D333.

their engines on the basis of the highest output which can be demonstrated on the test bed: and say so. This is brake horsepower (b.h.p.) and means that the engine is not driving a gearbox and its own ancillaries. For our purpose it means nothing. A manufacturer will then provide power curves: these will include the b.h.p. curve, with or without continuous and intermittent rating curves, shaft-horse-power curves (i.e. driving gearbox, etc.) possibly with intermittent and continuous ratings, and–we hope–propeller-law curves: the useful peak output of the engine lies at the intersection of the prop-law and engine curves, as shown in Fig. 43. Again, quite correctly, manufacturers may rate a given unit at different powers for differing usages; an engine used in conjunction with a stern drive to propel a planing runabout is far more lightly loaded than one coupled to a heavy reduction gear as an auxiliary in a heavy yacht. So one popular British diesel is sold as developing over 50 h.p. at 4000 r.p.m., with the manufacturer's proviso 'for approved high-speed applications only'; as an auxiliary it is rated at 35 h.p. at 3000 r.p.m., which it will churn out for decades. This maker clearly differentiates between usages, and it is the fault of the purchaser if he errs. On this point it is as well to note that the 'test bed' rating is pretty close to the declared automotive rating, so that a unit listed as giving 100 h.p. in a car will really give 75 h.p. continuous marine rating.

Converting Road Engines

We now arrive at the concept of converting automotive engines: builders ask, 'Manufacturers do it, so why can't I?' The answer essentially is: 'If you know enough about it, you can'. The UK magazine *Practical Boat Owner* has published some articles by John Watney on the subject, and Adlard Coles Ltd has published a useful book[1]; there are certainly several American books on the subject and maybe an Australasian one. The prime differences to consider are the replacement of the radiator by a heat-exchanger and associated water-circulating pump, plus a system of cooling. This may involve simple keel cooling, in which the hot water from the engine is piped around a closed circuit outside the hull and so dissipates its heat to the sea; this method is better suited to steel hulls than ferro ones, because there is always vibration present in the system which, over a period, can lead to failure of the hull/pipe watertight seal; on a steel hull this joint can be welded, and will last as long as the system. The better method is likely to be the fitting of a conventional marine heat-exchanger cooled by a simple seawater circuit; a single skin-fitting admits the water, which is then discharged into the exhaust system.

Consideration may have to be given to the fuel pump, for that on a road vehicle normally only has to pull fuel more or less horizontally, while on a boat it may have a significant vertical lift.

The greatest difference between a road and a marine unit is the one most often overlooked by the amateur considering conversion: on the road all the power is rotary, the final thrust from the wheels being carried by the U-bolts holding the rear axle to the chassis. At sea the urge comes from the propeller, straight back down the shaft to the gearbox. So a road gearbox is designed to resist torque, or turning: a marine box must be provided with a thrust-bearing large enough to absorb the full output of the engine. To return to *Snow Maiden* for a moment: in this installation the prime-movers drive rotating belts and thence the propeller shafts, so the engines need torque-resistance gearboxes while the shafts themselves must have the thrust-bearings. The belt-drive system therefore overcomes some of the headaches of marine conversion and could well be given serious consideration, especially in sailboats, where the engine may fit in relatively high up yet permit a well-immersed propeller; Fig. 49 shows how this might be arranged, and compares it with a conventional installation which necessitates a steep shaft angle.

The conventional alternative is to ensure that the engine selected for marinization is of a type widely used for this purpose, and then to buy a suitable gearbox whose bolting flanges mate exactly with those of the prime mover. It is, of course, possible to use dissimilar flanges and fabricate a connecting bell-housing to compensate, with an intermediate shaft splined or flanged to the output of the engine and input of the gearbox as necessary; this comes to rather complicated engineering.

Gearbox Ratios and Propellers

Far too many yachtsmen believe that, having determined the correct horsepower for the speed they wish to achieve, all they have to do is to add any marine gearbox, shaft and propeller. All too often this happens, and all too often disappointment results. The drive, gearbox and propeller, however, are so closely interrelated that it is quite impossible to consider them separately, since the choice of propeller size is based upon the horsepower transmitted and the speed of rotation and these, weighted by the effective speed of the hull, determine the efficiency, i.e. the ratio between the power used to drive the ship and the power wasted churning water to no good effect. This can easily be visualized in the terms of, say, a very large outboard motor (e.g. 140 h.p.): place it in the stern of a planing hull and it will make it get up and go; place it on the stern of a heavy workboat and it will scarcely move it. On the whole, then, it can be stated that fast boats need fast

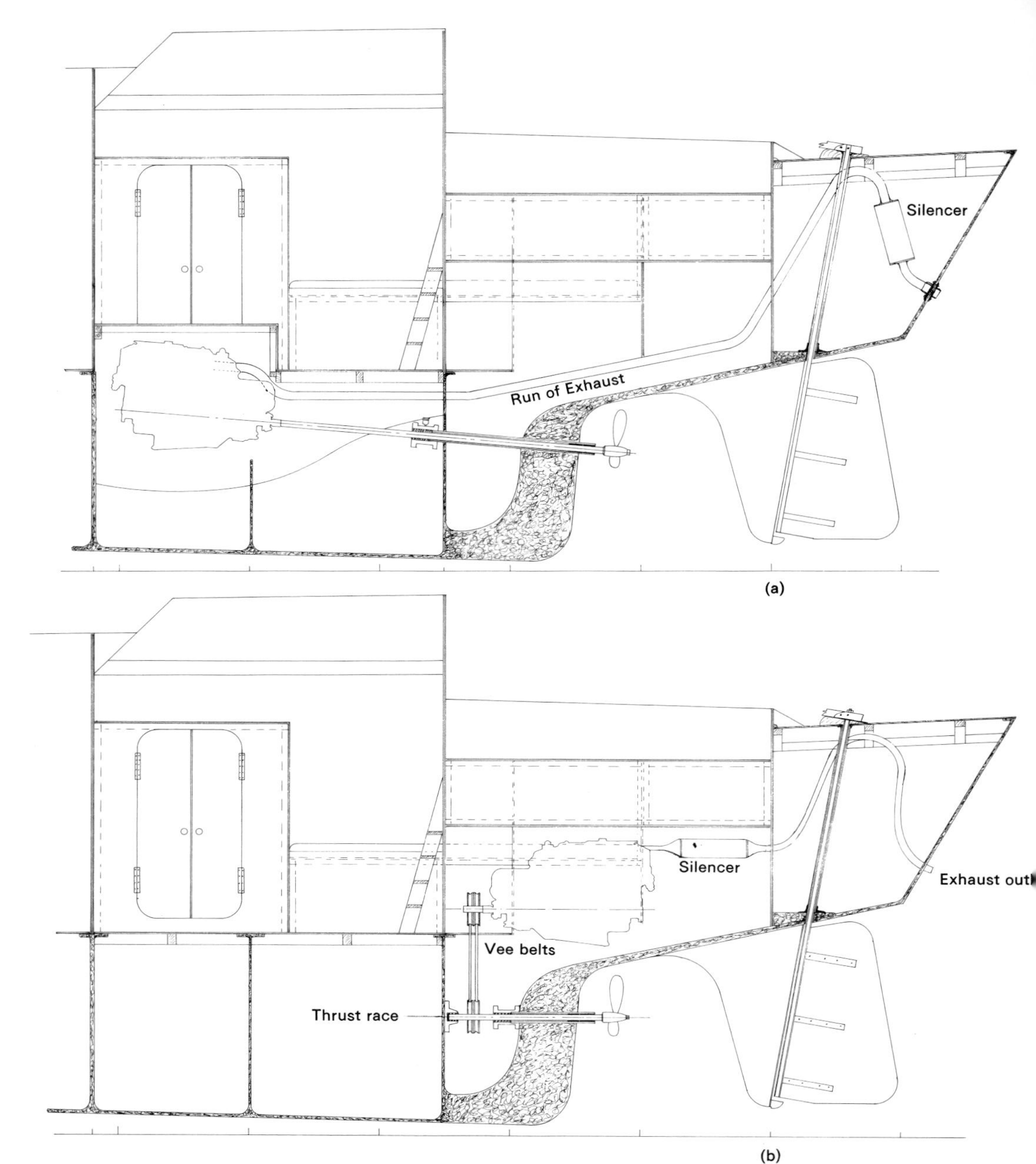

Fig. 49 Comparison of the space occupied by an engine driving (a) conventionally and (b) by vee belts; the former demands an awkward placement of the engine.

turning propellers and slow boats need slow ones. But for a given horsepower a slow propeller must be larger than a fast one.

For the average builder of ferro yachts the choice of gearbox is limited, but the man completing a workboat may well have a much wider range from which to choose. Thus, the sailing auxiliary of the average motor cruiser must choose between gear ratios of 1:1, 1·5:1

and 2:1, or approximations thereto, while the workboat can go on in steps of 0·5:1 up to 5:1 or 5·5:1. True, these latter ratios tend to be associated with large heavy-duty engines and craft over 75 ft long and are thus outside the scope of this book.

To illustrate the interaction let us revert to our 36 ft waterline yacht with its auxiliary diesel producing 36 h.p. at 3000 r.p.m., giving 8 knots maximum speed. Table 4 shows the calculations. In this instance the 3:1 reduction is included because it is available with this engine, albeit not 'off the shelf'. The reduction of propeller speed is seen to produce rapid reduction in slip (which occurs when the screw rotates madly, whipping the water into aerated foam and doing no good at all), the amount at 3:1 reduction being only 60 per cent of that on direct drive; concomitantly, the relative increase in efficiency is a massive 35 per cent. The cost is a doubling of propeller diameter, which means increased drag when sailing and a larger propeller aperture.

Table 4 Effect of reduction gearing on a high-speed diesel engine

Reduction ratio	Slip (%)	Efficiency (%)	Propeller size (in)
1:1	52	42	12 × 6
1·5:1	44	48	16 × 8
2:1	38	52	19 × 10
3:1	32	57	23 × 13

Allied to this is another problem, practically in terms of propeller blade loadings; in other words, the more power a screw must transmit, the greater the blade load; but if the blade is too heavily loaded it will simply shed load by cavitation. The calculations are out of place here, but the end results suggest that our 12 × 6 in (i.e. 12 in diameter, 6 in pitch) propeller, if of conventional form, will only be able to transmit 18 h.p. into drive, reducing our maximum speed to below 7 knots; the 16 in propeller will absorb 28 h.p. and give us 7¾ knots; the 19 in propeller will use the full 35 h.p. while the 23 in one could prove too lightly loaded for efficiency.

By contrast, consider the 50 ft trawler, using a medium displacement hull of 45 tons with an engine producing 220 h.p. at 2000 r.p.m.; Table 3 showed a speed of 9 knots in this condition. From Table 5 we see that there is little to be gained by increasing our reduction ratio above 4:1. Another calculation shows that this combination of speed and power needs a blade area of about 840 sq in, which is conventional on a 3-blade propeller of 52 in diameter, with a disc/area ratio of 0·41. The propeller loading of 6·3 lb per sq in is low.

From this general outline it will be seen that the correct matching of the hull, engine, gear ratio and propeller is a complex business

Table 5 Effect of reduction gearing on medium-speed diesel engine

Reduction ratio	Slip (%)	Efficiency (%)	Propeller size (in)	Thrust (lb)
1:1	60	35	22 × 9½	3000
2:1	47	45	34 × 16	4300
3:1	40	51	45 × 22	4850
4:1	35	55	52 × 26	5300
5:1	33	58	58 × 33	5500

involving a knowledge of various calculations and the experience to interpret their results in practical terms. Insofar that comparatively small changes of propeller can make large changes in propulsive efficiency, the need for expert advice is paramount. From the sailing man's point of view it is often better to opt for a smaller engine at peak efficiency than a larger one with half its power wasted. For the power enthusiast the correct combination can mean increased speed or reduced fuel consumption.

Propeller Shafts and Sterngears

Propeller shafts are made in a variety of metals: phosphor- or manganese-bronze, Monel, stainless and high-tensile steel. They tend to be characterized by a taper and keyway at each end, one to fit into the gearbox half-coupling and the other to carry the propeller. Their diameters are determined by correlation of their tensile strength with the engine torque to be transmitted, but for the average builder in ferro, who merely wishes to know roughly what size of shaft he should use for a given engine, Fig. 50 shows a simple relationship between shaft diameter and horsepower per 100 r.p.m.; note that the question of reduction gear has recurred.

The propeller shaft passes through the hull encased in a stern tube, which provides a gland on the inside to prevent seawater flooding back into the engine compartment and an outer bearing to carry the load of the propeller. Standard sterngears, comprising stern tube and propeller shaft, are widely available, cut to length as required, and usually comprise a bronze stern tube with bronze or stainless-steel shaft. The inside gland is normally grease lubricated, and all other bearings are of cutless rubber and lubricated by seawater.

However, a ferrocement hull poses three problems:

(a) Because it cannot be drilled (at least to the bore and length needed here), a steel core tube is normally welded into the mesh and mortared into place. This restricts the size of the stern tube.
(b) This tube and the surrounding hull are essentially ferrous and

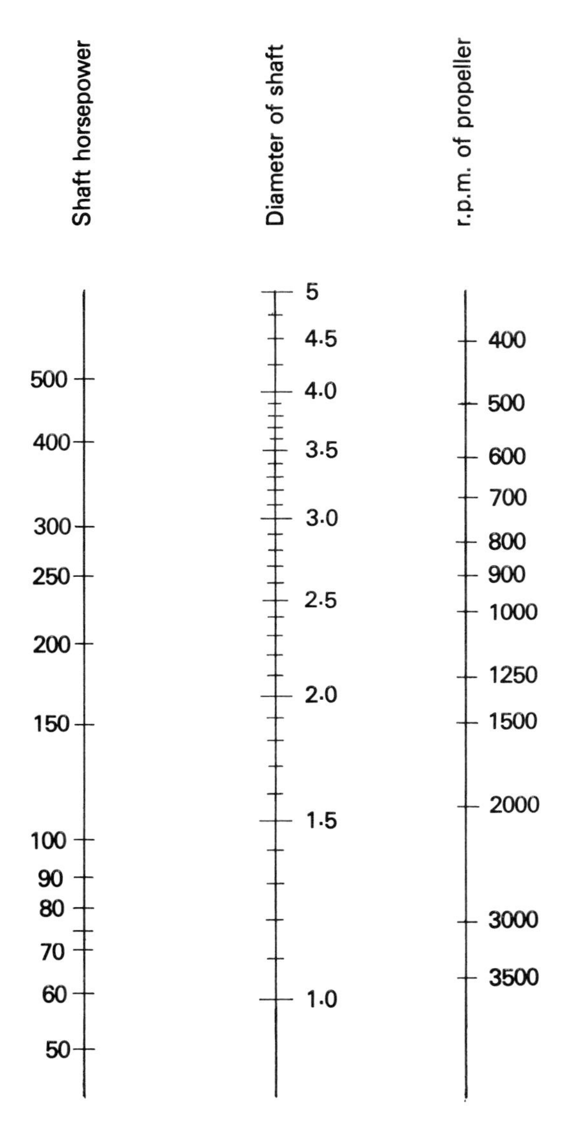

Fig. 50 Relationship between shaft diameter and horsepower.

thus subject to electrolytic interaction with yellow-metal sterngear.

(c) Ferrocement is by nature a poor conductor of heat, and the sterngear is encased in rather a lot of it (at least in the conventional single-screw installation).

Figure 51 shows the mating of a standard sterngear and a steel liner tube and it will be noted that the bore of the liner was selected to

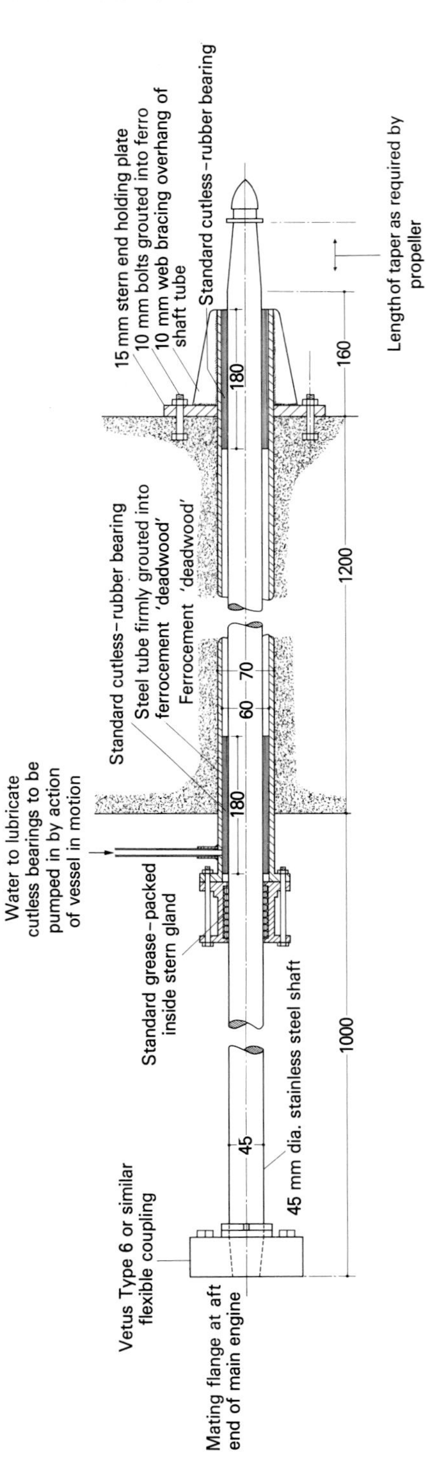

Fig. 51 Water-cooled sterngear with cutless-rubber bearings.

accept the largest part of the bronze gear, which is, of course, quite normal when the engine and gear size are selected before the liner tube is mortared in. A point which requires some thought is that the bore of the liner tube is liable to be out of true by quite an amount (up to 0·02 in is common in commercial tubes of about 3 in bore). Where the installation is of low power this can be tolerated by using undersize sterngear, for the problems of setting up a horizontal miller to reduce the eccentricity to machine tolerances are formidable. It will also be noted that the two coachbolts normally holding the outside gland and supporting the tube are working into nuts grouted into the ferro. It is unlikely that these will be available in a bought-in hull, and other solutions are needed: it is feasible to drill out oversize holes and grout in synthetic or timber plugs with high-resin grout, then drilling or tapping these for the coachbolts. The double-screw action of the opposing ends of the gear should prevent movement.

The simplest solution to the electrolysis problem is to coat the bore of the liner tube and the outside of the stern tube with four layers of epoxy tar. If there is space enough, the tube can be bound with plastic tape between only two coats. Preventing salt water from reaching the metals is always the safest protection. In a similar way, the length of exposed shaft between the sterngland and the propeller boss can be protected if there is any chance of electrolysis between dissimilar metals.

For such conventional sterngear systems the safest solution to the heat-conduction problem is a full-flow water system as shown in Fig. 51. A scoop-inlet, facing forward, brings seawater into the hull near the stern gear; thence it is piped into the inside cutless-rubber bearing by pressure generated by the forward motion of the ship, and so is forced along the stern tube and out through the outside bearing. Pressure maintains an adequate flow of water while the shaft is turning and so rapidly conducts away any heat built up by friction. It does not work in reverse, but few ships go astern for any length of time.

When the desire for more power is very strong and the liner tube is too small to accept standard sterngear, an oil-cooled system with white-metal bearings may be installed. This will almost certainly involve boring out the ends of the tube to within standard machine tolerances, and a reasonable overhang outside the ferro shell is needed, so that the bearings may be held in place with grub screws. An external cap with O-ring seals must be fitted to retain the oil and prevent ingress of sea water, and the hull must be drilled to permit the fitting of an outside tube to complete the oil-flow circuit. A small pump can easily be belt-driven from the shaft to provide the necessary impetus. (See Fig. 52.) Its obvious disadvantage is the need to check machinings and bearing fits, etc., especially under boatyard conditions, but its main advantage is that it permits an all-steel system,

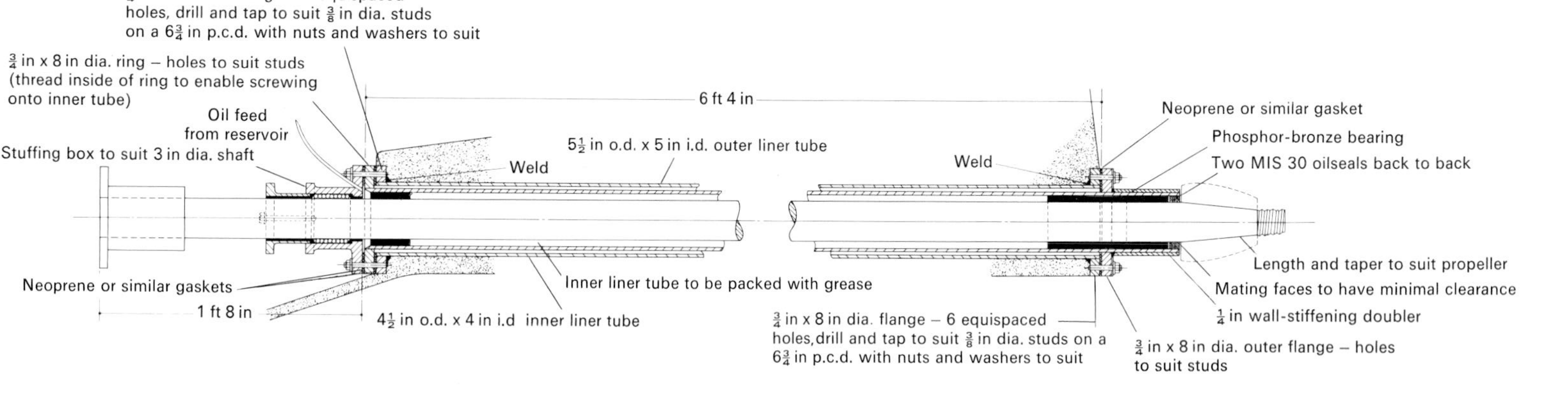

Fig. 52 Oil-cooled sterngear with phosphor-bronze bearings.

with a high-tensile propeller shaft to carry greater power than would be possible with other systems.

Twin-screw installations fall into two main classes: those in which the sterngear is largely enclosed in ferro, either completely to the propeller or partially, and those in which the shafts emerge through elongated openings in the hull and are supported, outside by a P-bracket or A-bracket, and inside by a combined gland and bearing, frequently flexible or capable of limited adjustment. This system is popular on fast motor cruisers in grp and plywood, but needs care in ferro by virtue of the greater difficulties of ensuring fully watertight seals in face of the vibration of the system. Much care is needed to provide the exit apertures, which must be drilled and cut out of the ferro shell with as little breakaway of the edges as possible; once the true shape has been established the raw edges of the ferro should be sealed; all exposed mesh should be tapped back or over into the inside of the hull, brushed and treated with rust preservative[2] and the edges closed with a resin grout, as in a repair kit. Matching timber pads about $\frac{3}{4}$ in thick should be shaped to the hull and aperture, giving the option of reducing the apertures further. It must be borne in mind that the shape of the shaft will displace the apertures vertically with respect to each other. Both pads should then be resin-bonded[3] to the hull and through-bolted. (See Fig. 53.)

The aft ends of the shafts will be supported by standard P- or A-brackets, according to the power to be transmitted. These must be bolted through the hull, and once again the use of bolting pads inside and out is advisable. The outside pads, of course, will allow adjustment of the positions of the brackets, although some modern P-brackets

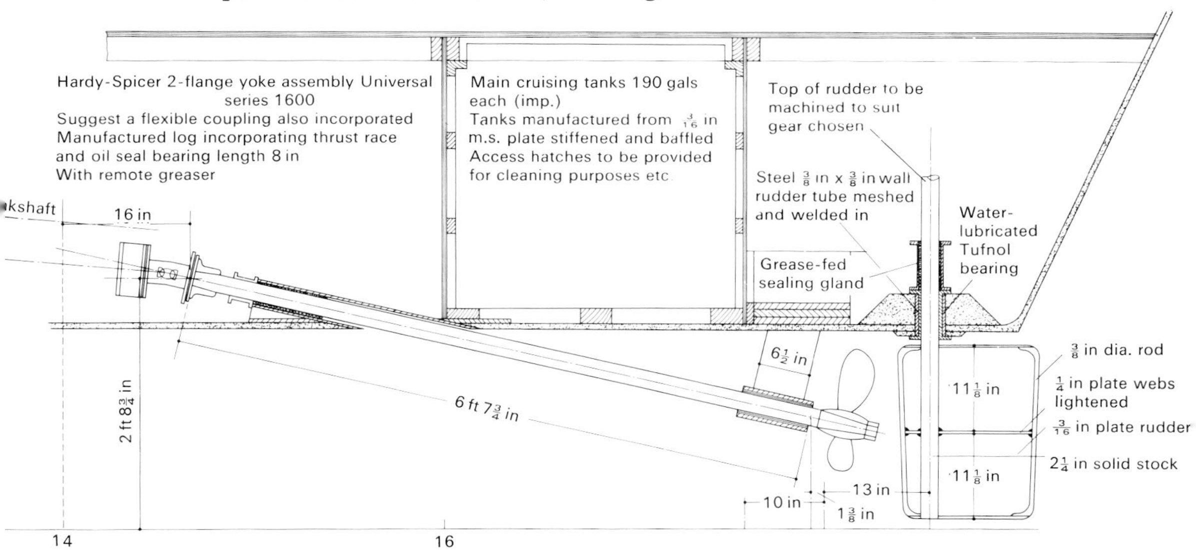

Fig. 53 Sterngear based on the flexible shaft log.

are adjustable. Unless made specifically, most brackets are bronze castings and carry cutless-rubber bushes in the bosses; complete lubrication is obvious here, and no further attention is required. The inner shaft-logs will also be bronze, grease-lubricated, and the shafts themselves will be exposed to the sea from the logs to the brackets: therefore they should be of stainless steel or bronze, and should be fully protected by epoxy tar, metal preservative and/or plastic tape. It should be remembered that, since yachts spend most of their lives on moorings, these shafts will attract marine growths and so will need antifouling treatment. The use of a plastic barrier, as advised, will inhibit any potential electrolysis between the metal of the paint and shaft.

Cathodic Protection

The shaft system just described is essentially inimical to the steel in the hull, and will attack it where possible. The systems described earlier are naturally safer in this respect; but all of them will terminate in a large bronze propeller, which will have the same effect. Theoretically, if the mortar cover on the hull is correct and the shell has been resin-sealed and epoxy painted, it should be quite inert and not subject to electrolysis. But it is better to be safe than sorry, so fit cathodic protection in the form of sacrificial anodes of pure zinc to the hull close to the yellow metal parts. Several firms[4] specialize in advising on the number, weight and placement of such anodes, and supply them as needed.

Engine Beds

It has been assumed that the hull being fitted out already has engine beds and stern-tube liner or core in place. If there is no provision for a stern tube, the chances of boring through several feet of mass-ferro are remote, and thus the concept of a centreline installation must be abandoned in favour of one or two drives at quarter beam. This was once quite common in sailing yachts, when engines were installed long after building and, provided that a full analysis is made of the space available, with special reference to the avoidance of fouling the rudder when hard over, the system can work well. An elongated hole can be broken through the hull in exactly the same way as for a twin-screw installation, with an adjustable or self-aligning shaft log inside and an A-bracket outside. If circumstances then dictate a central engine, the drive can be coupled by vee-belts or, if available, by one of the proprietary systems of hydraulic pump/motor drives. It should be remembered that a single screw will exert a turning effect on the stern by virtue of its own rotation, and one set out from the centreline will also exert a turning force by virtue of its position. Thus, a propeller which turns clockwise when viewed from aft will tend to force the ship's head to port: a propeller of any rotation set on the starboard side will do likewise. A clockwise propeller should therefore be installed on the port side, where the two head-turning forces will tend to neutralize each other.

The existence of a central liner tube has already been discussed in terms of its effect upon shaft size, and–by implication–on the diameter of propeller which can be used, insofar that it is most unwise to bring the tips of the propeller blades closer to the hull than 10 per cent of the diameter, e.g. a 24 in propeller should have its shaft 12 in + 2·4 in = $14\frac{1}{2}$ in from the hull. Moreover, in general terms the maximum distance between the front of the aperture and the centre of the blades (the point at which maximum clearance is needed) is seldom more than half the propeller diameter.

Data have been presented to give the builder reasonable choice of engine, shaft and screw; but the existence of the liner tube and of engine beds may restrict the choice. Irrespective of the beds, the liner tube will begin to dictate where the engine must be in the vertical plane and at what angle. Alterations or decisions, if the designed-in unit is unknown, lie along these lines:

(a) Use a double universal joint to change the angle; this might, for example, permit an engine to be set horizontally against an inclined shaft but will add up to 1 ft to the minimum clearance required between engine and sterngland.

(b) Reverse the engine and drive through a conventional vee box. This is feasible only if the liner tube is steeply inclined, so that the engine is nearly horizontal. It will raise the engine and so provide space for bed-width adjustment.

(c) Alter the attitude of the gearbox. Standard gearboxes can be of the straight-through variety in which the output shaft is in the same plane as the crankshaft, or the 'dropped' variety, where the output shaft is several inches below the crankshaft; many of these boxes can be reversed so that the drive is above the crankshaft. The relationship to the crankshaft is not really important here; what matters is the relationship between the output shaft and the engine mounting feet, and these gearbox variants allow a considerable range of choice in this.

(d) Raise the engine and use a belt drive, either with the conventional placement, i.e. gearbox aft, or reversed, i.e. gearbox forward.

What of the beds themselves? On the assumption that they are in place, one can expect solid ferrocement upstands with flat tops through which protrude bolts to carry timber cappings and/or to connect with the engine mounting feet. Generally, engine beds vary from 2 to 4 in wide according to the size of engine, and the cappings on the ferro should be from $\frac{3}{4}$ to $1\frac{1}{2}$ in thick, in good hardwood (afrormosia is favourite here). If the builder intends to install the designed engine, all he then needs to do is to lower the engine on to its beds, locating the hold-down bolts into the mounting feet, place about $\frac{1}{8}$ in of shimming beneath each foot and tighten down the nuts. All is then ready for connection to the sterngear and final alignment when the hull is afloat.

This arrangement is essentially a semi-rigid system, the timber helping the beds to absorb vibration; a rubber coupling, such as the Silentbloc or Vetus unit, can with advantage lie between engine and propeller flanges, although if the flange-sterngland distance is very small an all-rigid system is desirable.

The use of flexible mountings or vibration-absorption pads between the mounting lugs and engine beds is now common practice, but since they allow the engine to vibrate as a unit they must be associated with either a flexible coupling if the intermediate shaft (i.e. the part between the engine and the sterngland) is short, or a universal joint if it is long: and if its unsupported length is more than 20 times its own diameter, a pillow or plummer block must be provided. The whip induced in, say, a 3 ft length of 1 in diameter shaft rigidly coupled to a flexibly-mounted engine could wear out the inner bearing of the stern tube in a few hours, and the shaft itself would have but a short life. It should be noted that such mountings will raise the engine from 1 in to 4 in above its beds, according to size, but that the timber capping may be omitted, being replaced by square steel washer plates under the feet themselves to permit final shimming. Only with a double universal joint is this delicate final alignment of engine and shaft omitted.

When the beds are in the right place and of the right height but have no hold-down bolts (or those provided are in the wrong place so must be cut off), steel cheek plates must be provided. It is not difficult to drill through the sides of the ferro beds for a number of $\frac{3}{8}$ in bolts to hold the steel cheeks. A heavy plate welded across the top and a timber pad between it and the ferro provides space for the heads of short hold-down bolts, which should be caught to the steel with a tack weld to prevent them turning when the nuts are tightened. It follows that such an arrangement will lift the engine so that, used in conjunction with adequate timber pads and flexible mountings, it will permit a fair adjustment in engine height.

One of the problems of marine engines is that their designers seldom meet, and then they never discuss mounting feet; thus, the chances of finding two engines whose hold-down bolts are the same distance apart are rather slender. If the holes on the selected engine are further apart, or closer together, than the edges of the existing ferro bearers, some simple solutions are possible, as shown in Fig. 54. If the small

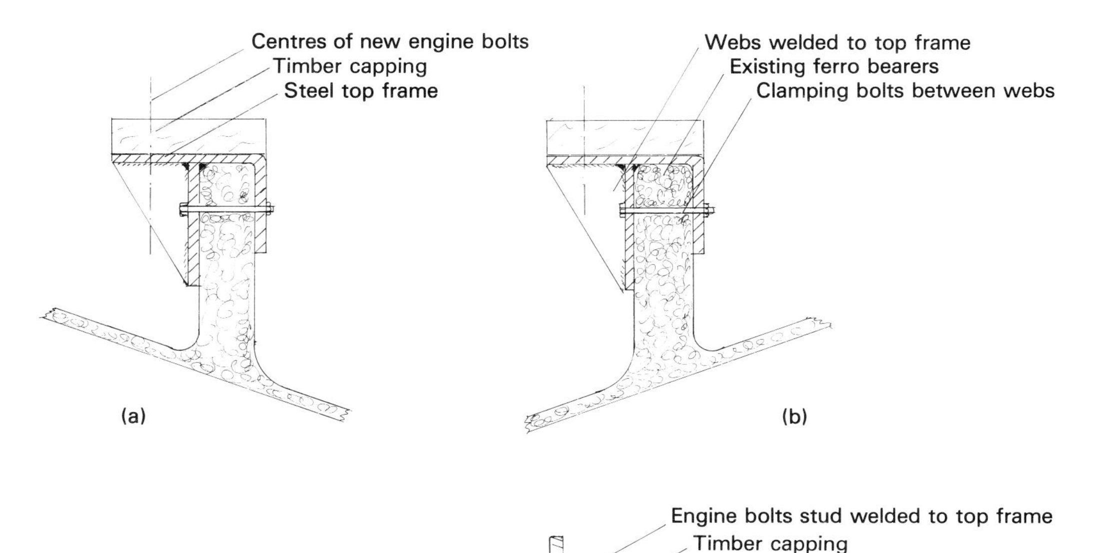

Fig. 54 Modifying existing beds

(a) Engine feet wider than beds
(b) Engine feet closer than beds
(c) Beds not quite correct and over-narrow.

The scheme shown in (b) will permit considerably smaller units to be fitted than originally designed.

support flanges at the hold-down bolts are correctly situated they will prevent the heads of the bolts from turning when the nuts are tightened. If the bolts are much wider than the existing bearers, additional full-depth hardwood bearers must be fitted, glued and bolted to the ferro. Since this situation presupposes a very much larger unit than originally intended, it should not normally arise. In the converse situation, with the engine much narrower than the existing bearers, it is also likely that it will need to be mounted below the bearer line; this can be accomplished as shown in Fig. 55, but the heads of the hold-down bolts must be tack-welded to the steel plate, for they will be quite inaccessible once the engine is set in above them. Shimming for alignment may prove difficult, but in this situation there should be room for a universal coupling between engine and propeller shaft.

A situation found perhaps rather more often in sailboats than in power craft is that in which the engine bearer tops continue outboard to the shell proper, forming a wide flat over solid ferro. From the

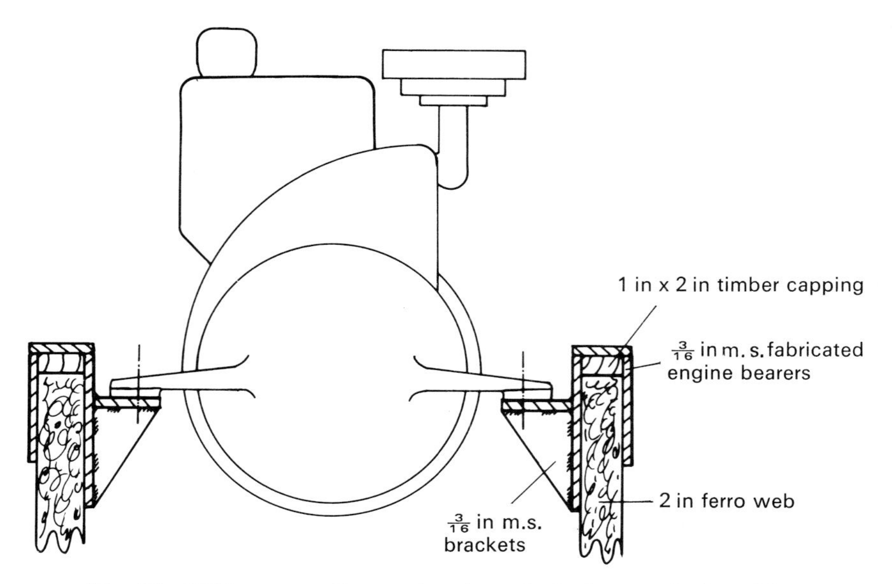

Fig. 55 Fitting a smaller engine than the beds were designed for.

aspects of vibration and support strength, as well as construction techniques, this has much to commend it in a reverse-garboard situation. If there are hold-down bolts mortared in, all is well, even if they are not quite right for the engine. But when there are no bolts one has a real problem, for the prospect of drilling down right through the hull to counterbore for the nut, and then having to seal all permanently against the ingress of water, is formidable. If there are floors or webs at the ends and/or in the middle of the floors, then the steel angle system can be flanged and bolted through them (given space for drilling). If not, the probable sole acceptable solution is blind-drilling down into the ferro, plugging with timber or proprietary products and using wood screws: in all cases here the use of a good industrial adhesive is advised; an epoxy-polysulphide such as Bostik 202A is probably the best answer, for its natural adherence to steel and cement is reasonable, especially if the surfaces are smooth, totally free from dust and de-greased.

Stern Drives

The association of stern drives and ferrocement hulls has before now been of little interest, because ferrocement hulls have tended to be heavy and thus of large displacement, while the stern drive has been essentially a high-speed job suited to high-speed hulls. But larger diesel stern drives are coming onto the market and the surface density of ferro is falling. Planing hulls are now a possibility, though perhaps only under controlled factory conditions. At the top end of the power range are units of about 200 h.p. and big outdrives, suitable for

40–60 ft pilot boats or similar. At the bottom end are 20 h.p. units suitable for canal or river cruisers.

The real trouble is the concept–an engine in front of the transom and a drive unit aft of it, with a substantial hole in the middle. At the present state of the art, producing a hole of 8–12 in diameter in a transom is undeniably a hazardous undertaking except at the mesh stage; even then, a substantial stress-collection ring is vital, for this hole is transmitting all the horsepower. The engine and the outdrive flanges must be bolted together and the bolt holes must match and must not leak; nor must the transom fracture under the loadings imposed. Fortunately the mechanical system is designed for solid wooden transoms, which may leave space for reasonable wooden pads on both sides of the ferro. Great care must be taken to ensure that every fit and tolerance specified by the manufacturer is met, and all the engineering work in terms of holes, etc., should be completed and then the whole coated with good resin sealer before the drive unit is installed.

Early stern drives hung the engine in cantilever from the transom, which has never seemed a sound engineering principle; later–and certainly larger–drives have normal bearers for the engines, and these must be in place. It is possible to fit adequate timber bearers by glassing them into the hull, especially when they can be locked between the transom and the bulkhead forward of it. But on the whole it is not really advisable to try to fit stern drives into a hull which has not been designed for them, except under the close supervision of a naval architect: the chances of producing a fracture failure of the ferro as the result of prolonged vibrational stresses are far too high.

The only outboards of real interest for use on ferro hulls are likely to be the Carniti diesel range, on small canal or river cruisers. As with stern drives–only more so–the transom must have been designed for the power unit; the mind boggles at the problems of trying to produce a standard outboard-well arrangement in a transom designed for another form of propulsion, and our advice is very simple: don't try. Apart from this the only problem is the crushing load of the clamping screws; it is essential that this be taken on adequate timber pads on both sides of the transom, since the grip on the aft face can damage the mortar as much as the screwing action on the clamp faces.

Ancillaries

Once the engine has been set firmly on its bed, attention can be given to its immediate ancillaries, first among which is its cooling water. If–as is now rather unlikely–cooling is by raw seawater, the runs of the inlet and outlet pipes must be sorted out to give the easiest leads. Both will require skin fittings with seacocks, so care must be taken to ensure that the fittings are firmly bedded on Neoprene or rubber washers, to reduce the chance of electrolysis between them (for they will be of brass or bronze) and the steel in the hull.[5] It is also necessary to ensure that they are so located that the cocks can be reached, even when the engine is hot: emergencies can arise. When the engine is cooled by heat exchanger and the cooling water is discharged through the exhaust system, only an inlet will be required; the above considerations still apply. It should be remembered that some larger diesels have water-cooled gearboxes; the point should be checked.

Controls

Control systems, fuel supplies, exhaust systems and the electrical circuits then need consideration. Of these, the fuel supply will depend greatly on the tank location, the exhaust will depend a great deal on the vessel and its engine, and the electrical system must needs be accorded particular attention.

The controls for the engine comprise essentially gearshift and throttle, perhaps with such refinements as trolling-valve control for prolonged low-speed running. In the simplest situation, the open boat, the gearshift will be manual, a simple lever projecting from the gearbox; and the throttle control will be a Bowden cable, perhaps to a simple thumb lever on the gear shift.

In a small sailing cruiser without a watertight cockpit, and in small motor cruisers, the same situation may exist, perhaps with the throttle control on a coaming or bulkhead near the helm.

Finally, completely remote operation may be achieved, and is now usual in yachts or workboats of any size; the methods available are (a) rod linkage, which is very positive but tricky to install, (b) Bowden cable, which is common even up to 250 h.p. units of high-speed type but which requires care in changing cable direction by the use of large bending radii, and (c) hydraulic, which is the most common in larger engines. There is one attractive little engine of 12 h.p. which uses electrically-actuated direct reverse, and still available–though of somewhat large proportions–are diesels which reverse directly by manual alteration of the valve gear; builders who opt for this type of drive must be assumed to know exactly what they are doing and in no need of advice.

Hydraulic systems certainly have a great deal to commend them and most modern engines are fitted with hydraulic gearboxes with small actuating levers (in place of the long ones of the manual box) designed to be coupled to hydraulic actuators. Installation of the copper piping calls for care in two ways–the minimization of the number of changes of direction, and the placement of the piping in positions where accidental damage is unlikely. The manufacturer's instructions regarding hydraulic fluid and the filling of the system should be adhered to scrupulously. The major ill with hydraulics is the inclusion of air bubbles, and it is vital that these be cleared from the system (this is known as 'bleeding'): fluids are incompressible and hence will transmit forces; air is compressible, and won't: thus, air in the system leads to a 'spongy' feel, culminating in total loss of operation.

The Bowden-cable system, e.g. Morse, Teleflex or Jaymo, has been mentioned and is probably the most suitable for smaller and/or faster engines. Apart from its radii, installation is easy. In the smaller sizes there is the choice between single and dual-lever control, the former combining clutch and gearshift throttle in a single control; this has some operational advantages, but can make it difficult to 'run up' an engine out of gear. Again, care should be taken with the manufacturer's literature and recommendations, to ensure that the system selected is powerful enough for the engine.

Considerable care should be taken to place the controls as conveniently to hand for the helmsman as possible, at the same time ensuring that accidental operation is impossible.

Fuel

The fuel system will comprise tank, pipes, filters and pumps: the pump will be fitted to the engine and driven from it, and be fully suited to its carburettors or injectors in a 'bought in' marine unit, or must be matched in a home-marinized one. The pump itself will determine the bore of the fuel-feed pipe, though the manufacturer's instructions should be sought, since some like to feed in via a taper down in the last couple of inches before the pump. The tank itself may be of metal or may be part of the hull: when the fuel capacity required is modest, and there is adequate space, there is much to commend the use of tanks from lorries or similar heavy vehicles,[6] though they should be bought new rather than secondhand. Construction is normally very robust, and capacities between 25 and 75 gallons are average. The next critical problem is the filling arrangement: here again, some of these tanks have long necks between tank and filler cap, and this is the type to acquire, for it is essential to have the filler cap above deck. Unless the cap itself is removable, the hole through the ferro must be larger than the neck itself; once the neck is in place the space can be made good with a resinous grout or epoxy filler. The alternative system is to use a proprietary flush-fitting deck filler and connect its underdeck spigot to the neck of the tank by a fuel-resistant plastic hose, secured by Jubilee clips; this is the only acceptable solution where the tank neck is short, and has the advantage of eliminating any transfer of vibration between tank and deck. Be wary of tank vents, and be sure that the vent is both adequate and exhausts above deck, preferably overboard; ideally, the vent should rise well above the deck, bend over at the top and come down again to within a few inches of the deck. It must be located where it cannot be damaged, such as beside a bulkhead or deckhouse.

Where the fuel requirement is high, as in an ocean cruiser or work-boat, the hull will be used as a bunker, and here we really do begin to court disaster unless the greatest care is taken. There are two sources of trouble: low, wide tanks and fuel osmosis. In a hull of trawler form the obvious place for fuel is in the double bottom, between the shell and the cabin sole; the space is otherwise unused and the fuel weight is low down. However the tank is liable to be wide and shallow, so that when it is only partially filled there will be a marked effect on stability: a somewhat technical subject designated 'free-surface effect', this may be visualized in terms of the surge of fuel from side to side. Multiple fore-and-aft baffling is essential, or the total subdivision of the space into several tanks connected internally. Where the bunker capacity is large (e.g. in *Trixie* the main tank holds 10 tons), the use of internal walls and external, valved, connections is advisable. There will need to be either separate or branched fillers which will come far enough above the deck to permit the use of proprietary screw-on hose connectors from mobile tankers. A typical arrangement would be a 4 in bore pipe ending 15 in above deck with a standard pipe thread outside for the hose, and a spun-steel cap to seal it when the tank is full. Such pipes will need to be very firmly mortared into the deck and may with advantage be placed *in situ* at the meshing stage to ensure perfect fit and seal.

In the raw state most ferrocements are not fuel-tight, and diesel (or even worse paraffin) will leak right through the intermolecular spaces of the structure. Where the mortar has been a wet one, for plasticity, the excess moisture drying out will leave substantial 'passageways' for fuel, which will leach through a hull in only a few months. Thus the shell must be sealed, using either a proprietary sealer such as Armorglass, Boscoprene or several coats of epoxy resin, preferably bonded by a scrim of glass fibre: for large tanks a woven cloth of 18 oz per sq yd is adequate. The real danger points are the filler pipes and the fuel exit pipes, especially the latter for they are under pressure. The tank should be cored for these at the mesh stage, to ensure accurate holes. After removal of the cores the shell should be de-dusted, de-greased and epoxy sealed; the pipes should also be epoxy sealed on the outside and eased into position with the aid of wet resin or grease. It is important not to use a hammer at this juncture, nor any action which will tend to break the sealing surface–although, of course, a tight fit is vital. The flanges should then be screwed on and bedded to substantial Neoprene gaskets. If the system is so large that the flanges must be through-bolted, the bolt holes should be drilled before sealing of the tank begins, and checked for fit; care should be taken to ensure that these holes are sealed throughout

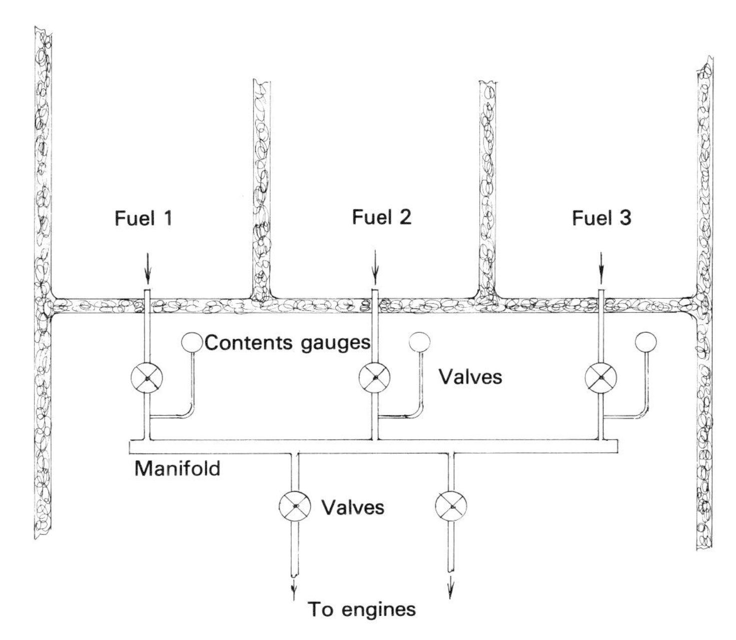

Fig. 56 Schematic diagram of feed-off for two engines from three tanks; the valve-and-manifold system permits complete operational flexibility.

their lengths. It cannot be too highly stressed that there is no margin for error here and no chance to take out a fitting and replace it– experience shows that osmosis leaks always occur when this happens, and once fuel has got into the matrix of the mortar it is almost impossible to remove it. Figure 56 shows a typical fuel-draw-off arrangement with three tanks feeding a large manifold from which two engines pull fuel; it is expensive in its use of valves, but it is safe.

A compromise system is possible where there is, perhaps, a single engine feed from wing tanks; here the front of each tank is sheet steel firmly bonded to the deckhouse upstand at its top end and to a matching upstand in the hull deadrise: the careful selection of mastic fillings and resin sealers is mandatory, but a fuel-tight joint can be secured. All fuel connections can now be safely welded to the steel sheet and hence the sealing problem of the connections is avoided. The shell itself must still be correctly sealed, of course. Figure 57 shows a half section of a small trawler in which this system is employed.

Exhausts

There are two types of exhaust: wet and dry. Dry ones demand a funnel and have a great deal to commend them where they are possible; the silencer can be in the funnel and thus much reduce the space used

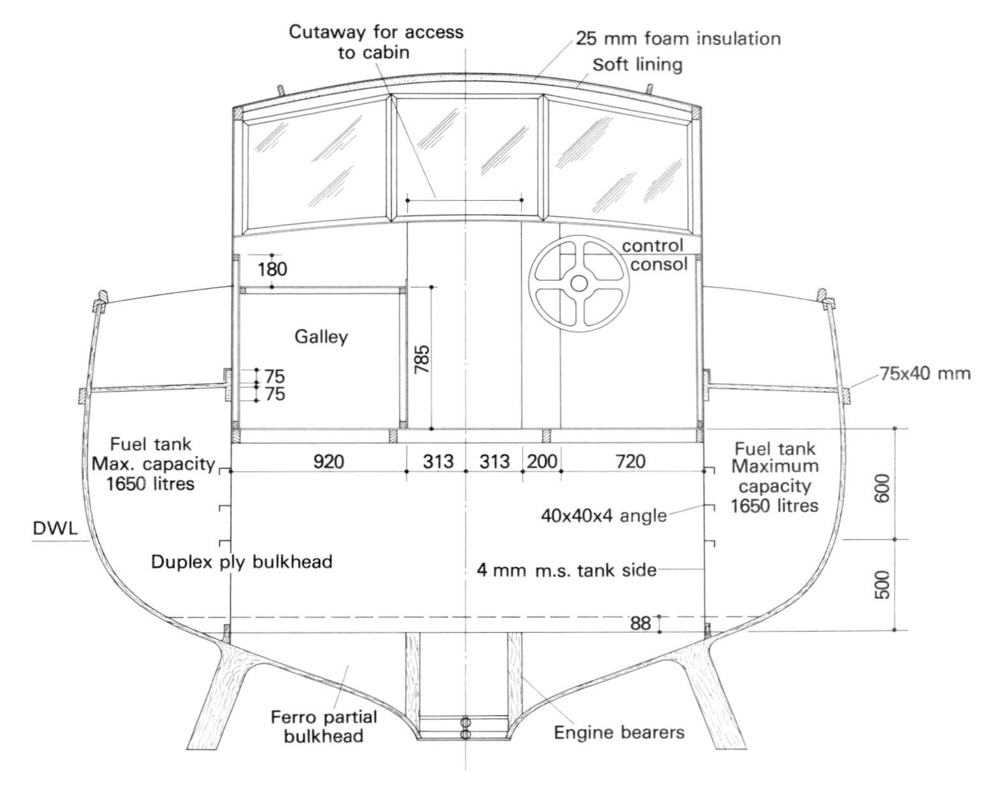

Fig. 57 In Yara 121 *the hull forms wing tanks, but these have steel fronts to facilitate plumbing.*

in the engine room, but the lead from the manifold to the silencer needs to be most carefully designed and thoroughly lagged. The usual problem is that the funnel wants to be forward with the bridge and the engine is aft; and there's a lot of accommodation between them. But many solutions are possible, and more so as the impact of the design of modern liners and ferries is felt in yachts, especially with regard to funnels and masts.

Wet exhausts are by far the more common, the outlet being in the side of the hull or in the transom. In a sailing vessel it really is wisest to bring the exhaust aft into the lazarette, swan-neck it up to deck level and then down to a low point on the transom, as shown in Fig. 49. In this way the chance of feeding seawater back along the exhaust pipe to the block is almost eliminated; such a risk is manifestly present in a sailboat, which will be moving at many attitudes to the sea with its engines silent; a power craft is less liable to such damage because the pressure of its exhaust gases will normally prevent water ingress. Nevertheless, a simple exhaust run to a point near the waterline could well produce trouble in a boat rolling heavily at its moorings. So even in a powerboat there is much to commend transom exhausts–including the ability to secure a clean, straight run, with consequent reduction of back pressure. In these installations it is customary to follow a 5 degree declivity in the line and to feed the cooling water from the heat-exchanger direct into the line at or near the manifold. In considering the placement of outlets it should be remembered that a diesel of 150 h.p. or so will have an exhaust of 4 in diameter, while one of 250 h.p. will be around 6 in. Moreover, the size of the silencer itself must be considered at an early stage, for the latter engine could well demand a unit 22 in in diameter and 45 in long. Flexibility in the exhaust line is essential, the more so if the engine is on flexible mounts and/or the outlet is bolted to the hull; vibration will fracture a rigid line.

Two final comments: few stainless steels take kindly to a hot mixture of seawater and exhaust gases, so stick to mild steel or cast iron (best if available); and stern exhausts, especially large ones, are unsightly in a trawler or canoe stern, where a dry system is advisable. There is much to study in this, as in the whole engineering side of fitting-out, and ferro hulls maybe have more problems than most. But there are solutions, and advice in detail is available, especially from naval architects who specialize in ferro. So press on, think clearly ahead, and make the engineering a credit to the ship and the fine materials of the hull.

Notes

1. Warren, Nigel (1977) *Marine Conversions*. London, Adlard Coles Ltd.
2. Strong contenders here are: Unitrol by Unibond Ltd, Camberley; Universal Protective Coatings; Boscoprene.
3. FerroJoin: MacAlister Carvall Ltd.
4. E.g. M.G. Duff and Partners, Chichester, Sussex.
5. Seacocks in nylon-based plastics are available up to 1 in bore.
6. If the vessel is built to Classification, the acceptability of this solution should be confirmed.

Chapter Eight **Layouts and Living Quarters**

The only way to write a chapter on layouts in a book such as this is to dismiss the subject very briefly indeed. The whole question of design for living afloat covers such a vast range of possibilities, especially when considered in conjunction with the history of yachting within this context, that it could well form a book of its own; certainly it is far beyond the scope of a single chapter. In review one may comment that, whereas in the early decades of this century yachts tended to be large with rather few berths, they later passed through a phase in which builders vied with each other to cram the maximum number of berths into the smallest hull and are now slowly returning towards the 'large hull with few berths' concept. The major difference perhaps between these two versions of the basic thesis is the use of light colours and plastics instead of stained mahogany and crimson leather, with the resultant feeling of even more space.

However, it is still unhappily true that owners, and even some professional designers (from choice or at owner's behest, maybe), pride themselves on cramming in the maximum number of berths (or cabins in the larger craft) that the hull will take. On paper these schemes may well seem most ingenious; in the solid they lose their glamour a little and sometimes need most drastic modifications to enable them to be made useable. But in the building yard, as the owner proudly demonstrates to you, everything works. After a few days at sea, when every berth has its quota of bodies, all wanting to move about at the same time, the 'art of living afloat' may well be reduced to a simple battle for survival. One of the most civilized 35-footers the author sailed on was described by its owner as a 'berth at each end with a bar in the middle'. In short, the crew did not eat where they slept, had room to stow their gear and a little privacy.

Privacy

Privacy is likely to be a commodity in the shortest supply on a small yacht and one which, on an overnight cruise or a modern ocean race, is hardly necessary. But many ferro yachts are conceived for long ocean voyages, and it is under these living conditions that the need for privacy makes itself felt. Its lack eventually leads to tensions and strains among a crew which started well together, leading to friction, reduced co-operation and hence to poor seamanship. Hard living is all right in a warship, where tight discipline takes care of morale, but one cannot run a yacht like a warship. As if to point both ways in this argument one might cite the 73 ft schooner *Pallas Athene*, on paper a rash of small cabins each full of berths; however, she is designed for very long distances and to be handled by a small crew. Thus each watch of four shares a miniscule sleeping cabin, which truly gives no privacy; but this arrangement leaves the deck saloon, lower saloon, library and forepeak (a spacious area) as 'privacy areas' in which those crew members who are neither on watch nor asleep can more or less get away from each other, albeit briefly. Such an arrangement would not work on a charter yacht, but then few charter yachts make really long voyages. On such duty the 4-man crew cabins would be converted into 2-man quarters, with adequate wardrobe and stowage volumes.

Berths

It follows that the many varieties of layout to be contemplated, covering both power and sailing yachts from 30 to 70-odd feet in length, together with small working craft, are–as stated at the outset–well beyond our scope. All that can be considered are the basic essentials. It is known (and all too well understood by professional designers) that the layout on which the whole design was initially based, and around which the hull form was conceived, will be redrawn a couple of times before fitting-out begins; and that if the owner does his own fitting-out the end-product will resemble none of the drawings. Indeed, in some hulls there is much to be said for mocking-up parts of a sketched layout in cardboard and scrap, to help visualization in three dimensions. But certain basic facts should be borne in mind when planning. First: it is reputed that the number of men more than 6 ft 3 in tall has increased six-fold since the 1920s. Second: the average human being is uncomfortable in a berth less than 6 in longer than his height. Ergo: a yacht with more than four berths needs at least one 6 ft 9 in long and all should be 6 ft 3 in clear; a 7 ft berth is not stupid and any under 6 ft are strictly for children. Now people are not really growing longer and skinnier; they are growing larger all round.

So the 18 in shelf which was hopefully called a 'sea berth' in the ocean racers of the immediate postwar era will now scarcely carry sails, let alone a crew man. Berths should be about 2 ft wide in the middle, preferably not less than this at the head, and certainly not less than 12 in at the foot; except where two berths are joined for more than their final 2 ft 6 in, as in a forecabin, when their combined width may be a foot provided that their individual lengths along their centre lines is more than 6 ft 3 in.

Double berths are fine in harbour, but can be uncomfortable in a seaway, especially when the ship is rolling. They need two people in each, or a central bunk-board to prevent a solitary occupant from being thrown out. Athwartships berths should be restricted to canal and river cruisers.

Wooden–plank or ply–berths need 4 in cushions, but those with sheet rubber, webbing or canvas tops are quite comfortable with cushions only 2 in thick.

The average person needs a minimum hip clearance of 18 in above an uncompressed cushion to turn over comfortably: note this most carefully when planning quarter berths, which should have a minimum of 2 ft 6 in inside the cabin proper, with adequate headroom. To sit up in bed requires 3 ft 3 in headroom above the cushion, although less is permissible if the overhead contact area is well padded.

A comfortable settee, that is one which crewmen can sit on for reasonable periods to eat, drink, talk and read, should be 14–16 in above the cabin sole and 14–18 in wide, with some form of backrest about 14 in above the cushion and a minimum of 3 ft 3 in head clearance. Soft webbing seats may be very nice to sleep on but can be acutely uncomfortable for sitting.

For a reasonable voyage an average person needs about 15 cu ft of space to stow his personal belongings–clothes, boots, books, cameras and so on.

Galleys

A clever cook can produce *ad infinitum* for four people from two burners and a grill, but an oven relieves the monotony. A crew of 6–8 begins to need three burners, grill and overn, while 8–12 need four burners, grill and oven. Allow space for a stove of the right size, swung in gimbals if you expect to travel heeled; and allow the cook room to move, to open his oven door clear and to dodge the lot when it is shot at him, all piping hot, by a high-speed tack made without warning. Give your galley plenty of ventilation, especially via an over-stove extractor vent, but try to avoid draughts: apart from blowing out the gas flames and hence possibly leading to explosions, they can give the cook pneumonia and play havoc with soufflés.

An average yachtsman can get through 4 lb of comestibles per day, easily. So your 8-berth ketch crossing the Atlantic must find room for nearly half a ton of food: this takes up a lot of space. He will also use 4 pints of water, excluding ablutions, or a gallon if he is allowed to wash/shave in fresh water: eight men on a 30-day passage will be looking for 240 gallons, which weighs rather more than a ton and needs no less than 36 cu ft for its stowage. So our crew with their food and water, but with no margin for error, will add nearly $2\frac{1}{2}$ tons to the overall displacement and could easily see the boot-top 4 in below the waterline, with an attendant loss of ultimate stability unless designed for from the start.

Toilets

A man not born to the sea stands up to pull up his trousers. So in the loo he needs something approaching standing headroom over an area some 30 in square, measured at waist level. Given 3 ft 4 in+ above the toilet itself, which may be set on a plinth up the ship's side, and a width of 30 in, one has the basic dimensions for a very basic loo: it can be improved upon.

The data presented above are necessarily both minimal in their approach to sizing and brief in their outline of the problem; it is the intention only that they should serve as a guide in planning.

Fixing Bulkheads and Joinery

Within this context one must consider both the placement and erection of main bulkheads, and any outline plan should give serious consideration to provisions for fixing bulkheads already existing in the hull. For example, some shells are built on widely spaced web frames, which can form obvious and useful take-off points for bulkheads; others, based on pipe frames, may well have plate grounds already welded to some of the pipes to form bases for timber work. There is much to be said in favour of web frames from the aspect of bulkhead construction, and newer, purpose-built vessels are being designed with webs in the correct positions for main bulkheads. On average the webs will be about $\frac{3}{4}$ thick and 3 in deep, so permitting the construction of duplex bulkheads made from two sheets of $\frac{1}{4}$ in marine ply or equivalent hardboard separated by a framework of $2 \times \frac{3}{4}$ in hardwood rails; these may well be half-jointed to give a lattice not greater than 2 ft 6 in square, the spaces so formed being filled with glass-fibre wool, mineral insulation wool or styrene-foam sheeting; on no account should air gaps be left to promote rot, and it is advisable to coat the framing with wood preservative. The resultant bulkhead is light and strong and possesses reasonable properties of sound and heat insulation–certainly markedly better than a single sheet of ply. Attachment to the web frame is by through-bolting, with careful bedding between the sheets and the ferro web. At the time of writing MacAlister Carvall, a firm specializing in products for the ferrocement boat industry, produce a filler for hulls (FerroFill) which may prove invaluable in surfacing-up the webs to take the ply since it has a good adhesive effect; for use where little or no surfacing is needed their gap-filling FerroJoin would be applicable. Another useful adhesive in this class is Bostik 2024, which combines epoxy resin and polysulphide rubber; other gap-filling resinous adhesives are available and more are being developed each year, so that it is impossible to have an entirely up-to-date picture; the builder should check what materials are available to him at the time of operation. However, it is probably worth while to sound two warnings:

(a) Check all the data carefully: the 'best' adhesive, i.e. that giving the strongest bond, may well require pressures or temperatures outside the scope of the building ambients; many fine adhesives are largely unusable because they need high temperatures (e.g. 75 degrees) to bring their setting times below 12 hours.
(b) Having selected an adhesive, be certain that you know how much to mix for a job and how long application will take; most of them have working lives of 1–2 hours when mixed (they all tend to be 2-part mixtures), so that too great a mix will lead to wastage, while too little will involve a second mix, which takes time at a moment when time is vital.

Figure 58 shows a section through such a bulkhead at the web joint, while Fig. 59 shows the junction between such a bulkhead and a

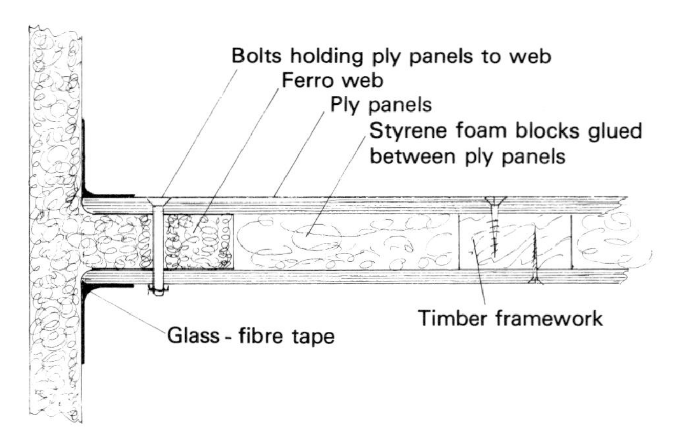

Fig. 58 Section through a duplex bulkhead attached to a hull web in ferro.

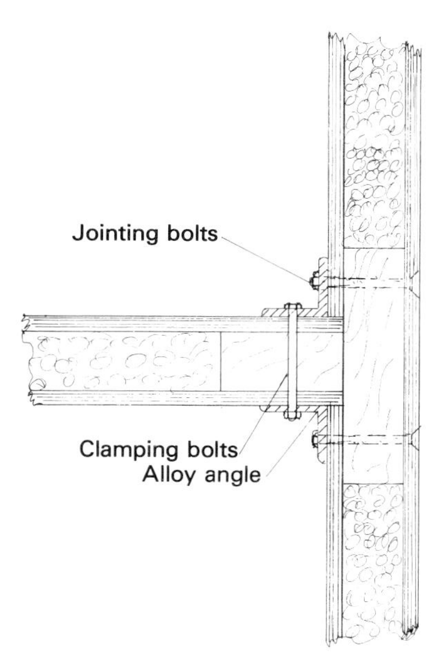

Fig. 59 Junction between longitudinal and transverse duplex bulkheads.

longitudinal cabin wall built on the same principle; it will be seen that the tee joint produces vertical rigidity enough, perhaps, to carry a small mast. Reinforced with steel angle, adequately fastened to appropriate deck beams and floors, as shown in Fig. 60, it will support a substantial mast.

When the hull is pipe-framed, with simple steel-plate grounds welded to the pipes, it is normal to fit a heavier, say $\frac{5}{8}$ or $\frac{3}{4}$ in (according to the size of boat), sheet-ply bulkhead, as shown in Fig. 61. It is advisable to seal the gap between hull and bulkhead with a rubber-based sealing compound, such as those mentioned previously, and it is altogether better to complete the joint with glass-fibre tape. A range of resins is available which will adhere to concrete, grp and wood, but all will need the concrete to be cleaned free from dust and grease by washing with carbon tetrachloride or similar cleaning fluid; some will need a special primer applied to the cement; in any event it may be anticipated that epoxy resins will be preferred to polyesters or urethanes. In general, the method is to coat both ferro and timber with the resin, applied with brush or roller, then lay in a length of glass-fibre tape 6–8 in wide, tamping well into the joint and rolling it well into the resin; then lay in a narrower tape, 4–5 in wide and work in a second coat of resin, ensuring that the tapes are fully impregnated ('wetted out' is the technical term) but that any excess which drains down is removed: here a thixotropic resin is useful, though rather more difficult to use.

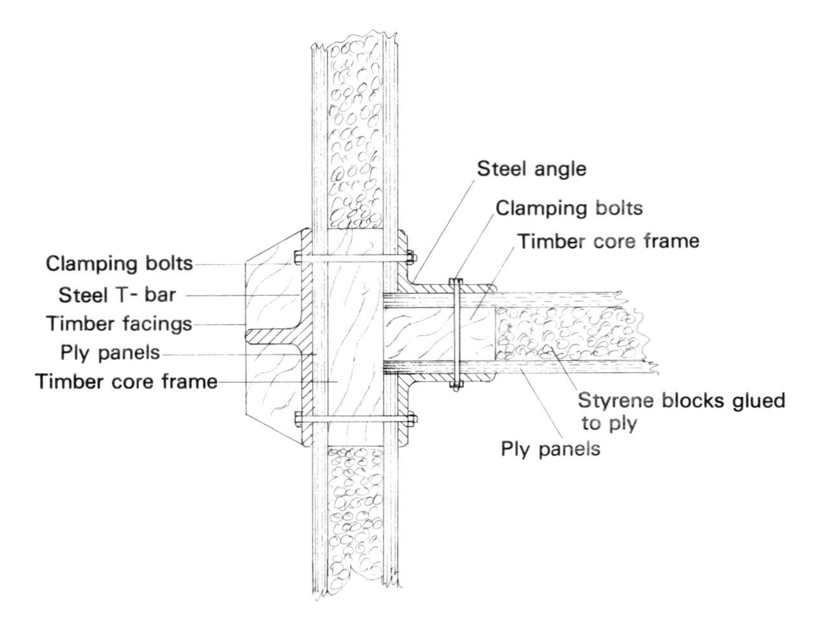

Fig. 60 Reinforcement of duplex bulkhead joint to support a mast; in these schemes a pair of such joints face each other across a passageway.

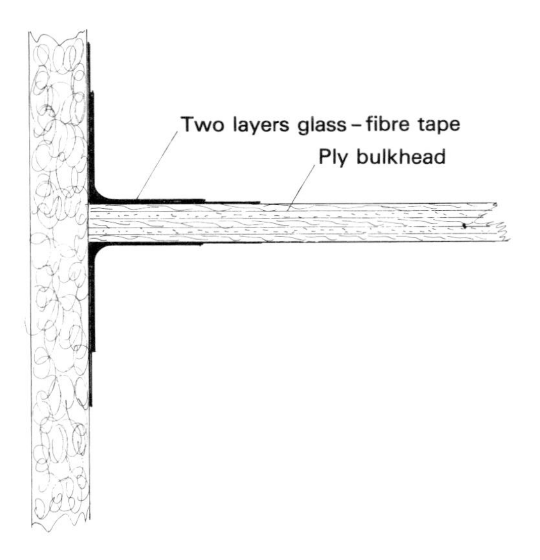

Fig. 61 Single-sheet bulkhead glassed to hull of small boat.

Building duplex bulkheads on a pipe-frame-and-grounds basis is more difficult, for more strain is imposed on the grounds and their welds. Probably the best solution is to build a complete frame of, say, $3 \times \frac{3}{4}$ in stock inside the pipe frame, making halving joints of each ground and sealing these joints with metal/wood adhesives. The exterior $\frac{1}{4}$ in ply panels can be glued and screwed to these wooden frames, but must be fully bolted through each ground. In view of the additional strains involved it is wise to seal the joint doubly with two layers of glass-fibre tape. Figure 62 shows the completed job.

The final–and most difficult–situation arises when the bulkhead position chosen does not coincide with existing framing. This is an adhesive and glass-fibre job and the duplex bulkhead, giving as it does a relatively large adhesion area and the spreading of load, is certainly to be preferred. Great care must be exercised in marking the position of the frame on the hull, checking so far as possible to ensure that it is square to the centreline and vertical; the latter can be checked out with a plumb line (if the craft is in stocks on an even keel), but the former needs a large square or simple triangulation. Having determined the line of the frame, the builder must make a template of the true hull shape at the marked position. A rough frame of odd scraps should be nailed together so as to conform reasonably to the hull contour and to give a flat surface on one side. With this frame held firmly against the hull the builder can use a simple scribing block to mark off the curves at the points which touch the skin, and can then cut the wood away to the marks. Repetition of this process will lead to an accurate fit of pattern to shell; it is, of course, necessary to make only one half, but to check that it fits to the opposite side. Any significant differences should be noted, so that when the bulkhead is completed it will fit snugly. The bulkhead may be made up completely off the ship and then lowered into place to check finally for fit. Once this is ensured it can be removed, or twisted into the centreline and its

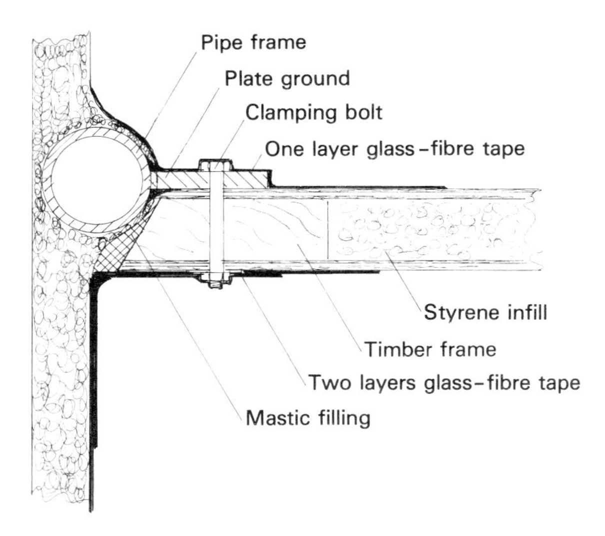

Fig. 62 Duplex bulkhead on pipe-frame grounds, also glassed in.

edges coated with adhesive, e.g. Bostik 2000 or 2024. The contact area of the ferro should be de-dusted and de-greased, then coated with the appropriate adhesive primer and a coat of adhesive. The bulkhead is then twisted or lowered back into place: it is useful to use wedges between its top and a strongback across the deck, forcing it down into the hull and so ensuring good contact pressure while the adhesive sets. Once this has happened the edges should be bonded in with two layers of glass-fibre tape, as previously described.

A similar procedure is followed for partial bulkheads, except that rather more is likely to be needed in the way of bracings to hold the timber firmly against the ship's side and provide the required glue-line contact pressure. Care must be taken, when wedging braces against the opposite side of the shell, not to cause shell distortion. In such circumstances a contact adhesive has much to commend it (e.g. Bostik 2402 with primer 9252), but it should be remembered that these glues offer no 'slide margin', so that one must make the fit dead right first time. Any handyman who has used contact adhesive to place a Formica top on a table will be all too well aware of this problem. However, as a solution it cannot be ignored.

With bulkheads and partials fitted to the hull, the longitudinal furniture framing should be installed rapidly, especially where–as in the case of longitudinal cabin bulkheads–it tends to brace the free ends of the partial bulkheads. The procedures for attaching longitudinal bulkheads to the deckhead are identical with those described for transverse bulkheads, with something of a hope that there will be longitudinal webs simulating beams (correctly 'intercostals') in the desired positions.

With a craft large enough to have cabins on each side of a central corridor it is logical to build the longitudinal bulkheads on to the cabin soles. This is permissible so long as the soles are so arranged that substantial areas of them can be removed to give access to the bilges beneath them. On the whole soles are better in planks than in ply, for in this form they lend themselves better to removal and relaying. The plank scantlings will depend greatly on the length to be spanned, which should not exceed one metre. On a small craft planks of $3 \times \frac{3}{4}$ in will be adequate, while on a larger one 4×1 in will be correct. A fishing or working craft may well need thicker sole planks to meet the requirements of licensing authorities; certainly any soles in fish or cargo holds will need $1\frac{1}{2}$ or 2 in thick planks to meet UK statutory requirements, and similar sizes to meet the laws in other countries. In general terms all floorboards will be of good-quality softwood such as deal, Oregon pine, Virginia pine or kauri, as available, but in some areas, especially saloons and wheelhouses, a well-laid sole of teak, afrormosia or danta, planed smooth and very lightly oiled, can be both practical and attractive; any temptation to polish should be avoided on seagoing craft.

Linings

Hulls in most materials need lining to prevent or reduce condensation; ferrocement hulls are less prone to sweating than those in glass-fibre or steel, but more so than those in natural timber–as distinct from ply, which is very prone to show condensation. The inside of a ferrocement hull will certainly need sealing with one of the proprietary sealers now marketed for the job; these tend to be based on epoxy resins or polysulphide rubbers, or a mixture of both, the rubber-based sealers making a notable contribution to the lining/anti-condensation solutions. Indeed below the berth levels two coats of polysulphide or chlorinated-rubber paint will normally be all that is required. In addition to those sealants discussed in the foregoing pages, rubber-based resinous paints are made by most of the larger paint manufacturers.

Above the berths, on the deckhead and in the coachroof, as applicable, a substantial lining is needed. Where the topsides are straight or very nearly so, it is feasible to fit timber studdings of about 2 × 2 in scantling hard to the shell, jamming them to hold them in place and–preferably–gluing them with one of the adhesives mentioned above. On such studwork the builder can screw a lining of ply or hardboard or even-spaced planks, leaving an air-gap between hull and lining. This last-named scheme is more a workboat idea now than a yacht arrangement, although it has the great virtue of permitting real ventilation–not necessary for the ferro hull but much needed by the timber. More normal nowadays is a lining of hardboard, or of ply–faced with Formica or similar easy-care plastic in galleys and work areas–with the shell-lining gap filled with a heat insulator. Sheet styrene is both popular and cheap, though, being stiff is not easy to contour; polyurethane foam sheets are also reasonably cheap and, being more flexible, are easier to fit. Both materials, however, are liable to burn or melt, and certainly any craft built to the rules of a licencing authority (e.g. the White Fish Authority or the Department of Trade and Industry to name two common British ones) will need this shell-lining gap filled with mineral or asbestos wool or glass-fibre teasings; in short, with fire-retardant materials. The reasoning here is obvious, especially since the urethanes give off highly toxic smoke when burning; but the fact is that a fire in the hull sufficiently severe to burn through the ply panelling (and ply does not combust readily) so as to ignite the foam would be correctly deemed out of control, with an 'abandon ship' situation, reinforced by toxic smoke from the berth and settee cushions (which are not covered by rules!). This shows the faulty reasoning of the rules. Unfortunately, such thinking seems to be all too widespread among licensing and classifying bodies throughout the world; in some parts it is certainly engendered by the application of big ship thinking to small-craft practice; in the example cited, for instance, a big ship may be presumed to have a properly trained fire-fighting crew, who will have room to move away from the fire, re-group and re-equip and then go forward to do battle with the flames: such luxuries cannot exist on a 50-footer. In parenthesis it may be commented that there is no harm in this thinking *vis-à-vis* the problem of linings as quoted, though in truth it has led to some very dangerous craft when applied structurally.

But back to our subject: the smaller craft cannot afford the space occupied by hard linings of the type described, especially if there are no web frames to break up the accommodation. From the aspect of insulation a foam sheet some $\frac{3}{4}$ in thick is adequate, and as before one is forced back to styrene, urethane and pvc. Styrene tiles are commonly used in houses, offices, restaurants, etc., ashore to insulate ceilings, and can be used on deckheads afloat; the general rule is that these tiles are reasonably safe provided the adhesion is more or less total, i.e. the whole back face of the tile must be covered with glue, not simply the corners and centres as instructed for domestic use; moreover, covering the face of the tiling with two coats of fire-retardant paint will certainly help. The softer foams will mould better to the contours of a well-curved hull and can easily be fitted around ports and other openings. As with styrene tiles the sheets must be glued all over, so it is advisable to use sizes which can be handled conveniently. Clam and Bostik 2402 are examples of contact adhesives used for polyurethanes and rubbers or latexes, but nitrile-based glues are needed for flexible pvc. In the planning stage the quirks of the adhesives should be noted and any instructions followed; for example, polysulphides are not good adherents although they are excellent in adhesives; ergo, it may prove difficult to glue, say, flexible pvc sheet to the hull after the application of a polysulphide sealant. Prechecking on data always reduces the risk of accident or later problems.

Insulated soft linings such as flexible pvc or polyurethane need flexible coverings, such as sheet pvc, abla or heavy moquettes. These must be carefully tailored to fit and then glued to the foam underneath. It is not an easy task and all mistakes show up glaringly, so there is much to be said for calling upon the help of a professional upholsterer. Pvc and imitation leathercloths are certainly easy to care for, but fabrics are much nicer to live with, especially in tropical conditions; they are rather more difficult to apply, and need somewhat more aftercare. Duplex materials, such as foam-backed nylon/cotton mixtures are easier to apply, being foam to foam, but are rather difficult–though not impossible–to acquire. Remember, you will have to live with these finishes so long as you have the boat, so choose wisely and make a thoroughly professional job of their application.

Chapter Nine **Domestic Engineering**

Ports, Windows and Holes

It is always to be hoped that the hull fit-out is that for which the craft was designed; for if the designer was a professional it may reasonably be assumed that things will fit where they are drawn. Equally, it would be reasonable to assume that windows and portlights will be located to suit the accommodation and that, because they are large apertures, they will have been fabricated into the vessel at the time of casting. A decision to cut a large aperture in a ferrocement structure should not be taken lightly, for it is no mean undertaking; alternatives must always be considered. However, the task is not impossible, at least in the materials most likely to be encountered. In selecting the location the builder should study most carefully the positions of any vertical frames, especially pipe and web frames: webs cannot be cut; pipes can, but their cutting can engender structural weakness, and produce incipient corrosion centres. Rod frames are merely a nuisance, but since they are apt to be in mild steel while the more closely spaced horizontal rods are liable to be in high-tensile steel, they present few problems.

Once the aperture has been clearly marked, closely spaced holes about $\frac{3}{8}$ in diameter should be drilled around the circumference, using the standard heavy-duty masonry bit, probably with tungsten-carbide cutting edge. These holes are then opened one into the next with a hacksaw: builders of boats in conventional grp will know well those short, very tough blades which fit the power hand-saw units and will trim a sheerline without self-destruction; these tools are most useful in connecting the circumferential line of holes and so cutting away the ferro panel to make the new aperture. It should be remembered that ferro panels normally weigh between 10 and 15 lb per sq ft, so that a window 6 in deep and 24 in long will mean that a ferro panel weight up to 15 lb will begin to detach itself and fall as the final cuts are made. So care must be taken to ensure that it cannot fall or otherwise cause damage: one simple method is to drill two holes in the middle and insert long bolts, which will enable the cutter's mate safely to hold the panel as it becomes detached from its parent structure.

When the panel is removed the aperture will be delineated by a complete circumference of half-holes, and jagged ends of mesh and rods; this must be ground back to the fair line using a carborundum grinding wheel on a heavy-duty portable drill. A great deal of cement dust will fly everywhere and should be contained where possible by polythene drapes. By the same token the grinder should wear overalls and an effective facemask to prevent inhalation of the dust: a low-quality mortar will line the lungs as effectively as a high-quality one and produce silicosis just as quickly.

Once the hole is completely ground, any remaining ends of the mesh should be riveted back into the main structure and the whole then sealed with a good epoxy sealer; any areas from which the mortar has broken away beyond the fair line should be made good with a resinous grout.

The port to be fitted must be bolted through, which means drilling more holes in the main fabric, all close to the edges just repaired and sealed; it therefore follows that the ports should have the widest flanges practicable and that a lot of small bolts may do less damage than a few large ones. As has often been stated before, mortar is happier when the crushing loads of boltings are spread and cushioned, so that both the spigot-flange and the bezel ring should be separated from the hull by timber or Neoprene pads. The material for the port frames needs thought: all too often the temptation to buy brass ports from ship-breakers' yards is a very real one because substantial financial savings can be made; but brass and steel are well apart on the electro-chemical table, so that electrolysis is a threat–and it is the structural steel which disappears, not the brass. The solution lies in using a double-seal coat on the ferro, bedding really good timber pads inside and out in epoxy tar or similar bedding compound (taking care not to use oak or a timber with an acid sap), bedding the port-metal itself in epoxy and using Monel bolts.

An alternative combination which has had Lloyds' approval is aluminium frames and stainless steel bolts, a typical fitting arrangement being shown in Figs. 13 and 14 in Chapter 4. Most custom-made ports and windows will be in aluminium, which must be of a seawater-resistant grade such as N8 or DS54, normally containing $2\frac{1}{2}$ per cent manganese. Good bedding compounds, ferro sealing and timber pads remain necessary.

The really competent woodworker can, of course, make up his own window frames in timber, using a sealing spigot on the bezel ring; Fig. 63 shows a simple scheme, but it must be pointed out that this can work only if the aperture has straight sides and sharp corners. If any other shape is chosen it is virtually impossible to fit the sealing ring: all the vertical joints will be exposed to moisture and will ultimately leak, leading to rotting of the timber.

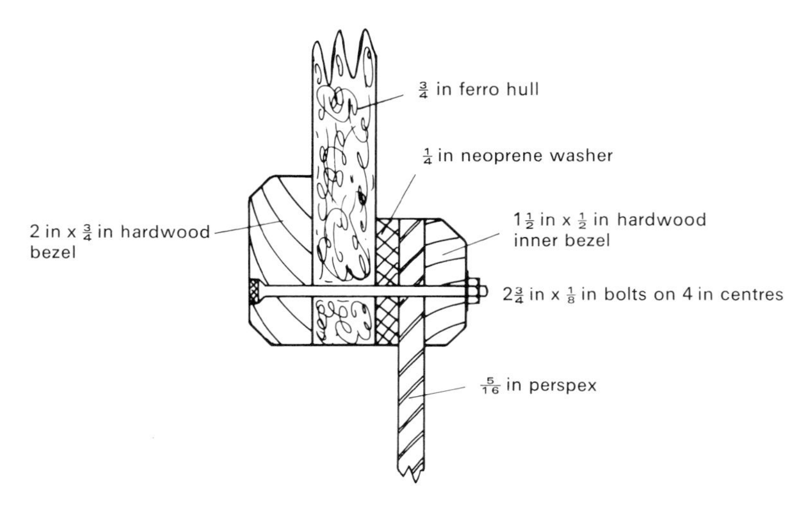

Fig. 63 Wooden-frame window in ferro hull.

Vessels for use in tropical conditions need more ventilation than those for colder climes, and the use of opening portlights in the hull commends itself. When this expedient is adopted it should be remembered that there is some loss of strength compared with a fixed light, and smaller apertures are advisable. Great care needs to be taken to ensure that the closed light is really watertight. and from this aspect the round portlight from the shipbreaker has intrinsically the right design, although the rubber sealing ring will almost certainly need replacement.

Whenever possible hull lights should be so designed that the transparent section is flat, so permitting the use of glass rather than Perspex, Lucite or similar plastics. Some classification societies will accept laminated glass, but most prefer or require armour glass. Insofar that the material must have a resistance to sea pressures comparable to that of the main hull, such a requirement seems eminently reasonable. It is quite probable that, by the time this book is in the hands of its readers, some of the newer transparent plastics such as Oroglass will have proved acceptable in hulls–some may prove better than glass, which will shatter if struck hard enough; certainly they will permit curves, but whether they will have the resistance to abrasion and the dimensional stability of true glass remains to be proven.

Classification societies rightly demand that windows in hulls, whether opening or fixed, be provided with deadlights, i.e. cast or pressed metal plates which screw down over the glass to make a watertight seal. While it is always to be hoped that these deadlights will never be used, since their prime function is to seal the hull in the event of damage to the glass, their presence must constitute an insurance.

In general terms it is not advisable to use opening ports in sailing hulls, no matter how large, for there will always be the possibility of a port being left open, or so inadequately closed as to be forced open by the sea, when the vessel is well-heeled, driving perhaps to windward. In such a circumstance the yacht could well ship a dangerous quantity of water before the opening was discovered.

In designing windows and ports in the superstructure or above the main deck line, the question of appearance is added to the practical considerations of those in the main hull. Windows in ocean-going craft must be seaworthy; there are good grounds for being even more emphatic regarding vessels operating in the shorter seas of coastal waters. The thickness and framing of ports and windows must be related to their size; where possible, larger side ports should be provided with ply or hardboard storm shutters, to relieve the glass of the need to withstand sea impacts; screens or forward-facing windows which cannot be battened down in gale conditions should be altogether stronger than side ones and, where possible, be angled or curved to minimize impact loadings. A typical example of an elegant solution is shown in Plate 9 (Chapter 5) where the large front of the deck saloon is almost semi-circular, raked forward and protected by the overhang bridge.

Hatches

Within the scope of this work it is necessary to consider only three hatches: the sliding accommodation hatch; its hinged counterpart; and the simple cargo or fish hatch. From the aspect of ferro decks the main distinction is the presence or absence of a ferro upstand, in much the same way that deckhouses were so categorized. And in much the same way the constructional methods described earlier can be employed for hatch making. As before, it is easier to construct wooden hatches without ferro upstands, but by the same token it is more difficult to keep them watertight. Equally, there are a great many ways to make timber access hatches, and it is certainly not the intention to examine and compare them; representative ideas alone must suffice. Figures 64 and 65 show sections through typical hinged and sliding hatches with and without ferro upstands.

Commercial vessels may need accommodation hatches with openings well above deck level in order to meet statutory requirements; these will necessarily be hinged, and will follow the precepts laid

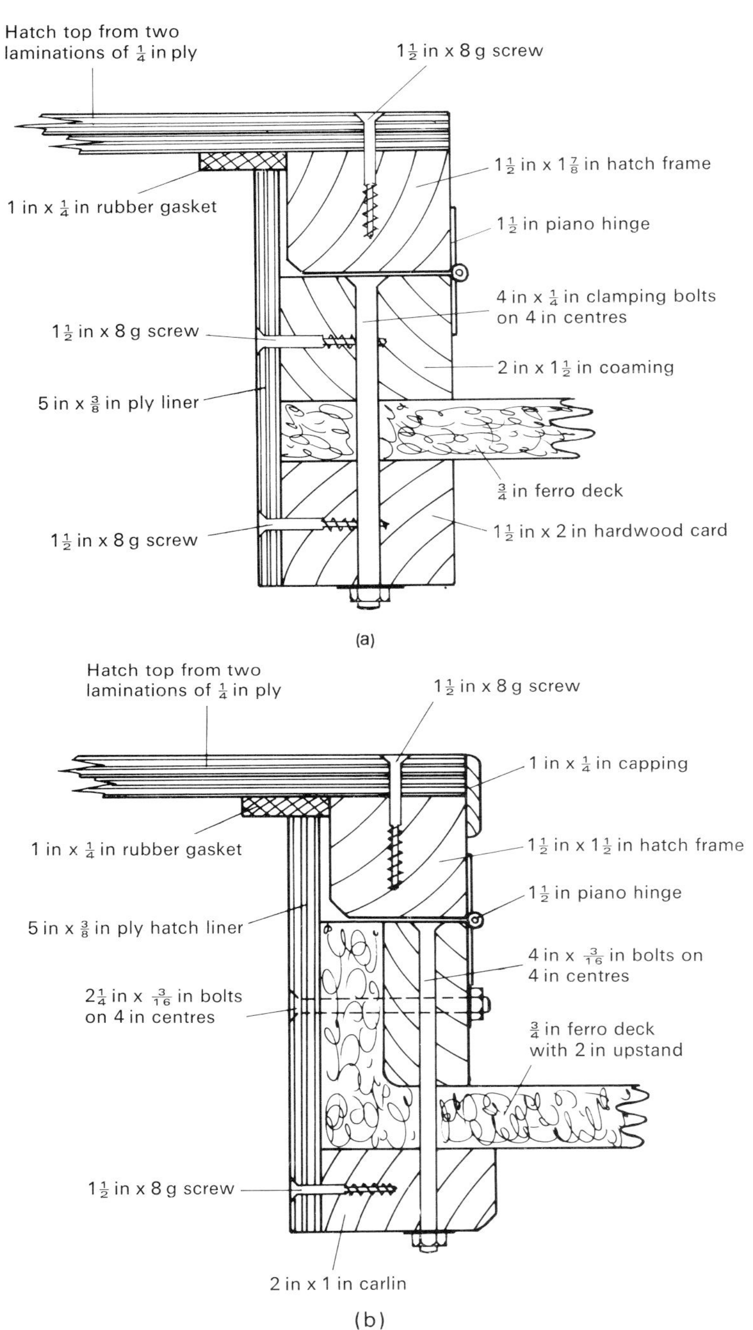

Fig. 64 Sections through a hinged hatch in timber (a) with and (b) without ferro upstand.

down for hinged hatches on ferro upstands. It is recommended that they be placed adjacent to deckhouse structures to give the hatch support when open.

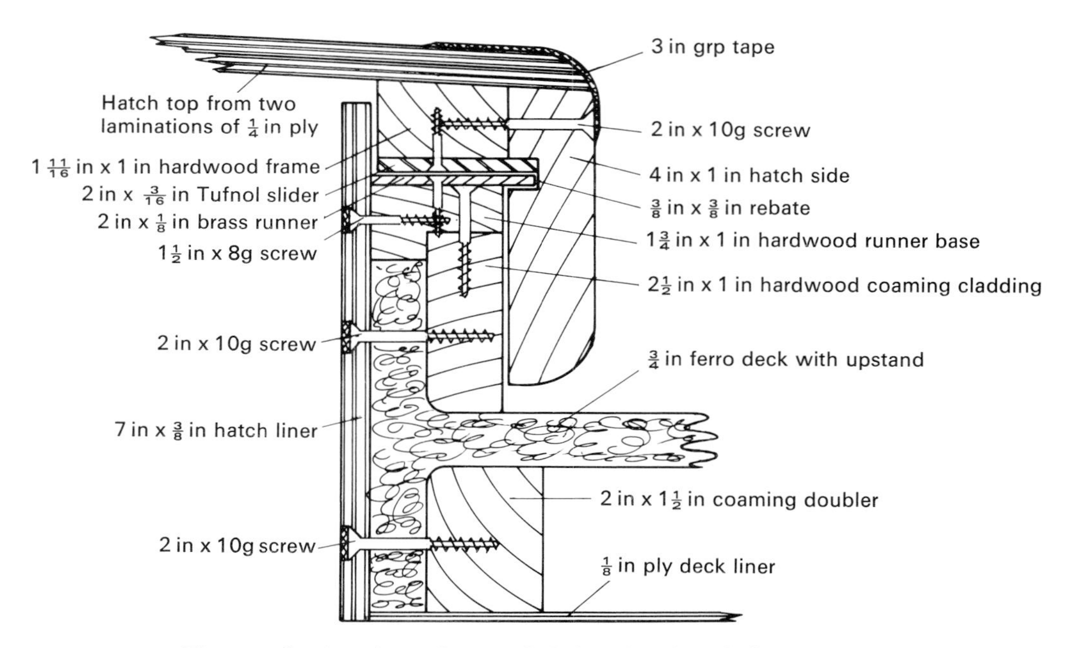

Fig. 65 Section through typical sliding hatch with ferro upstand.

Cargo or fish-hold hatches are considerably more complicated, requiring as they do an inner ledge for the hatch boards plus external brackets for the cover hold-down wedges. A simple solution is shown in Fig. 66, with an all-round boundary strap carrying the wedge brackets, and the ferro upstand providing the hatch-board ledging. When no ferro upstand is provided it may prove difficult to obtain classification; the only possible solution would appear to lie in an all-steel hatch of conventional pattern bolted through the deck on a heavy timber pad; the coaming should project below the deck edge. Figure 67 shows the joint scheme. How long such a solution would remain truly seaworthy is open to conjecture.

Ballast

Very few ferrocement motor yachts require ballast, and those which do are perforce of such proportions that the choice and stowage of ballast presents few problems, although they may well call for professional solutions. Insofar as a motor yacht with enough displacement to need ballast must have a very full body, consideration must be given to the effect of ballast placement on stability and motion. Normal reaction would be to place it as low down as possible, as in a sailboat; if the bilges are very soft (which is unlikely) or the superstructure is very high, so that the craft has a long roll period and a

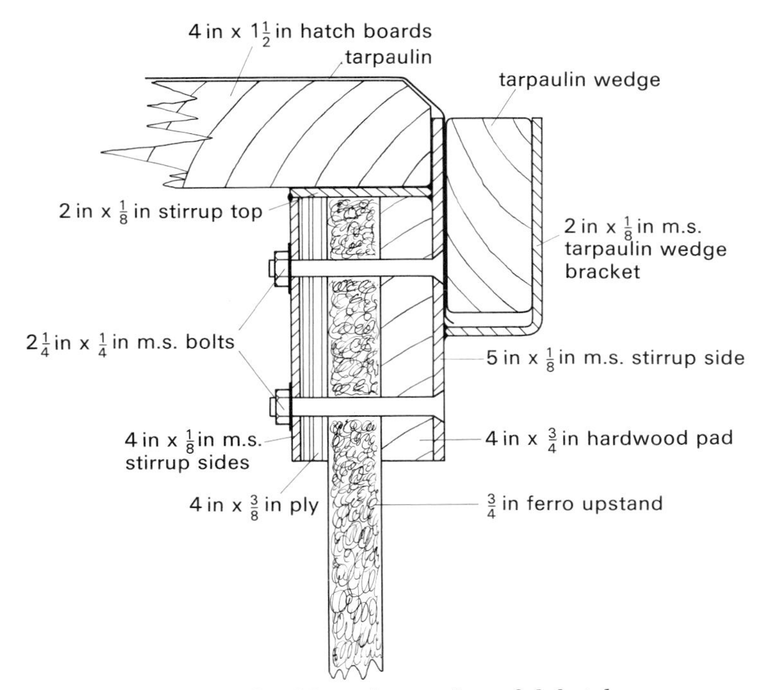

Fig. 66 Steel-bound top to ferro fish hatch.

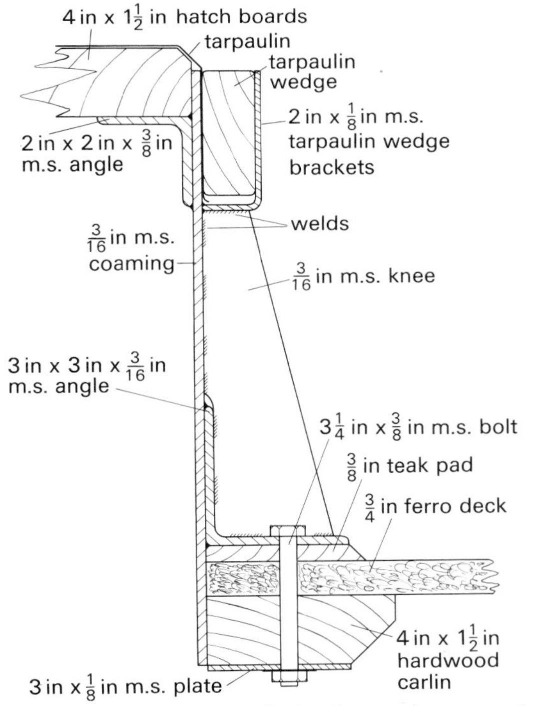

Fig. 67 When there is no ferro upstand the large, deep-coaminged hatch needs structural care in design and execution.

large roll angle, then ballast low down shortens roll period and decreases roll angle. But if the bilges are fairly hard and the superstructure is low the roll angle is smaller and the period short, giving a sharp, jerky roll; low, central ballast exacerbates this condition, producing a most uncomfortable motion. In such a condition the ballast should be set up in the bilges to increase roll angle and period, the longer, slower roll both being more comfortable for the crew and placing less strain on the ship and its gear. Apart from such considerations, it is necessary only to ensure that the ballast cannot move, however severe the sea conditions.

In ferrocement sailboats the problem is almost invariably that of achieving sufficient stability and an adequate ballast ratio, largely because the superficial weight of the hull itself is high compared with grp and timber, and often with steel in the smaller sizes. To combat this designers are forced to increase designed displacement, usually by filling out the garboards and softening the bilges. But in providing space and displacement for more ballast they reduce the form stability and so need more ballast–a case of 'back to square one'. The situation is exacerbated by the high cost of really dense ballast materials, which leads so many builders to less adequate solutions. If to this combination one adds the fact that many ferro designs are sparred and rigged for climates less boisterous than that of Northern Europe, and that builders use solid pine spars to reduce costs, so placing a rig of high capsizing moment over a hull with inherently small stability, it is surprising that more of these craft do not capsize. Certainly, one 40 ft cutter so scared the author that he crossed the Solent close-reefed in a force 2/3 breeze. The pros and cons of heavy rigs have been the subject of calculation in Chapter 6.

It is therefore axiomatic that to achieve the greatest righting moment the centre of gravity of the ballast must be as low down as possible. This, of course, is why, during the great forcing-house of yacht development that was the turn of the century, yachts moved their ballast from inside the bilges to below the keel. The concept that a sailing yacht terminated in a ballast casting bolted on to the main hull members remained well established until the 1950s, when the massive popularity of grp hulls saw the return of inside ballast, it being easier to cast the hull with a ballast trough than to devise a workable external ballast-keel arrangement.

As an aside, it is intriguing to ponder upon the growth of the worship of ballast ratio and, at the same time, the claims for spuriously high ratios. A light-displacement yacht with good beam, high, hard bilges and a lead casting on the bottom of a deep fin will be altogether more stable, and a better seaboat, than a heavy-displacement craft with slack sections and internal iron/cement ballast, even though the latter may have a ballast ratio well in excess of the former. It seems just one more example of the danger of 'a little learning'. By the same token, a ballast ratio of 60 per cent (sometimes claimed) can be achieved in a cruiser only by lightening the whole structure to near danger point, or reducing the accommodation to the barest minimum acceptable to the rules; and always in the light-ship condition, i.e. without crew, water, food, etc.

From the foregoing it seems therefore that we must begin by seeking the best solution from the requirements of the vessel, then work back from this–the most costly–towards the point at which cost and efficiency find harmony. How heavily this must be weighted by cost alone must be related to the value which the builder places on his life and the lives of his companions.

Experience of racing yachts in the first half of the present century showed that maximum stability was provided by a lead casting bolted to the outside of the hull. The cost escalation of lead drove many to cast iron, although often the delivered cost of an iron keel, cast in a foundry in the Midlands and delivered to the coast, could well approach that of a lead one cast in the boatyard, as was customary. By the mid-1970s, however, the demand for sail-carrying power in modern ocean racers had swung the pendulum so hard the other way as to produce ballast castings of uranium (considerably heavier than lead) at unimaginable cost. Thus, the ferrocement yacht will achieve its best sailing performance with a ballast keel cast from lead and bolted to the outside of the hull; and the second best will be an iron casting bolted externally. Consideration of the mechanics involved shows clearly that the hull must be built to accept a casting, with the sharpest possible corners to mate with the sharp edges of the top of the casting. As with engines and deck equipment it is advisable to insert a timber pad between the casting and the ferro hull. The casting must be bolted on, which means bolt holes through the base of the ferro keel, and keelbolt floors to spread the wringing strain throughout the hull; if these are solely in ferro they will need tubular cores to take the bolts, set into the meshing before mortaring; it will certainly be difficult to ensure watertightness. Hardwood floors set into the hull with glass-fibre tape will reduce this problem.

But ferrocement hulls are like grp hulls and lend themselves better to internal ballast; there is a fair choice of materials: lead castings, iron castings, lead dust, steel blasting shot, steel scrap, boiler punchings and mortar, or various combinations. If the inside of the shell is smooth and the keel trough is subdivided by ferro floors, as it should be, then it is a fine idea to ballast with lead castings. The secret is to grease the hull so that a pattern of the trough subdivisions can be made in plaster, each pattern having its cast-in lift handle. These patterns will then allow lead to be cast, in the yard, in a more convenient form than a single keel, and each casting will be relatively small. The same procedure can be followed to produce iron castings, but these will need a proper foundry.

While this technique enables one to get the ballast as low down as possible, it does presuppose a knowledge of its correct lateral distribution. If the vessel is built accurately to a professional design there should be little problem; but if there have been changes in layout, engines, tanks, etc., made without calculations, then it is wise to allow for a reasonable amount of trimming ballast, i.e. small pieces or dust which can be placed as needed to secure designed fore-and-aft trim.

The weight and weight-distribution variations to which ferro hulls are prone favour ballasting when afloat, for trim can then be assured. The easiest way to achieve this is with lead dust, which often comes in 28 lb bags, and is thus convenient to handle. However, although the particles are very small it is difficult to achieve a packing density greater than 550 lb per cu ft in comparison with the 700 lb per cu ft of a good lead casting. But it remains an improvement on cast iron at 400 lb per cu ft. So we will achieve our ideal solution by casting some 70 per cent of our total ballast requirement in shaped lead blocks and trimming when afloat with the remaining 30 per cent as lead dust. But if the bottom of the keel is wide and flat it will be simpler to cast our lead into ingots of about 100 lb each, pack them as carefully as possible, i.e. to achieve maximum density, and fill the interstices with lead dust; because the space to be filled will be higher than before, a 50/50 mix of ingot and dust may be obtainable, giving a ballast density of 625 lb per cu ft.

Moving further away from the ideal one comes to the mixture of iron ingots or steel bars packed round with lead dust; iron castings average about 400 lb per cu ft while steel bars should approach 480 lb per cu ft. A packing ratio of 50 per cent is most unlikely to be exceeded, giving an overall density of 510 lb per cu ft with steel bars and 470 with cast iron when filled with lead dust.

Until quite recently, steel plate was de-scaled by blasting with fine steel shot (now it is cuprous slag, which is very light), and the used shot, reduced by its action to powder form, could often be bought quite cheaply. It has, however, surprised many who have used it, for even with so small a particle size one cubic foot seldom weighs more than 300 lb. If this material becomes available for use in place of lead dust, our mixes will give overall densities of 500, 450 and 400 lb per cu ft with lead, steel and iron solids respectively.

At the bottom end of the scale is mortar, with a density of 140 lb per cu ft, giving mixes at 420, 310 and 270 lb per cu ft when combined 50/50 with lead, steel and iron ingots respectively. The difference between the last mix (which is much beloved by ferrocement boat-builders) and pure lead at 700 lb per cu ft speaks for itself. In practical terms it means that the righting moment of the iron/mortar keel will be less than two-thirds that of the lead casting in an average boat, because its centre of gravity will be significantly closer to the waterline by virtue of the greater volume occupied by equal weights. For comparison, one ton of ballast will occupy the following volumes (cu ft):

Lead casting	3·2
Lead ingots + lead dust	3·6
Steel bars + lead dust	4·4
Lead ingots + iron dust	4·5
Iron ingots + lead dust	4·8
Lead ingots + mortar	5·3
Iron casting	5·6
Steel bar + mortar	7·2
Iron ingots + mortar	8·3

It is interesting to note how far down the table pure iron castings come, which means in effect that many other combinations are to be preferred. That the iron/mortar mix occupies 2·6 times the volume of lead equally shows its shortcomings. It may well be the cheapest solution, but it could also prove the most disastrous. Where the displacement and draught of the yacht is known, it is a reasonable assumption that the basic righting moment should be 30 per cent of displacement × (draught minus 1 foot). Thus, a 10-ton yacht drawing 6 ft should have a ballast moment of $3 \times 5 = 15$ tons-ft. So if the use of low-density ballast raises its centre of gravity by 1·25 ft, (as it easily might), the ballast weight should be increased to $15/3{\cdot}75 = 4$ tons. These are, of course, very rough rule-of-thumb techniques, but they will give the builder a first approximation.

Tanks

The storage of fuel having properly been covered in the chapter on motive power, only water need be considered. The need to arrange for adequate supplies has been mentioned, as has the weight–something all-too-often overlooked. So here we need examine only the methods of storage. When high-density ballast is used at the bottom of a substantial keel trough there is frequently enough space left beneath the cabin sole to contain all the water (and often the fuel) needed by the yacht in normal cruising. It may here be worth recapitulating that 1 ton of water equals 224 gallons and occupies 36 cu ft.

Without doubt the neatest solution to the storage problem is the plastic bilge bag; not only does it conform to the shape of the bilge but it collapses as its contents are drained, so greatly reducing the free-surface effect–that swilling about of water in half-empty tanks which can have so deleterious an effect on stability. These bags are not cheap, but they are certainly an excellent device. Metal tanks–galvanized steel or tinned copper–would be even more expensive, requiring carefully made patterns to ensure a snug fit into the ferro. Once the ballast has been securely pitched or cemented into place, the hull itself can be used to contain water. All cement surfaces must be thoroughly sealed with epoxy resin; large tanks might well have a glass-fibre scrim added to hold the second coat of resin. Recent years have seen several new sealing compounds reach the market, notably Armoglaze and UPC (Universal Protective Coating). Manufacturers' literature should always be sought and instructions followed explicitly. Where any doubt exists the builder should seek advice from other builders, for there are records of a special ferrocement paint which peeled off differentially (and was irremovable elsewhere), of special fuel-tank sealing rubber which dissolved in diesel, etc. It is certain that some finishes are marketed before the completion of full-scale field trials.

When the hull is to become a tank it follows that the top must be sealed, normally with steel plates. These will need to be bolted down all round and bedded on rubber or Neoprene gaskets to ensure complete watertightness. Unless a ledge to receive the tank top has already been cast into the hull, together with provision for holding-down bolts, this solution is unlikely to be workable. Yachts which must carry very large quantities of fuel or water must perforce use the hull for tankage and will have had all the requisite ledgings and fastening points cast into the hull at mortaring. Against integral hull tanks is the risk of hull puncture allowing seawater into the fresh-water tanks; and, of course, of the leaking-through of diesel in the event of a sealing failure.

Finally, when organizing the tank top the builder should remember to fit substantial manhole covers, to allow for both inspection and cleaning. The size required will much depend upon the space available and the distances to be reached from the access, but if possible the hole should exceed 18 in across.

Equally important is the plumbing: the inlet should be large and preferably welded into the tank top to ensure complete watertightness; the pipe should lead to deck, and the filler cap should be remote from that for fuel, clearly marked and preferably colour-coded–blue for water and red for fuel are common codes. A breather pipe of not less than $\frac{3}{8}$ in bore should run alongside the filler pipe: ideally this will emerge by a coachroof side or cockpit coaming, so that it can be taken several inches above the deck then bent down again almost to deck level; in this way, the chance of seawater entering the breather and thence finding its way into the fresh water will be minimized. The draw-off lead should lie as close to the deepest part of the tank as practicable, thus ensuring that the tank really is drained when the pumps run dry. Terminating the hose in a filter or strum box has merit, for it may reduce the intake of any unwanted matter which may have entered the tank or settled out of the water.

Plumbing

The choice of a pumping system will depend on the size of the vessel, its crew and water supply–and the owner's pocket. In a small cruiser of say 30 ft, with a 40-gallon bilge tank feeding taps in the galley and toilet, hand pumps would be normal and quite adequate; there are many on the market. But a large vessel, distributing water to half a dozen cabins plus galley and saloon with long pipe runs and lifts of up to 15 ft, will need an electric pumping system such as the Bee or Crowell.

In larger craft, designed for long-range cruising often with several passengers plus a crew, large tanks are needed but conservation remains important. To extend the water supply in the Caribbean an owner will often rig an awning, or arrange his upper deck to catch rain water, which will be piped into its own tank and distributed via its own circuit for washing, etc. In other parts of the world seawater is pumped through for domestic use, and some vessels are complicated by the presence of all three circuits–sea, rain and fresh water; there is no doubt that seawater is excellent for flushing toilets. Colour coding of all pipes and outlets is essential: coffee made with seawater tastes vile.

At the time of writing a growing number of harbours have introduced legislation prohibiting the discharge of raw sewage into the sea: by 1980 it is expected that it will be illegal to discharge sewage or septic tanks within 20 miles of any coast. The days of the simple sea toilet are therefore numbered, and builders of new craft would be foolish to install devices which may have to be replaced. It is certain that the growth of anti-pollution legislation has been hastened by the introduction of a range of self-contained toilets which can often be folded, sealed and carried ashore to prescribed sanitary stations. The chemical toilet has been around a long time and the name Elsan comes immediately to mind; such toilets have been mandatory on craft using such rivers as the Thames, which has provided drinking water for decades and is closely monitored. But the original devices are being outmoded by these new machines with a self-contained internal flush system and a seal arrangement which overcomes the problem of the unpleasant odour associated with the older units. Even newer is the incinerating WC.

The larger and more sophisticated yacht will use a variety of toilets ranging from one of the above through standard domestic low-flush suites to all-electric systems. All will discharge into a septic tank which must be large enough to cope with the demands likely to be made upon it, and should be so arranged as to permit being pumped out when well offshore or into a shore-side sanitary installation. The design and installation of such systems is normally carried out by professionals called in by the naval architect and builder.

Associated with the toilet are handbasins, baths and showers; again, the variety of handbasins is large, but often they are too small for comfortable usage: 15 × 10 in is a useful size for a handbasin, measured across the basin itself, inside the flange. Plastic and grp basins grow in popularity and are light, but are more subject to scratching than vitreous-enamelled ceramics. By contrast, baths are very difficult, perhaps because they fell from popularity as showers captured the imagination. The standard domestic bath is nearly always too large for a yacht, but a few small ones have become available in various plastics as part of the development of equipment for the modern micro-home. Showers proliferate, the biggest problems aboard usually being control of the water used and the pressure head required. A teak grating atop a grp water-sump makes an attractive and practical base to the shower area, and a plastic closure curtain, if there is room for it, helps keep the compartment dry. In setting out a loo compartment it should be remembered that the minimum usable size for the average human is 2 ft 6 in square.

The need to ensure cleanliness with rapid drying demands easy-care surfaces throughout toilet compartments. Larger yachts tend to use ceramic tiles, as in domestic installations, but smaller craft will find plastic tiles, purchased in sheets, or simply plain materials such as Formica, quite acceptable; it should be remembered, however, when plastic-faced ply or hardboard is used, that all joints and edges require waterproof seals. Plate 15 shows some ideas on the subject.

Galleys

Earlier mention was made of the need to ensure that the galley facilities were adequate for the number of people normally likely to be aboard a yacht, and the need to give the cook adequate room to operate was stressed. But with thoughts of plumbing much in mind it is appropriate to examine briefly such items as sinks and stoves. For the smaller vessel there is now a wider choice than ever before; one attractive unit comprises a 2-burner gas stove and sink all in stainless steel ready to drop on top of an open-top cupboard approximately 48 × 18 in. When these items are installed separately and where space permits, a double sink is popular, so that crockery washed in one can be allowed to drain in the other; the domestic plastic-covered dish drainer which can be fixed to the bulkhead is often better for draining and more compact; but it should be fitted with a door of plastic mesh to prevent dishes being cascaded across the cabin. Builders are also warned about circular sinks: do make quite certain that these are not exactly of the right size to jam your plates, for so many have this unwanted facility.

The supply of water to sinks has been dealt with. Waste water can usually be allowed to exhaust to sea, although some river authorities

Plate 15 Bathroom in a large cruiser; the opening portlight shows clearly.

may have local prohibitions. There are seldom real problems on power craft, but on sailboats, subject as they are to changes of attitude, care in the placement of sink outlets is essential. Ideally, they should be close to the waterline and fitted with an air-vent, for it is most disconcerting to find one's sink stopper fired into the galley as the ship goes about and the air in the waste pipe is suddenly compressed: this always seems to happen just as the sink has been filled with hot water, which promptly disappears; this habit was quite a feature of one production yacht. A screw-in stopper would, of course, have prevented it, but sinks so fitted are rare.

Propane or butane gases are common stove fuels in Europe and have much to commend them, not the least of which is the availability of a wide variety of equipment for them. The gases are not indiscriminately interchangeable but if the appropriate regulator is fitted when cylinders are changed it is unnecessary to change burners. Much is often made of the fire hazard of gases, especially since these two are heavier than air and so will sink to the bilges and collect if allowed to escape. No fuel can be inherently safe, by definition, but most accidents arise from poor installation or careless use. If the cylinders are stored on deck and their locker has top and bottom vents so that any escaped gas can flow overboard, if the supply lines are of seamless copper pipe, and if any flexible connections are made with one of the Neoprenes approved for petrol-based gases, the system as such will be safe. Note that plumbers use a 'goo' called Loktite to seal gas joints.

Alcohol and paraffin stoves have their devotees, notably on opposite sides of the Atlantic. The former seem totally reliable and the American firm of Hillier used to supply one with a reasonable oven; but the flame seems to lack heat because of the low flash-point of the fuel. Pressurized paraffin cookers based on the Swedish Primus principle suffer from the same fault–you need a fuel of even lower flash-point to preheat the feed tubes; the current favourite is methylated tablets. While modern fuels and most careful filtering (use four layers of nylon stocking to filter) have drastically reduced the absolute dependence on the pricker which was once the bugbear of the Primus cooker, jet clearance is vital to ensure reasonable ignition and to prevent flare-up. In addition to a variety of camping units, Taylor's Para-Fin Ltd make excellent paraffin stoves with ovens.

Cooking by electricity is spreading to Europe from the USA where the national use of 110-volt equipment has helped by reducing the fatal-shock risk inherent in Europe's 220–240 volt system. Of course, most small craft have 12-volt electrical systems, and a 12-volt cooker would use a very high current. But on a large craft, especially one using fridge, freezer, dishwasher and washing machine, etc., a galley supply at domestic mains voltage is essential if the cost of equipment is to be kept within reasonable limits.

Electricity is 'dry-heat' cooking, and only for operation in hot climates is an extractor fan essential. Gas and paraffin (hydrocarbon fuels) give off large quantities of water vapour as a by-product of combustion, so that flue systems are very desirable, especially in cooler climates where this vapour will be encouraged to condense everywhere before natural convection can disperse it. An efficient extractor vent should therefore be fitted above the stove, and on larger installations this should be motorized.

Heating and Ventilation

On the whole, yachts under 40 ft are unlikely to have any heating system other than the galley stove; from 35 ft or so upwards, motor cruisers grow increasingly likely to have some form of heating, with the ducted hot-air methods top of the popularity stakes. An older generation of yachts favoured solid-fuel heating, usually in the form of a round, cast-iron bogie stove burning coal or coke. While difficult to light and undeniably messy, often with a flue problem when sailing hard in inclement weather, these stoves had the major merit of pulling a draught through the boat and out of the flue, thus providing excellent ventilation. Modern developments such as the Esse stoves, burning coke or charcoal behind closed doors, are a not unreasonable substitute, although charcoal is often difficult to obtain. Heaters burning diesel fuel are not without merit, albeit inclined to be smelly, and are also ventilated by exhausting through a flue. Conventional gas and paraffin heaters are convenient but produce great quantities of water vapour; both can be dangerous when the ship is heeled and should never be used in a seaway unless adequately gimballed.

The smaller the yacht the more difficult it is to ventilate–and the more it needs ventilation. Four bodies in a 20-footer's cabin consume a lot of oxygen and exhale a lot of carbon dioxide; inadequate ventilation can insidiously turn a comfortable fug into a lethal atmosphere, especially when the growing staleness is masked by tobacco smoke and the danger-signs of drowsiness attributed to alcohol. A simple mushroom vent on the foredeck, into the forepeak, and another in the forehatch, plus louvred cabin doors (preferably open) can make the difference between life and death. The irreversibility of this latter process suggests that it be accorded considerable respect.

Apart from the needs of the crew the ship herself must breathe. It is certainly true that a ferro hull will not rot, as timber will, if bathed in stale, damp air; but over a long period the condensate will absorb salt and become aqueous sodium chloride, ready, willing and able to corrode any steel which should lose its protective galvanizing or cement cover. Again, most of the interior joinery will be of timber, which will therefore be prone to decay if improperly ventilated. In areas where foam is glued to the ferro, or there is an adequate seal of polysulphide rubber or epoxy tar, the hull will come to no harm; if lockers are provided with vent-holes and under-berth stowage is accessible through open front access, all will be well. Problems seldom arise when the yacht is in use, for movement of people produces movement of air; but long periods of disuse produce stagnant air and set up a breeding tank for decay spores.

Larger craft will need various forms of forced draught, ranging from simple motorized extraction from two or three selected points, with reliance on natural air flow to them, to fully ducted systems. The size of ducting, fan diameters and capacities, etc., are essentially the province of the specialist ventilation engineer, whose services should be invoked in the planning of such systems.

Vessels of almost any size will carry an engine, frequently tucked away in the very bowels of the hull. And this engine (or engines) will need a great deal of air, preferably cold: it needs air for combustion of fuel and a flow of air around it to assist the cooling water by convection. Architects determining power requirements for craft building for tropical use know that a 'tropical derating' factor must be applied to take account of the ambient; a normal horsepower loss would be 1 per cent per 10 degrees C above 30 degrees C, and many small-craft engine bays, even in northern climates, will reach 55 degrees C through inadequate ventilation. Small wonder then that the engine runs roughly and fails to develop its anticipated power. A builder installing a new engine from a reputable maker should receive an installation manual which will specify the minimum air-flow requirements, but where this is not available a very rough rule is to double the combustion needs. Thus a 2 litre engine turning over at 2500 r.p.m. will require a little less than 5000 litres per min or 175 cu ft per min; an air intake of only 4 in diameter would therefore gulp air at 450 cu ft per min. Reduced thus the demand seems small, and indeed is indicative of the ease with which an adequate flow can be achieved; but it is remarkable how often this minimum is not even approached.

There are four ways to provide this air:

(a) Rely on a natural flow of air.
(b) Force air in and rely upon natural exhaust.
(c) Use forced exhaust and rely upon natural inflow.
(d) Use forced inlet and outlet.

Method (a) is normal in most small craft and is often inadequate, while method (d) is really restricted to large engines in undersized engine rooms, so the norm will be a choice between (b) and (c), the former tending to create a pressure build-up and the latter a pressure drop; insofar as a pressure drop gives a more controllable system it has much to commend it, but it is perhaps more dependent than (b) on ensuring an adequate supply in low-pressure conditions. Whatever system is chosen, ducted inlets and outlets are really necessary for good engine operation.

Lighting and Wiring

Lighting falls into two sections, external and internal. External comprises navigation lights as required by law according to the class of vessel and its service, and builders of power craft could well conform with the statutory requirements for merchant shipping closest to their yacht, since so many yachts have navigation lights which lack visible range. Sailing yachts tend to rely on masthead lights or bicolour lamps on pulpits, since sails often obscure the port and starboard lights. It has been argued that the modern sailboat should not bother about statutory sidelights since they are seldom visible from another vessel, but builders of new craft should make serious efforts to rectify this situation so far as possible. A few years ago, the market saw miniscule fluorescent lamps with red and green covers designed to mount on the main spreader roots: with a good light output and a mounting well above the water, even when heeled, at least the weather light should be visible.

Most navigation lights operate on 12 or 24 volts and the circuits are therefore vulnerable to potential losses caused by salt deposits on terminals, etc. Unbroken leads from battery to lamp are not really feasible, and plug points on deck are normal; fully waterproof rubber-enclosed fittings are absolutely essential, and cables well oversize are advantageous.

Fluorescent lighting, with its considerably lower power demand than incandescent-filament lighting of comparable luminosity, is obviously a major advantage on battery-operated circuits. Accommodation lighting layouts are so essentially a combination of aesthetics and utility that it would be out of place to discuss them here; only one should remind owners and builders that they must ensure that internal lighting does not blind the night helmsman, when the hatch is open or closed. Oversize cabling should always be used, to reduce transmission losses (so low a voltage can be sensitive, especially when provided by a near-spent battery), and the switches should be of a type not subject to contact-spring loosening. Most yachts will use dc circuits, and thus only have to earth at the alternator; but larger craft may well be wired for a domestic voltage ac ring main, and here it is essential to use a 3-wire earth-return system; the hull is non-conducting and so cannot be used as the earth-return circuit; indeed, a ferro hull should be provided with a really adequate earthing plate below the waterline, close enough to be kept clean of fouling and with really adequate electrical connections. It can also be connected to act as the discharge terminal of the lightning conductor.

Classification societies take great interest in electrical circuits and equipment, especially when voltages above 24 are used; owners and builders are therefore advised to have their electrical schemes prepared by professionals experienced in the field. Since marine atmosphere is conductive, and not so far removed from the electrolyte of a battery, these cautions are fully justified. Particular attention is paid to fuses and fuse ratings, although the modern inclination towards miniature circuit-breakers (MCBs) is accepted and offers advantages, especially for the speed at which a momentary overload can be cleared and the circuit remade.

Also worthy of study are the battery stowages, which should hold the cells snugly but allow good access for maintenance, as well as having exhaust facilities, for the hydrogen given off when cells 'gas' on overcharge is, of course, explosive. Many yachts have their batteries in open cases, which, while certainly providing ventilation, give no means of ensuring that the hydrogen is led away from hazards.

Electronics

One short word embraces a considerable array of equipment, generally classified as aids to navigation or communication, although two other divisions may concern the builders of ferrocement craft, namely aids to ocean racing and fish-finders. Navigational aids essentially comprise the compass (which is *not* electronic), echo-sounder, log or speed-and-distance meter, radio direction-finder and radar; the last two are unlikely to be found on power craft under 35 ft and sailboats under 50 ft. There are many makes from which to select, and deliveries tend to be rather protracted; on the whole, each is as good as its rival, and none is better than its installation. Radar, especially, can suffer from a masked scanner, mismatched coaxial, light reflections on the screen and inept operation. Communication aids involve radio-telephones of two categories, namely those for emergency use only and those for social contact. All new RT equipment except VHF must be for single-sideband working (to permit greater usage of the limited transmission spectrum available), although the cheaper double-sideband units are allowed on existing stations. Owners with RT transmitters must have a crystal calibration certificate to ensure accurate frequency working and must possess a valid operator's licence.

The spectacular array of instrumentation devised to help the ocean-racing man to sail well without actually being able to are rightly the province of the specialist. The arguments for and against are not for this book, in which one can say only–as before–that inept installation is all too easy and can negate any advantage.

Fish-finding equipment is even more specialized and tends to fall into the province of the larger fishing vessels, where its installation is always carried out professionally.

This section really must be brief or form a book in its own right; it can only conclude with the warning, often given already but never more appositely than to electronics: 'If you're not sure of what you're doing, don't do it'.

Chapter Ten **Deck Layout and Finishing Work**

With the interior layout organized and ideas clarified on rig and power units, attention can be turned to the exterior of the vessel, to consider deck gear and deck layout, rudders and steering system, painting, rubbing strakes, rails, bulwarks, cappings and all those odd jobs which seem never-ending when a boat is apparently complete 'except for...'.

Deck Equipment

With the exception of canal and river cruisers, all ferro craft will need anchors, chains and warps; and once these exceed a certain size, winches or windlasses will be required to handle them.

Anchors fall into three basic types: fisherman, patent and stockless. The last rely for holding largely upon weight rather than shape, and owe their popularity to the ease with which they will stow in a hawse pipe; their use is mainly confined to large commercial craft, say from 200 tons upwards, and will seldom be of interest to the builder in ferro. Fisherman anchors are characterized by having the stock set at right angles to the flukes, the theory being that the stock will lie on the ground and so cause the flukes to dig in: this anchor is reasonably efficient in most holding grounds, but its stock/fluke configuration makes it difficult to stow, except in sizes small enough to permit easy removal of the stock. While it needs more weight than patent anchors of comparable holding power, it is a very useful general-purpose job, and most yachts should carry one for emergency use and some kedging jobs, etc.

Patent anchors may be broadly classified under their early trade names, CQR and Danforth, although other manufacturers have devised similar tools. The CQR or plough anchor is characterized by its heavily curved 'ploughshare' flukes, which drive into the ground as they are pulled forward by the chain. The Danforth is characterized by flat flukes markedly triangular in shape; these dig into the ground, as before, the two sharp points giving the flukes a good bite; this is not strictly a stockless anchor, but the stock is, in fact, below the flukes, and is in the same plane, not at right angles to it. Each of these patent anchors works better in some ground than in others, so that, in theory, one of each should cope with any type of holding. However, most yachtsmen have their own preferences, often based on ease of stowage.

In common with other classification societies, Lloyds produce Tables showing preferred sizes of fisherman and patent anchors; part of these are reproduced in Table 6 for guidance.

Allied to anchor weights are the sizes and lengths of chain and warp which should be carried, and Lloyds' rules have been incorporated in

Table 6 Anchors, chains, hawsers and warps

Equipment number[1]	Anchor weight[2]		Chain[3]		Warp[4]		Hawser[4]
	Stockless (lb)	Patent (lb)	Length (fm)	Diameter (in)	Length (fm)	Circumference (in)	Circumference (in)
400	42[5]	32	30	$\frac{5}{16}$	30	2	$2\frac{1}{4}$
600	70[5]	52	30	$\frac{3}{8}$	30	$2\frac{1}{4}$	$2\frac{3}{4}$
800	84[5]	63	45	$\frac{3}{8}$	45	$2\frac{1}{4}$	$2\frac{3}{4}$
1000	112	84	90[6]	$\frac{7}{16}$	45	$2\frac{1}{4}$	3
1200	126	96	90	$\frac{7}{16}$	60	$2\frac{1}{4}$	$3\frac{1}{2}$
1600	200	150	90	$\frac{1}{2}$	60	$2\frac{1}{2}$	$4\frac{1}{4}$
2000	320	240	105	$\frac{9}{16}$	75	$2\frac{1}{2}$	$4\frac{3}{4}$
2400	420	315	105	$\frac{11}{16}$	75	$2\frac{3}{4}$	5
2800	500	375	120	$\frac{3}{4}$	75	$2\frac{3}{4}$	5
3200	600	450	120	$\frac{13}{16}$	75	$3\frac{1}{4}$	$5\frac{1}{2}$
3600	625	475	150	$\frac{13}{16}$	75	$3\frac{1}{2}$	$5\frac{1}{2}$
4000	715	540	150	$\frac{7}{8}$	75	$3\frac{1}{2}$	$5\frac{1}{2}$

[1] The equipment number is given by $L(\frac{1}{2}B + D)$ plus $\frac{3}{4}(l \times h)$ for craft with full-width deckhouses or $\frac{3}{8}(l \times h)$ for part-width deckhouses, l and h being length and height. L is overall length at mid-freeboard, B is greatest beam and D is depth from sheer to underside of keel. Thus an average 40 ft sailboat will have $L = 38$, $B = 11$, $D = 9$, giving an equipment number, N, of

$$38(\tfrac{11}{2} + 9) + \frac{3(16 \times 1{\cdot}5)}{8} = 560$$

[2] The rules call for two anchors.

[3] Non-ferrous shackles should never be used.

[4] Warps are for making fast alongside, hawsers for mooring; the difference in circumference should be noted by owners anticipating replacing chain with rope.

[5] It is anticipated that these would be normal fisherman anchors.

[6] This seems spuriously high; 60 fathoms should be adequate.

Table 6. Vessels seeking classification must conform, but it follows that the man building an ocean racer or a fast powerboat will not want to carry the weight of chain specified. In these classes there is a tendency to use hawser rather than chain; this is acceptable only if there remains a substantial length of chain at the anchor itself, for most anchors rely on the weight of chain at the stock end to give the horizontal pull on the shank for which they are designed. Hawser does not give this, especially the lighter ones which float, hence the need for some chain: a useful guide is one-third chain, two-thirds hawser. Yachts intended for use in coral sea should not use hawser–coral will cut it to ribbons.

A final comment on Table 6: these are essentially Lloyds' figures for yachts and bear no relation to those promulgated by other classification societies, especially statutory bodies such as the British Department of Trade and Industry or the Australian Docks and Harbours Board; builders needing licences from such bodies should obtain a written statement from an authorized member of the appropriate department giving his views on the day the question was posed.

However, consideration of the weights of anchor and chain to be handled even on a small yacht (our 40-footer is expected to carry $1\frac{1}{2}$ tons of chain), indicates that a good anchor winch is essential on vessels over 30 ft long. The basic choice is between manual, hydraulic and electric operation: manual winches are satisfactory for equipment numbers up to 600, especially if at least one regular crewman is tough; a competent skipper can power up the chain bight in such a way that the crew can bring in the chain hand over hand, but a good winch will help once the chain is 'up and down'. Hydraulic winches are excellent and less liable to problems than electric ones when on a salt-swept foredeck; but they do require at least some motor running to drive the hydraulic pump, and the need for good holes through ferro structures to carry the hydraulic pipework blunts their charm in the craft we are considering. Of course, electric winches need good hefty cables, but these can often be run where pipework would be inadvisable; it must be remembered that a 1 h.p. dc motor requires 62·5 ampères of current at 12 volts, which calls for a power cable of stout cross-section. A wide selection is available from manufacturers all over the world, so there is no shortage of choice.

It is common practice for power craft to ride to their anchor winches rather than to a Samson post and thus the greatest care must be exercised in the fastening. Winches normally have adequate bolt holes, so it is up to the builder to ensure that the structure will sustain the loads. The winch itself should be mounted on a substantial hardwood pad, shaped to give a really snug fit on the ferrodeck and bedded to it with mastic. The bolt holes through the ferro should be as clean as possible, since only the mastic between pad and deck can fill any bolt/ferro gaps. A similar pad of hardwood, at least as large as the other, should be fitted to the underside of the deck; if possible, the winch should span a deck beam, even though this will divide the underdeck pad. The bolts should have steel plate washers at least six diameters square under the nuts, which should be of the self-locking variety. It is normal for the chain to fall from the aft side of the gipsy into the navel pipe and thence to the chain locker; thus, the location of the navels must be determined early, since they may pass down through the forecabin. If the tops of these navels are flanged on to the top of the winch pad, and the holes in the deck itself are grouted, it is unlikely that they will leak.

If both chains are to be stowed in the same chain locker, it is advisable to provide a substantial vertical division between the piles, otherwise they will assuredly inter-tangle at a critically difficult moment. It used to be good seamanship to make fast the bitter end of the chain with cord, which could be cut if an emergency dictated slipping it to save the ship; a shackle could be difficult and time-consuming to undo. Small craft built to classification rules cannot use such commonsense devices because the chain-locker bulkhead must be watertight, so that if the chain is made fast to prevent inadvertent loss, the ship may founder, being unable to slip its mooring.

In addition to the anchor winch the average yacht will have a stemhead roller or hawse pipe (this must be fitted before mortaring), mooring fairleads, and cleats or bitts; aft there will be more fairleads, cleats or bitts, and really large craft may sport a warping capstan to help when coming alongside or mooring stern-to. There are no hard-and-fast rules about sizes of these fittings, and builders should either seek professional advice or study craft of similar size and type. The basic rule is: if in doubt, use the larger size. Once more, it is necessary to stress that through-bolting must be adopted, with timber pads above and below decks; and also that galvanized steel fittings are less liable to cause electrolytic action than stainless steel ones. On lighter craft, where appearance is important and some weight-saving an advantage, the wide range of equipment now available in light alloy offers attractive alternatives up to considerable sizes–one Dutch manufacturer has made aluminium bitts for 5000-ton liners.

It is doubtful whether any subject–unless it be ladies' hats or football teams–engenders more controversy than sail-handling equipment in ocean racers, with views ranging from maximum simplicity to 'a winch for everything'. While the days of plentiful manpower and multiple pulley blocks are no longer with us, the sight of 25 winches on the deck of an ocean racer must daunt the man whose sea experiences always revolve around severe gales and pitch-black nights. However, as yet very few ferrocement ocean racers are being built–well, serious enough to warrant so many winches–and those which are will be nursed by competent designers and skippers. The average yachtsman must seek his own compromise between extremes. Smaller family

Plate 16 The deck of Pen Duick VI, *a modern ocean racer, showing the tremendous complexity of winches–a problem if floodlighting fails.*

yachts will certainly be glad to bring the halliards back to winches at the cockpit front, and to have one pair of substantial sheet winches for the headsails. It is better to forgo a second pair to ensure that the first are really man enough for their main task, which is likely to be considerable with a big genoa in a fresh breeze. One spin-off from the current winch mania is the proliferation of supplies, so the choice is wide–almost too wide for the average yachtsman. However, many yachting journals publish periodic reviews of winches, and many wholesalers tabulate their stocks in terms of the area of sail which each will safely handle. All one can do here is to reiterate the perennial cry–make sure it's bolted down properly with a pad underneath to help spread the load.

For interest, Plate 16 shows a modern deck layout.

Rubbing Strakes, Rails and Painting

Most craft need a rubbing strake around the line of the main sheer, to help fend the hull from quayheadings, etc., when coming alongside; in this position it is not always as well placed as it would be in other areas of the freeboard, but it is the most satisfying aesthetically. When a lower strake or strakes could be useful, as in canal cruisers or fishing-boats, they tend to be additions to the main sheer rubber rather than substitutes for it. Figures 68 and 69 profile a canal cruiser and a workboat respectively, showing how experience has developed the layout of these extra strakes.

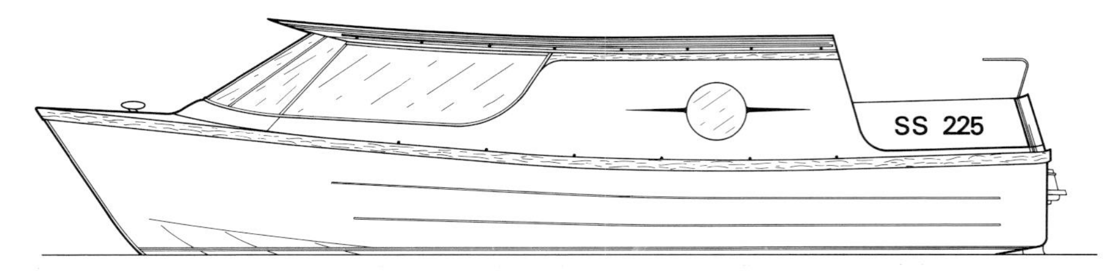

Fig. 68 Profile of a small canal cruiser showing horizontal rubbing strakes.

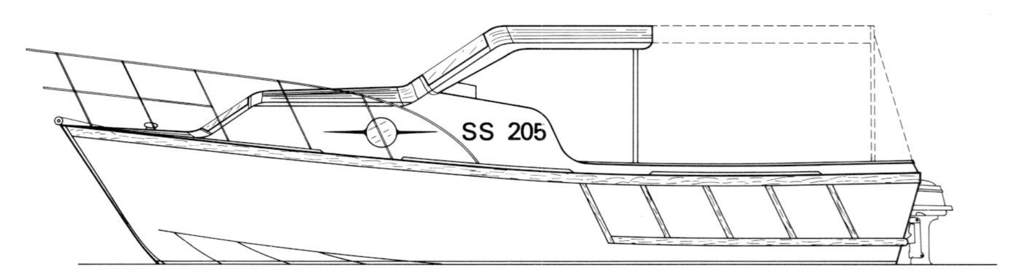

Fig. 69 Profile of a small fishing-boat showing diagonal rubbing strakes.

Essentially the choice of materials lies between timber and rubber, the latter being available in a wide range of styles and qualities up to grades quite suitable for 50 ft working craft. The smaller sizes of rubber are often very decorative, in a variety of colours and with contrasting inserts, but on the whole these are too small for ferrocement usage; the larger sizes tend to be available only in matt black finish, but what may be lacking aesthetically is certainly compensated for by durability. Such rubbers are heavy, must be through-bolted and need careful handling by a small team. The real problem is to ensure a clean, smooth line, for it is all too easy to allow the rubber to lie in a wavy line; despite its weight and strength, it lacks the rigidity of timber; thus the bolts should be spaced as closely as circumstances permit, normally 4–5 times the width of the rubber. The difficulties of drilling so many holes through the ferro hull are considerable, but it is not really possible to prejudge the position of these bolts and so set them into the hull prior to mortaring.

Timber strakes are easier to fit nicely, and call for relatively fewer bolts because of the inherent rigidity of the material. But timber always needs maintenance, be it paint, oil or varnish, and in this respect may have less appeal than rubber, especially on working craft. Teak or afrormosia strakes may be left bare, or given a coat of tung oil (which is best rubbed in by the bare hand), so reducing the amount of finishing needed. Oak and mahogany are also popular, the former suiting dark hulls and the latter suiting light ones. Unseasoned oak is very flexible and can often be bent round curves which would demand the steaming of seasoned wood, but oak sap is acid and liable to corrode the bolts; thus it is advisable to use hot-dip galvanized bolts and coat these with epoxy tar before driving them. In all events the timber should be well bedded in mastic and the heads of the bolts should be sealed with wooden dowels.

While the temptation to use ferro bulwarks is ever present, often, regrettably, purely on financial grounds and quite irrespective of suitability, the choice of the guard-rail system should be dictated by the craft as a whole. Motor cruisers built on trawler lines certainly carry ferro bulwarks well, and have the displacement to do so. Even so, it is sobering to recall that those on *Trixie* (65 ft) weighed more than $1\frac{1}{2}$ tons; a contrast may be drawn with the ultra-modern *Jensen 85* (Fig. 70) where weight is at a premium: aft of the main saloon the deep-rail effect is achieved with light alloy panels on alloy stanchions; forward it is provided by tightly stretched canvas, the whole structure weighing little more than $\frac{1}{4}$ ton.

When ferro bulwarks are fitted they must be capped, and the thoughtful hull builder will have provided adequate nuts at 1 ft intervals to receive hold-down bolts. When these are totally absent the builder is advised to use a timber channel, made off the job and through-bolted, as shown in Fig. 71.

The usual alternative is to use timber toe-rails and alloy or stainless steel stanchions, with lifelines of plastic-covered wire. The problems of drilling ferro have repeatedly been mentioned, and it is probable that a combination of rubbing strake and toe-rail will appeal, as shown in Fig. 72. Assembling this unit in long lengths on the ship will be anything but easy; however, the saving in bolt holes makes the effort well worth while. It is, regrettably, unwise to bolt the stanchions

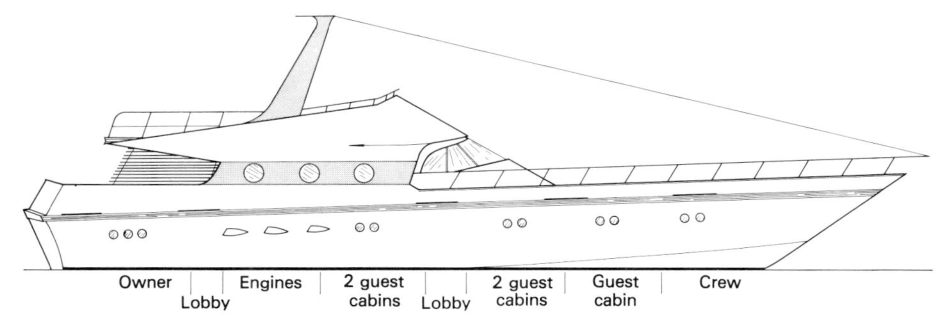

Fig. 70 The Jensen 85 *is a large, fast cruiser for the super-luxury trade; structural strength with minimum weight must be combined throughout to keep the power demands as low as possible.*

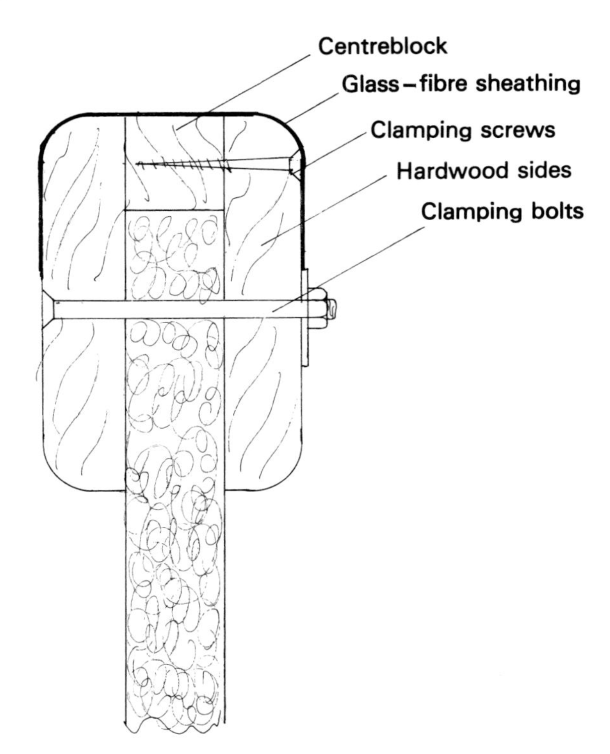

Fig. 71 Application of timber channel to top edge of ferro bulwark.

to this timber assembly, for if a heavy blow should damage the timber the work of repair would be excessive.

Nobody who has contemplated making a first-class job of painting a large ferro hull can fail to be daunted by the prospect, from the aspects of both the labour involved and the cost of paint. A 60 ft yacht with an average freeboard of 4 ft will use up to $1\frac{1}{2}$ gallons of enamel per coat, and will need four coats or more. Yet this is the final task, the one, perhaps, on which the acceptability of the yacht may succeed or fail. Of course, if the plastering has been faulty initially there is not a great deal the painter can do; if the mesh was unfair the task is hopeless.

'To grind or not to grind? That is the question.' And every authority on ferrocement hulls seems to have a different view. Certainly, if the bare, untreated hull has been standing in the open for many months while fitting-out progresses the surface will have acquired a patina of sulphur dioxide, soot and grease, so that it does no harm to go over the hull with a belt-sander. It is obviously going to be a tiring job, working on vertical or overhead surfaces, so it is probably unnecessary to advise caution against excessive pressures. Care must be taken not to expose the mesh, although it will be necessary to remove excess

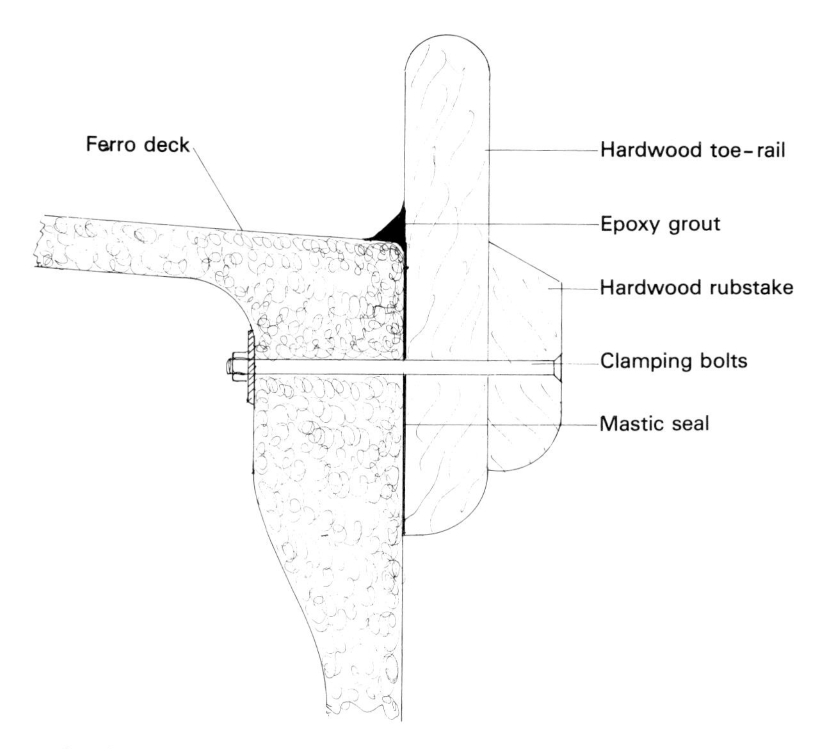

Fig. 72 Combination toe-rail and rubbing strake which reduces the incidence of through-hull bolting.

mortar build-up. It also follows that the sanding process may well show up any voids which have not previously become evident and thus reduce the labour of checking over the entire hull, tapping with a small hammer and listening for the characteristic dullness of a void. Once more it pays to remind the reader that protective clothing, goggles and face mask must be worn when grinding, since eyes and lungs are irreplaceable.

Voids should be filled with resin or resin-rich cement grout[1] according to size, it being hoped that none is large enough to require a full sand/cement mortar.

Once the surface has been prepared to this stage it is essential to ensure that every trace of loose mortar is dusted from the surface before paint is applied. From this point on there is a choice of finishes, of varying costs, but in essence all must be based upon effective sealing of the cement, usually with a resin. International Paints and MacAlister Carvall both supply surface sealing compounds developed specially for ferro; other manufacturers may also have done so or will do so. Epoxy tar is acceptable for this purpose, but could be more expensive than the new custom-made filler/sealers. Whichever material is selected, the manufacturer's instructions should be followed closely. There is much to be said for beginning with a test area well below the waterline, to try material and techniques; should application or curing problems manifest themselves the builder can check his method again and, if still dissatisfied, report back to the manufacturer. This warning is sounded because new products are coming in to the ferro industry without adequate trial, and one at least has proved disastrous. However, whatever the shortcomings of most of the marine industry, it is pleasant to find that paint manufacturers bend over backwards to provide competent service and advice to amateur and professional alike.

Normally the sealing coat is allowed to dry hard before being sanded down to provide a key for further painting; but if it is deemed advisable to use two coats of sealer the second can be applied over the first without rubbing down, provided the interval between coats does not exceed 30 hours. Once the seal coat has been prepared for further painting it is advisable to strike in the waterline and boot-topping. This will involve getting the hull onto the ground which is as even as possible and chocking it with a spirit level in the attitude in which the craft is designed to float. When this can be done on a flat level floor as, for example, in a car park, the waterline can be marked in with a pencil or chalk set on a pole exactly the correct distance above the ground. If such niceties are not available the builder must measure down from the sheer at a dozen points along the hull, using measurements taken from the lines, due allowance being made for deck thickness, etc.

It is unlikely that either method will produce anything but a rather wavy line, so that a clean one must then be struck in with the aid of a long, straight batten. The boot-top should next be struck in, preferably with a scriber, at several inches above the waterline; depths vary with taste, and–more practically–with any variations in freeboard expected from differing loadings, but an average for yachts would be one twelfth or 8 per cent of the minimum freeboard. When the yacht sits on the hard she looks best if this boot-top provides a nice colour contrast between the topsides and the bottom. In the water, of course, this effect is lost; and since weed fouling is most prolific close to the surface, where the sun's rays penetrate readily, it is far more sensible to take the antifouling straight up to the top of the boot-top line. True, some of the older, stronger, antifoulings do not take kindly to exposure, and should be totally immersed within eight hours of application; but the newer ones, developed for racing yachts and craft which dry out on moorings, will accept exposure to air in this way, and are amenable to scrubbing.

Topsides should be painted before the bottom; any paint runs and splashes will then be painted over; furthermore, the painter will not constantly be in contact with the antifouling which is–or should be–toxic. For the best quality finish the topsides should receive four coats of epoxy resin paint, each applied within 30 hours of the preceding one without rubbing down between coats; the final coat should be left to harden before being sanded down with wet-and-dry sandpaper, used very wet. Once the desired surface has been achieved in this way, with the resin pigmented to the appropriate undercoat tint, the final gloss is achieved with two coats of polyurethane enamel, the first being rubbed down wet after being allowed to harden for a few days.

A less expensive solution is to use polyurethane undercoats throughout, or one of the special lower-cost coatings developed for ferro. If the surface after sealing still exhibits hollows of reasonable quality these can be filled: MacAlister Carvall's FerroFill has previously been mentioned in this context, but a good-quality trowel cement can be as effective. Fillers need a rough surface to ensure that they key into the preceding layer; and they should be allowed to harden properly before being rubbed down. By this combination of filling and rubbing down, and by using different colours between undercoats so that high spots show through readily, it is possible to bring a ferro hull to as good a finish as can be achieved with timber or grp, given that the original plastering and mesh fairness warrant such effort. The owner or builder must decide how far he is prepared to go in the search for finish perfection.

Below water the owner should select an antifouling recommended for his cruising water. Ferro is unlikely to suffer from marine borers, but the surface is basically porous enough to permit the attachment of barnacles and grasses, both of which reduce performance markedly. For almost a century antifouling paints were based on copper salts which leached out under the action of salt water, producing a poisonous film. Copper is not the best material with which to cover steel or ferro hulls, for the two metals form an electrolytic couple; however, the interposition of a substantial non-metallic barrier, such as the epoxy sealer, much reduces this effect and two coats increases the protection afforded. Antifoulings based on mercury and antimony have been tried, but the newer plastic developments such as International TBT seem to be more effective than their more dangerous predecessors. Owners based in warm climates should note that some of these new coatings can be applied under water, the painting team wearing masks and standard Scuba gear; since these areas often lack tides suitable for drying out, and are still rather short of slipping facilities, these techniques may prove invaluable.

Ferrocement decks present a problem: they are normally reasonably rough and thus provide a natural non-skid surface. But it is unwise not to seal the mortar, thus reducing the non-slip effect. The preferred solution will be to apply sealer, without pre-grinding if at all possible, then two coats of waterproof undercoat followed by a topcoat of polyurethane gloss containing coarse sand; if thought necessary this can be sealed by a further coat of gloss, heavily thinned and without

Chapter Eleven **Steering Gears and Rudders**

Before launching his creation, or if he has been fitting-out afloat (which always seems a sensible move, for it is usually easier to have heavy equipment craned overside than up into the air), before committing himself to sea in it, the builder should give his handiwork a long, hard appraisal to see what he may have forgotten, lest it be something rather vital. The omission of some major item is certainly not unknown, especially in projects which have come to fruition over many years; usually it is one of those odd things which have never quite fitted into the mainstream of the completion programme.

Alike with authors: looking back through this book one discovers the happy sight of one's ferro creation, ready for the sea, glistening with paint and varnish, shipshape and Bristol fashion except for one small item: no steering gear! Nowhere in what has gone before has the subject of rudders and their control systems received an airing; thus, this most important matter must be examined in the detail it deserves. It is not a simple subject, for in any range of ferro yachts we shall discover:

(a) Transom-hung single rudders.
(b) Single rudders hung behind keels or skegs.
(c) Single rudders hung in cantilever.
(d) Twin rudders in cantilever.
(e) Rudders in timber.
(f) Rudders in steel, both hollow and in single plate.

Transom-hung rudders are found on a limited number of craft nowadays; these are usually developments of traditional designs such as smacks and pilot cutters, or they come on the sterns of modern ocean racers and are of quite sophisticated design. Figure 73, although taken from a wooden boat, typifies the construction of a conventional

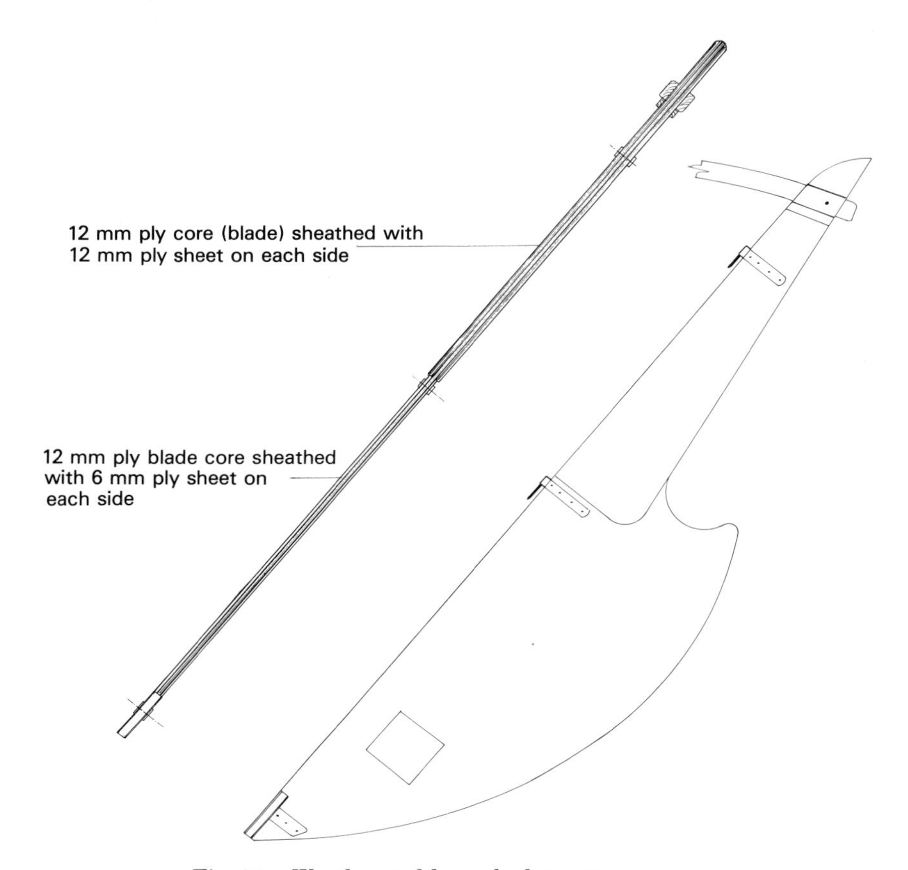

Fig. 73 Wooden rudder to be hung on a transom.

transom rudder for a 26 ft smack yacht. Owners looking longingly at it and thinking of the advantages of being able to unship the rudder on moorings or when stern-on would do well to remember that these assemblies tend to weigh in at about 8 lb per foot of boat length–the one drawn weighs over 200 lb.

The single rudder hung behind a skeg or keel is by far the most common; sailboats with more than one rudder are rare–in fact Lord Riverdale, an expert on twin keels, is perhaps the only modern naval architect to use the system, which could well make sense in the context. Single-screw power craft have single rudders, as do a fair proportion of twin-screw ones.

The first question to need an answer, if one has not already been provided by the architect, is the requisite area. This could be a complex subject, well beyond the scope of our builder, but most designers relate rudder area to the lateral area of the hull itself, occasionally modified by speed when the vessel is a fairly fast power yacht. The builder who is unsure of the helm balance of his yacht could well opt

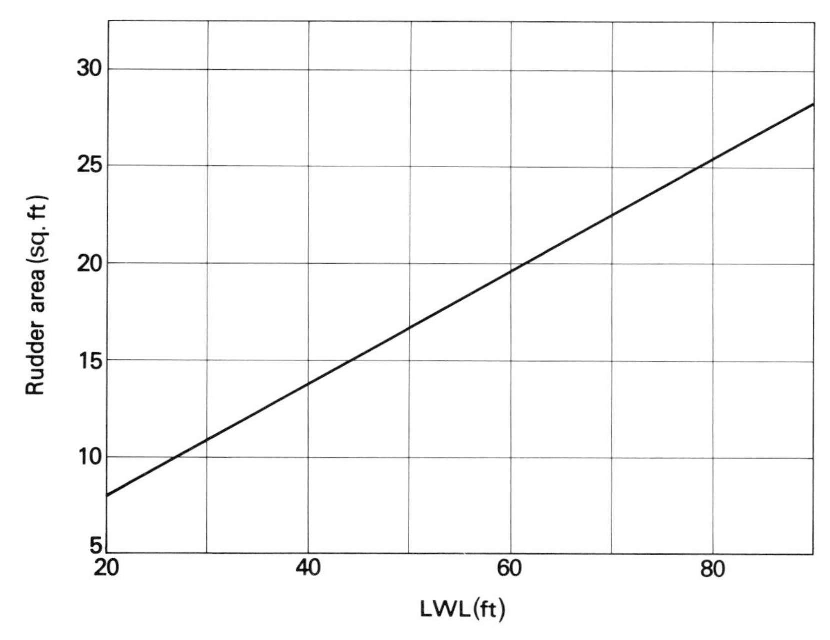

Fig. 74 Correlation between rudder area and waterline length in ferro hulls when the speed/length ration ($V/\sqrt{L}$) does not exceed 1:5.

for a wooden rudder rather larger than normal, so that he can reduce the area by experiment. Figure 74 has been developed from a number of sources to relate rudder area to waterline length, assuming an average shape of lateral plane.

The pros and cons of balanced and unbalanced rudders are liable to be argued extensively. Balance–the placing of part of the area ahead of the stock–can much reduce the helm torque required; but if the rudder is close to the propeller, even a small amount of balance can lead to rudder-snatch once the helm angle exceeds a few degrees. Therefore balance should be approached with caution, and in any event the area ahead of the stock should not exceed 8 per cent of the total area except when specified by the architect. It should be noted that balanced rudders are difficult to build well except in the double-plate configuration of aerofoil chord shape.

An important factor in rudder design must be the ease with which the rudder can be fitted to the ship or removed from it. Early designs for small cruisers often demanded that the vessel be tipped on to its nose so that the rudder, permanently attached to its stock, could be inserted into the rudder tube; the bottom of the hollow stock then received the lower pintle, bolted through the heel of the skeg. Simple, effective, but not easy to deal with.

More recent developments show the rudder blade fixed permanently to a tubular stock; a solid central stock is threaded from above down through the rudder tube and its bearings and out through the bottom of the hull; the rudder blade being held into its position between hull and heel, the solid stock is driven through the tube on which the blade is based and then into the heel fitting, where it serves as pintle. Bolts through tube and stock hold the rudder firmly in place, while a substantial Tufnol washer between blade and heel fitting provides a water-lubricated bearing surface. Figure 75 shows the design of such a system as developed for *Yara 121*, a 40 ft motor-sailer. It will be noted that a wooden blade is used; heavy though this is, the natural buoyancy of the timber reduces the loading on the lower pintle and eases the steering load simply by reduced friction.

A rudder can be made in this way from a single steel plate, and the method is popular in cheap steel coasters. In small sailboats, especially when the rudder is balanced, the slightest irregularity in the leading edge of the blade can set up considerable vibration; amplified through a reasonable length of steel-tube tiller, the result can be acute discomfort for the helmsman. On a power craft with, for example, hydraulic steering, this vibration is unlikely to trouble the helmsman; but it will still exist and may lead to early failure of components by fatigue. Chord-shaped stiffeners are often welded to plate rudders, not only to strengthen them but also to reduce this vibration, and almost all classification societies lay down rules to cover the system. Interestingly, at least one (Italian) prefers the plate rudder to the more robust glass-sheathed timber blade, although this may largely arise because its surveyors are more accustomed to steel coasters than ferrocement yachts.

But, the reader will expostulate, why should not a ferrocement yacht use a ferro rudder? Indeed, some designers have been known to draw them, and certainly a number of owners have built them. This is a bad use of a good medium, and does the technology more harm than good; perhaps this is always true, for when an enthusiast becomes a zealot he becomes antisocial. No, a ferro blade is altogether too heavy. It must be solid, which in itself poses uncertainties in ensuring that there are no cavities; thus, while the weight of steel and timber in the unit shown in Fig. 75 just exceed the buoyancy of the volume when immersed, giving a downthrust of some 20 lb, an aerofoil ferrocement replacement would have a balancing loading of 160 lb or more, according to the chordal area (in air it would weight some 300 lb). Of course, a steel-plate rudder built to the requirements of a classification society would be every bit as heavy, if not more so, and have maybe fewer redeeming features.

Classification societies, often rightly maligned for being out of touch with modern yachting, really go to town on rudders and steering gear, and Lloyds' rules for the diameters of stocks, pintles and steering heads are voluminous, detailed and worthy of study. It is not possible to reproduce here all the many tables of data provided, and the builder

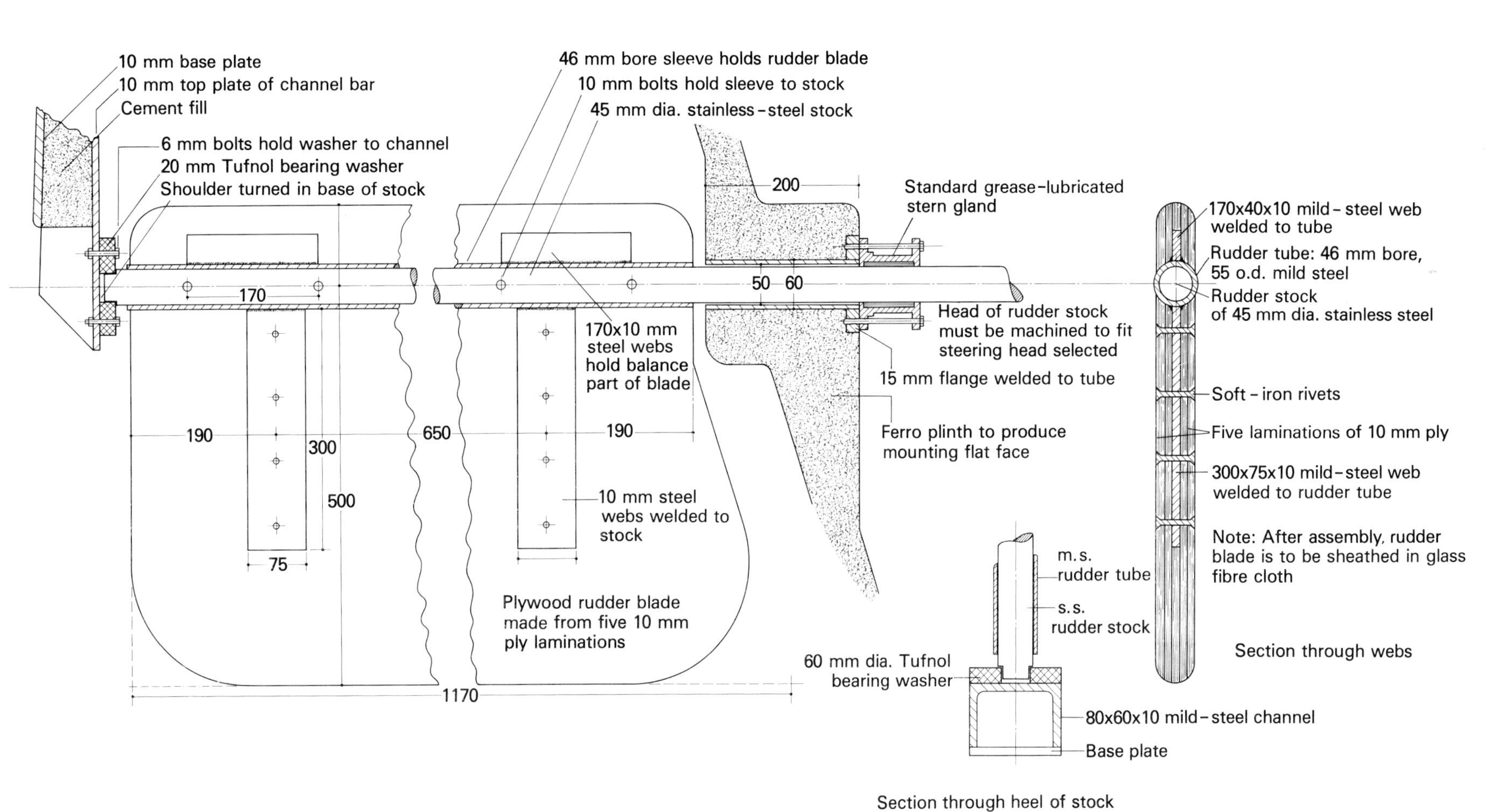

Fig. 75 Construction of rudder and stock system in Yara 121; *the blade is supported at top and bottom and can be removed without tipping the hull.*

of a ferro yacht is referred to their *Rules for the Construction of Reinforced Plastic Yachts* for more comprehensive advice, until this is replaced by *Rules for Ferro*. It is a slim, portable volume, and eminently readable, unlike the rules for steel ships, which must remain the province of the professional. The dichotomy within this organization shows in the difference between the simple vulgar fractions used for sailboats (even in the metric section) and the complex two-places-of-decimals layout for powerboats. Indeed, so simple and effective is the outlook on stock diameters, and associated pintles, that it is reproduced here in full (Table 7).

Table 7 Diameters of rudder heads and pintles for sailing and auxiliary yachts

Length (ft)	Head diameter (in)	Pintle diameter (in)
20	$1\frac{1}{4}$	$\frac{7}{8}$
40	$1\frac{7}{16}$	1
60	$1\frac{7}{8}$	$1\frac{3}{8}$
80	$2\frac{5}{16}$	$1\frac{5}{8}$
100	$2\frac{3}{4}$	$1\frac{7}{8}$
120	$3\frac{1}{4}$	$2\frac{1}{8}$

Note. These figures are for mild-steel shafts; where other materials are used, which is unlikely in ferro hulls, corrections should be applied.

Power craft pose more complications, for the stressing is much affected by the speed; indeed, it is considered more important than the size of the vessel (although this must be reflected in the blade area). Thus, one begins by calculating the area of the blade and then finding the centre of area; the product of area and the distance of this CA behind the centre of the stock gives the moment *AD* in Table 8, which is only part of Lloyds' data.

Cantilever or spade rudders have had some vogue in sailing craft,

Table 8 Variation of rudder-head diameter with area moment and yacht speed

Moment *AD*	Diameter (in) at various speeds					
	6 knots	8 knots	10 knots	12 knots	14 knots	16 knots
10	1·58	1·83	2·08	2·33	2·58	2·83
20	1·95	2·20	2·45	2·70	2·95	3·20
30	2·32	2·57	2·82	3·07	3·32	3·57
40	2·68	2·93	3·18	3·43	3·68	3·93
50	3·05	3·30	3·55	3·80	4·05	4·30
60	3·43	3·68	3·93	4·18	4·43	4·68

Note. AD is given in ft^2-ft.

and by ensuring an uninterrupted flow of water to a balanced blade have advantage in allowing the area to be reduced. They have lost now in popularity to deep, swept-back rudders mounted on long shallow skegs. Now Lloyds have evolved formulae for determining the additional stock diameter needed to accept the greater stresses of a cantilever rudder; the first allows for the twisting moment and the second for the bending moment. The first should be used to estimate the diameter for these new half-skeg rudders, since it takes into account the much greater torque imposed by the trailing blade.

Figure 76 shows such a rudder and indicates the parameters required by the formula:

$$d_1 = \sqrt[3]{\left[\frac{2A(1{\cdot}2V)^2}{2240} \times \frac{32D}{\pi}\right]}$$

where d = stock diameter
A = blade area
D = distance from centre of area to centreline of stock
V = speed in knots.

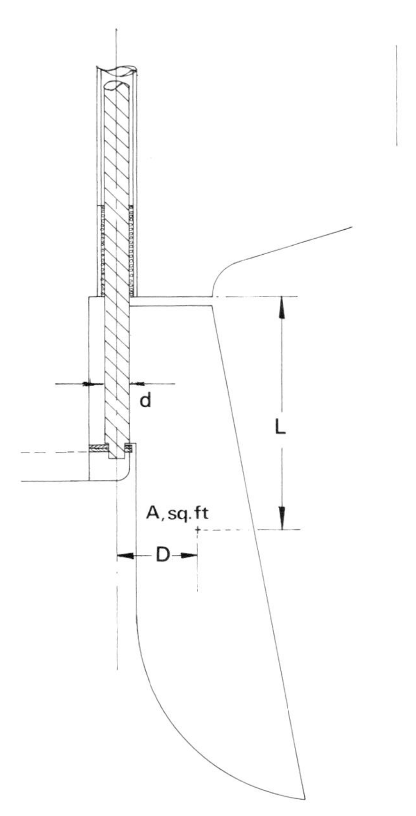

Fig. 76 Profile of a modern sailboat rudder showing measurements needed to determine stock size under Lloyds' rules.

Because this type of rudder tends to be used largely on fast offshore racing yachts capable of surfing, V should be taken as twice the square root of the waterline length of the yacht.

Power craft with twin rudders, and a few sailing craft, still use the unsupported cantilever, and compensation must be made for the bending moment imposed by this configuration: this is done by correcting the above formula thus:

$$d_2 = d_1 \times [\sqrt[3]{a} + \sqrt[2]{(a^2 + 1)}]$$

where $a = L/D$
L = distance from centre of rudder area to bottom hull bearing

This correction is considerable, and when applied to a normal type of balanced rudder with an aspect ratio of 2:1 will increase the stock diameter by more than 50 per cent.

Of course, all these calculations should have been made at the design stage, because the rudder stock must pass through the ferro hull via a tube already welded into the mesh before mortaring. And if that tube's bore is too small for the stock needed by the rudder selected, alternative arrangements must be sought. For example, it may be possible to replace a cantilever blade with a supported one, or it may be possible to use a stock of Monel metal or high-tensile steel to secure a diameter reduction.

Where space permits it is normal to use a lower bearing of Tufnol, since it is water-lubricated, but where the thickness of the plastic would produce an unacceptable reduction in stock diameter it is permissible to use a thin-shell phosphor-bronze or white-metal bearing with a total-loss grease system. An example of this system is shown in Fig. 77. The layout was, in fact, developed to meet a change in ruling which was promulgated after the basic tubes had been mortared into the hull.

The head of the stock may emerge on deck, the containing tube running throughout; there is no problem of watertightness, so the system is as simple as it can be. If the steering head is below deck level there is always the possibility of water leakage, so a standard grease-packed gland should be fitted.

Steering itself may be accomplished directly, by the application of a simple tiller to the rudder stock; or it may be effected remotely, normally by a steering wheel. Five main connections are normal:

(a) Direct by gear system, as when the wheel is pedestal-mounted immediately adjacent to the steering head.
(b) Morse/Teleflex or push-pull cable system.
(c) Hydraulic.
(d) Chains or wires in endless loops.
(e) Rod systems, such as Mathway and Whitlock.

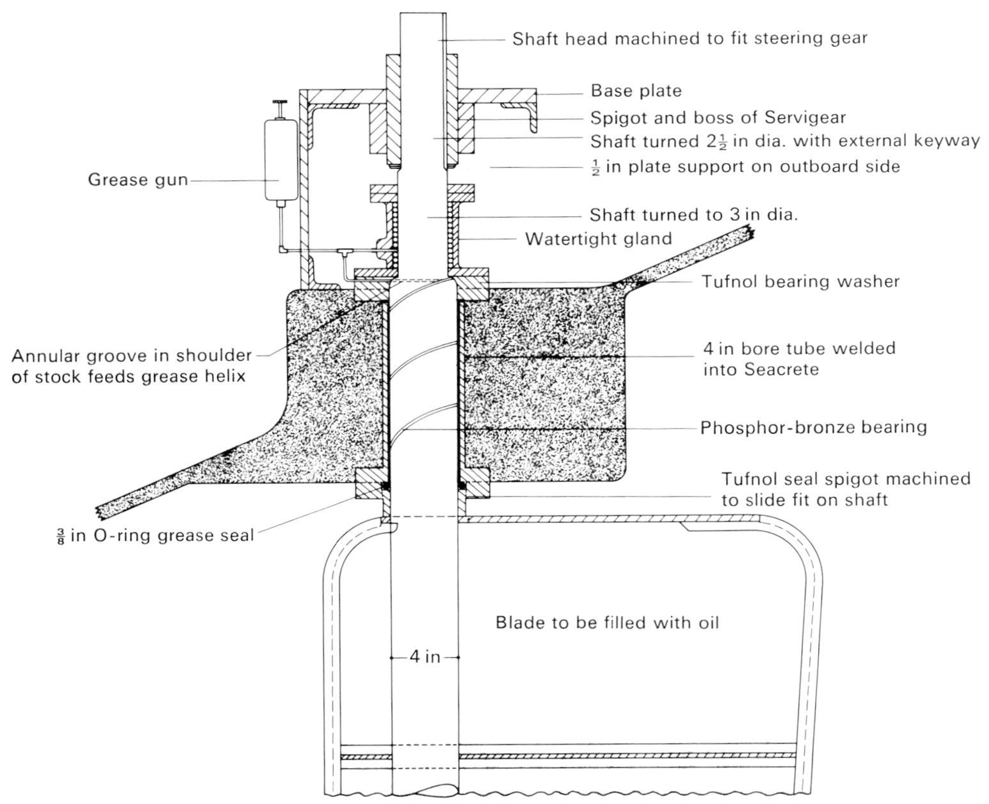

Fig. 77 Double-plate rudder with grease-lubricated phosphor-bronze bearing.

System (a) is really applicable to sailing yachts, for it brings the helm right aft. A variety of manufactured pedestals and gear is available, at a considerable range of cost, but the builder can fabricate a simple plywood plinth, and mount a crown-and-pinion gearing on top of the stock. It has the advantages of simplicity and feel, a feature notably lacking in the other systems.

Systems (b) and (c) are normally laid out by the supplying agent or manufacturer, who will gladly advise on the equipment which should be used. Both have the considerable advantage–in power craft– that two steering stations can be used; many larger yachts are designed to be steered either from a pilot station at the forward end of the saloon or from a flying bridge, according to the weather. Moreover, both systems allow for the fitting of an automatic pilot at the rudder head, which is useful, if not essential, on long voyages. Of the two push-pull cable systems, Teleflex is normally used only for small craft, but since both are distributed by the same organization the builder will have no difficulty in selecting the correct solution.

The main headache with hydraulics is the presence of occluded air bubbles in the lines, leading to malfunction ranging from sponginess

Plate 17 Steering consol in a 65 ft motor yacht with upper-deck control station in addition.

to non-operation; standard industrial air-bleeding procedures will cure the trouble. Both (b) and (c) have another common disadvantage in that the short travel normally provided by the actuating ram leads to reduced helm angles: it is normal to design for ± 40 degrees, since from 38 degrees onwards a rudder tends increasingly to stall rather than steer. But experience shows that the judicious combination of extreme helm angles and bursts of engine power can permit consider-

Plate 18 Steering consol in a 40 ft motor-sailer with 2-station control.

able manoeuvres at speeds normally below steering threshold. This facility is invaluable when docking or coming alongside. Normally, only the chain or wire system can be arranged to provide this facility. Its other advantage is low cost. Its disadvantages are cumbersomeness, tendency to slackness (leading to slow or poor response) and the twin difficulties of installation and maintenance. Standard steering springs are available to allow a measure of automatic compensation for wire stretch, while intelligent planning at the layout stage can minimize the installation and maintenance problems.

Rod-linkage systems are positive and reliable, with very little to go wrong at any time. But they need great care in planning, preferably at the ship-design stage, because one simply cannot bend solid rods round the sheer. They are thus perhaps best suited to working craft, especially those with the wheelhouse aft. However, the few manufacturers who specialize in steering systems maintain excellent customer-advice departments, so that builders with a penchant for such qualities will not lack for experienced aid.

The organization of steering consols and their layouts fall perhaps more within the province of the aesthetician than the engineer; Plates 17 and 18 show two solutions in different situations–a big power cruiser and a medium-size motor-sailer. With this thought we conclude our brief look at rudders and steering systems. Like all of the topics dealt with in this book, it has been given but a cursory examination, for–as with them all–it could form the subject of a book in its own right. Yet, were it to do so, the outcome would doubtless be too detailed and too abstruse for the builder of a yacht.

So it is with all the specializations considered, and an effort has been made to provide references and sources of more detailed information and advice. But if the result is the completion of more ferrocement hulls into the high-quality ships they should and can become, and if more and more builders are persuaded that so excellent a building material as ferrocement should be enhanced by a comparable standard of finish, the whole project will have been worthwhile.

Index